D1035026

Shapes of Power
The Development of
Ezra Pound's Poetic Sequences

Literature Advisory Boards

Studies in Modern Literature

A. Walton Litz, Series Editor
Princeton University

Consulting Editors
Joseph Blotner
University of Michigan
George Bornstein
University of Michigan
Jackson R. Bryer
*University of Maryland
at College Park*
Ronald Bush
California Institute of Technology
Keith Cushman
*University of North Carolina
at Greensboro*
Richard J. Finneran
Newcomb College, Tulane University
Daniel Mark Fogel
Louisiana State University
Carolyn G. Heilbrun
Columbia University
Paul Mariani
*University of Massachusetts
at Amherst*
Thomas C. Moser
Stanford University
Linda Wagner
Michigan State University

Nineteenth-Century Studies

Juliet McMaster, Series Editor
University of Alberta

Consulting Editors
Carol Christ
*University of California
at Berkeley*
James R. Kincaid
University of Southern California
Julian Markels
Ohio State University
G. B. Tennyson
*University of California
at Los Angeles*

Studies in Speculative Fiction

Robert Scholes, Series Editor
Brown University

Studies in Modern Literature, No. 95

Other Titles in This Series

No. 4
The Latin Masks of Ezra Pound
Ron Thomas

No. 36
*These Fragments I Have Shored: Collage
and Montage in Early Modernist Poetry*
Andrew M. Clearfield

No. 64
Poets, Poems, Movements
Thomas Parkinson

No. 72
*William Carlos Williams and the
Maternal Muse*
Kerry Driscoll

No. 76
*Yeats: An Annual of Critical and
Textual Studies, Volume V, 1987*
Richard J. Finneran, ed.

No. 79
*T. S. Eliot and the Politics of Voice:
The Argument of* The Waste Land
John Xiros Cooper

No. 94
*Faulkner's Poetry: A Bibliographical Guide
to Texts and Criticism*
Judith L. Sensibar

/ochc

Shapes of Power
The Development of
Ezra Pound's Poetic Sequences

by
Bruce Fogelman

811.09
P876f

East Baton Rouge Parish Library
Baton Rouge, Louisiana

U·M·I Research Press

Ann Arbor / London

Copyright © 1988
Bruce Alan Fogelman
All rights reserved

Produced and distributed by
UMI Research Press
an imprint of
University Microfilms Inc.
Ann Arbor, Michigan 48106

Library of Congress Cataloging in Publication Data

Fogelman, Bruce, 1955-
   Shapes of power : the development of Ezra Pound's poetic sequences
/ by Bruce Fogelman.
      p. cm.—(Studies in modern literature ; no. 95)
      Bibliography: p.
      Includes index.
      ISBN 0-8357-1883-2 (alk. paper)
      1. Pound, Ezra, 1885-1972—Criticism and interpretation.
   I. Title. II. Series.
   PS3531.082Z629   1988
   811'.52—dc19   88-9647
                                                          CIP

British Library CIP data is available.

The proper METHOD for studying poetry and good letters is the method of contemporary biologists, that is careful first-hand examination of the matter, and continual COMPARISON of one "slide" or specimen with another.

No man is equipped for modern thinking until he has understood the anecdote of Agassiz and the fish:

A post-graduate student equipped with honours and diplomas went to Agassiz to receive the final and finishing touches. The great man offered him a small fish and told him to describe it.

Post-Graduate Student: "That's only a sunfish."

Agassiz: "I know that. Write a description of it."

After a few minutes the student returned with the description of the Ichthus Heliodiplodokus, or whatever term is used to conceal the common sunfish from vulgar knowledge, family of Heliichtherinkus, etc., as found in textbooks of the subject.

Agassiz again told the student to describe the fish.

The student produced a four-page essay. Agassiz then told him to look at the fish. At the end of three weeks the fish was in an advanced state of decomposition, but the student knew something about it.

Ezra Pound, *ABC of Reading*

Contents

Acknowledgments

I wish to thank, first and most of all, Professor M. L. Rosenthal, whose guidance and friendship have contributed greatly to this study. My debt to *The Modern Poetic Sequence: The Genius of Modern Poetry,* by Professors Rosenthal and Sally M. Gall, and to Professor Rosenthal's other writings is greater than the references in the following pages indicate.

I also wish to thank the Department of English of New York University for a Penfield award, which enabled me to devote more concentrated effort to the completion of the initial phase of this study than would otherwise have been possible and to make fewer compromises than would otherwise have been necessary.

Thanks are due to others who have helped in various ways: to Princess Mary de Rachewiltz for reading and commenting on parts of this work, to Ms. Wendolyn Tetlow for offering attentive and helpful suggestions, and to Dr. Thomas McKeown for making his fine, unpublished study available to me. The faults and shortcomings of the following pages, however, are independent of my predecessors, my supporters, my sources, and my readers.

Staff members of the Beinecke Library of Yale University have also been tremendously helpful, especially Mr. Stephen C. Jones, Ms. Lori Misura, and Ms. Catherine Sharp, who enabled me to spend my time there efficiently and most enjoyably.

I wish to extend my gratitude to the Center for the Study of Ezra Pound and His Contemporaries in the Collection of American Literature of the Beinecke Rare Book and Manuscript Library at Yale University for permission to quote materials in the Ezra Pound Archives (marked "YC" in the text) and to Special Collections of the Joseph Regenstein Library of the University of Chicago for permission to quote materials in the Harriet Monroe Archives (marked "UCL").

Finally, grateful acknowledgment is given to New Directions Publishing Corporation for permission to quote from the following copyrighted works of Ezra Pound: *ABC of Reading* (Copyright 1934 by Ezra Pound); *Collected Early Poems* (Copyright © 1976 by the Trustees of the Ezra Pound Literary Property

x   *Acknowledgments*

Trust. All Rights Reserved); *Ezra Pound/Dorothy Shakespear* (Copyright ©
1976 by the Trustees of the Ezra Pound Literary Property Trust); *Ezra Pound
and Music* (Copyright © 1977 by the Trustees of the Ezra Pound Literary
Property Trust); *Ezra Pound and the Visual Arts* (Copyright © 1980 by the
Trustees of the Ezra Pound Literary Property Trust); *Gaudier-Brzeska: A Memoir* (Copyright © 1970 by Ezra Pound); *Guide to Kulchur* (Copyright © 1970
by Ezra Pound); "Hilda's Book" from *End to Torment* (Copyright © 1979 by the
Trustees of the Ezra Pound Literary Property Trust); Interview in *New Directions 17* (Copyright © 1961 by New Directions Publishing Corporation); *Literary Essays* (Copyright 1918, 1920, 1935 by Ezra Pound); *Selected Letters of
Ezra Pound* (Copyright 1950 by Ezra Pound); *Personae* (Copyright 1926 by
Ezra Pound); *Pound/Ford* (Copyright © 1982 by the Trustees of the Ezra Pound
Literary Property Trust); *Pound/Joyce* (Copyright © 1967 by Ezra Pound);
Pound/Lewis (Copyright © 1985 by the Trustees of the Ezra Pound Literary
Property Trust); *Selected Prose* (Copyright © 1973 by the Estate of Ezra Pound);
The Spirit of Romance (Copyright © 1968 by Ezra Pound); *Translations* (Copyright 1954, © 1963 by Ezra Pound. All Rights Reserved); Previously unpublished material by Ezra Pound (Copyright © 1988 by the Trustees of the Ezra
Pound Literary Property Trust); used by permission of New Directions Publishing Corporation, agents.

Abbreviations

ABCR	*ABC of Reading*
CEP	*Collected Early Poems*
EP/DS	*Ezra Pound/Dorothy Shakespear*
EPM	*Ezra Pound and Music*
EPVA	*Ezra Pound and the Visual Arts*
GB	*Gaudier-Brzeska: A Memoir*
GK	*Guide to Kulchur*
"HB"	"Hilda's Book"
"Int" Bridson	"Interview" in *New Directions*
"Int" Hall	"Interview" in *Paris Review*
LE	*Literary Essays*
LRA	Selections in *The Little Review Anthology*
Ltrs	*The Letters of Ezra Pound*
P	*Personae* (1926)
P/F	*Pound/Ford*

P/J	*Pound/Joyce*
P/L	*Pound/Lewis*
SP	*Selected Prose*
SR	*The Spirit of Romance*
Tr	*Translations*
UCL	Unpublished materials in the University of Chicago Library
YC	Unpublished materials in the Beinecke Rare Book and Manuscript Library at Yale University

Introduction: "Look at the Fish"

"Intense emotion causes pattern to arise in the mind—if the mind is strong enough."

Ezra Pound, "Affirmations: As for Imagisme"

In a well-known interview published in 1962, Pound remarked:

> I began the *Cantos* about 1904, I suppose. I had various schemes, starting in 1904 or 1905. The problem was to get a form—something elastic enough to take the necessary material. It had to be a form that wouldn't exclude something merely because it didn't fit.
>
> . . . Only a musical form would take the material, and the Confucian universe as I see it is a universe of interacting strains and tensions. ("Int" Hall 23)

Since then, critics have devoted increasing attention to Pound's work before *The Cantos* but have generally focused on its thematic continuities and its relation to the works of earlier poets, or else on its theoretical bearings.[1] Some have discussed his pre-*Cantos* experiments with the long poem but have restricted their examination, with few exceptions, to those later works that most obviously fit within this category: "Near Perigord" (1916), *Homage to Sextus Propertius* (1919), and *Hugh Selwyn Mauberley* (1920).[2] All of these appeared near or after the publication of the first sketches of *The Cantos,* however, and do not take us very far toward the experimentation that began "in 1904 or 1905."

But the strong concern with both traditional and newer forms that emerges in some of Pound's earliest critical statements should suggest to us that his exploration of structural possibilities in his poems and the formulation of the principles guiding his experiments were already well advanced long before the first drafts of *The Cantos.*

In fact, one of the central concepts informing Pound's working methods is present in his very first expositions of them and is clarified and refined in his later statements on aesthetics: emotion allied with intellect not only is or should be the basis of poetic expression, but is also the essential determinant of form.[3]

2 Introduction: "Look at the Fish"

In his earliest, unpublished speculations, his emphasis on emotion even to the exclusion of intellect is clear: "Poetry is of the sense and of the soul / The intellect . has no part therein" (YC).[4] On a leaf dated September 1907, he affirms that "as a poet ('doit etre lyrist') my strife is to express my feelings[;] as a dramatist to dissect and expound those of humanity" (YC). Somewhat later, in *The Spirit of Romance* (1910, compiled from lectures delivered in 1909), we are told that "poetry is a sort of inspired mathematics, which gives us equations . . . for the human emotions" (14) and "the mood, the play is everything; the facts are nothing" (16). And in another statement during the same period, Pound discusses the importance of sound—rhythm, in particular—to the precise conveyance of emotion and to the crucial relationship between the single verse unit and the composition as a whole. The passage merits extended quotation, since it also helps to explain what Pound meant by a "musical form" in his interview fifty-two years later:

> Rhythm is perhaps the most primal of all things known to us. It is basic in poetry and music mutually, their melodies depending on a variation of tone quality and of pitch respectively, as is commonly said, but if we look more closely we will see that music is, by further analysis, pure rhythm. . . . When we know more of overtones we will see that the tempo of every masterpiece is absolute, and is exactly set by some further law of rhythmic accord. Whence it should be possible to show that any given rhythm implies about it a complete musical form— fugue, sonata . . . a form, perfect, complete. Ergo, the rhythm set in a line of poetry connotes its symphony, which, had we a little more skill, we could score for orchestra. . . . the rhythm of any poetic line corresponds to emotion.
>
> It is the poet's business that this correspondence be exact, i.e., that it be the emotion which surrounds the thought expressed.
>
> . . . It is only when the emotions illumine the perceptive powers that we see the reality. (*Tr* 23–24)

Of course, what "emotion" signifies here is hardly a matter of simple self-expression, for this is what Pound militated against both in his poetry and in his critical decrees: "The only kind of emotion worthy of a poet is the inspirational emotion which energises and strengthens, and which is very remote from the everyday emotion of sloppiness and sentiment" (*EP/DS* 325).

As his poetics developed, Pound's emphasis shifted toward an insistence on the alliance of emotion and intellect, most notably in his key formulation of the image in 1912 as "an intellectual and emotional complex in an instant of time" (*LE* 4). In a later essay on Eliot (1917), he distinguishes "intellect" from "intelligence"; the latter, inseparable from emotion, is an essential force in poetry: "The supreme test of a book is that we should feel some unusual intelligence working behind the words. . . . I have expressly written here not 'intellect' but 'intelligence.' There is no intelligence without emotion. The emotion may be anterior or concurrent" (*LE* 420–21).[5] Pound here anticipates Eliot's distinction, in a 1921 essay, between the "direct sensuous apprehension of thought, or a recreation of thought into feeling" in the metaphysical poets and its absence in later poets who "do not feel their thought as immediately as the odour of a rose" (*Selected* 246–47). Pound's discrimination between the force of intelligence infused with emotion in art, on the one hand, and sentimentality and intellect, on the other, is clarified in a statement he made in 1918: "Good art is the expression of emotional values which do not give way to the intellect. Bad art is merely an assertion of emotion, which intellect, common-sense, knocks into a cocked hat" (*LRA* 269). Other such statements from this period and later abound.[6]

In his emphasis on the primacy of emotion, Pound invokes a tradition in aesthetics that evolved ultimately from Aristotle and Longinus, along with Dante, Richard St. Victor, and other medieval theorists and has more recent antecedents in the critical writings of Coleridge, De Quincey, Poe, Emerson, Pater, De Gourmont, and Yeats.[7] Parallels may be found in the theories of Pound's contemporaries—notably in Eliot's concept of the objective correlative—and, naturally, in those of his successors.[8]

Correspondingly, among Pound's many ideas about the function and the proper procedures of criticism is an emphasis on "the feel of the thing." Early in 1919, for instance, he wrote to his father, "My music crit. all based on general feel of the thing. Good crit. probably is based on general feel. Rest all manner of one's exposition" (YC). In another statement of that year he concludes that "we test a translation by the feel, and particularly by the feel of being in contact with the force of a great original" (*LE* 271) and that translation is one form that criticism can take (*LE* 74). Much of Pound's criticism reflects this focus.[9] Ten years later he wrote in the preface to a still unpublished collected edition of his prose that one of his motivations is to provide a corrective example for current critical misdirection:

> At any rate I am contending that a method exists and that the method can cure certain forms of critical grossness, particularly that of letting in every grubby handed professor to muddle art with pseudo philosophy. The grossness of the vulgus is in never being able to isolate any subject of discussion. Incapable of treating philosophy as philosophy or art as art. (YC)

Pound's final pronouncement on the matter may very well be his description in Canto LIX of the Chi-King as "less a work of the mind than of affects / brought forth from the inner nature"—a description equally applicable to *The Cantos*.

But perhaps the most crucial formulation of Pound's critical and poetic practice is a statement published in the "Affirmations" series of 1915, midway between the earliest poems and the first volume of *The Cantos,* during the Vorticist period. The pressure, or energy, of emotion is objectified through its presentation in "pattern-units," which develop into an "arrangement of forms":

Intense emotion causes pattern to arise in the mind—if the mind is strong enough. Perhaps I should say, not pattern, but pattern-units, or units of design.
. . . The pattern-unit is so simple that one can bear having it repeated several or many times. When it becomes so complex that repetition would be useless, then it is a picture, an "arrangement of forms."
. . . One believes that emotion is an organiser of form, not merely of visible forms and colours, but also of audible forms. . . . Poetry is a composition or an "organisation" of words set to "music." By "music" here we can scarcely mean much more than rhythm and timbre. The rhythm form is false unless it belong to the particular creative emotion or energy which it purports to represent. (*SP* 374–75)

Ultimately, a structure based on an arrangement of such pattern-units has the potential to allow for great musicality and for a virtually unbounded inclusiveness; yet it can still sustain the volatility, intensity, and compression indigenous to shorter lyrics but impossible in traditional models of the long poem oriented according to the priorities of narrative, dramatic, or logical continuity. As this study will show, the juxtapositional succession and interaction of emotive pattern-units is a central organizational principle of Pound's poetic works and was already in its first, tentative stages of development in the earliest poems, "in 1904 or 1905." The long poem organized in this way has come to constitute, through Pound's and others' innovations, a genre that has recently been defined by Rosenthal and Gall as the modern lyric sequence: "a grouping of mainly lyric poems and passages, rarely uniform in pattern, which tend to interact as an organic whole. It usually includes narrative and dramatic elements, and ratiocinative ones as well, but its structure is finally lyrical" (9).

In its correspondence to Pound's own structural concepts and procedures, this formulation is particularly useful for an assessment of the continuity of Pound's work and the evolution of his practice in shaping extended structures. Other commentaries have made considerable advances in the explication of the poems and have pinpointed their crucial thematic continuities and philosophical orientation; the large debt owed to these studies in the following pages will be obvious. At the same time, it seems important to bear in mind that these modes of exegesis do not fully account for the kinds of poetic structuring we find in Pound's work. Indeed, an insistence upon rational modes of organization as the only valid bases of poetic unity can tend to limit our recognition of the patterns actually inherent in the works under examination and can dull our sensitivity to their virtual life as works of art. A basic premise that may help to avoid some critical detours to which the allusiveness and fragmentation of Pound's work can lead is that poetic structure depends not on narrative or other logical modes of development but on the succession of emotive qualities, their variations in intensity, and the relationships established among them (cf. Rosenthal and Gall 6–7).

What this study will undertake, then, is an approach to Pound's poems in terms of their emotive pattern-units (or "affects," in Rosenthal's and Gall's terminology—"radiant tonal centers of specific qualities, and intensities, of emotionally and sensuously charged awareness" [15]), and their use of these units as a basis of structure from the earliest short poems through the more extended and complex organization of later works. The attainment of an emotive coherence involved, for Pound, the exploitation of a number of structuring devices and a range of key, recurrent designs; an assessment of these strategies in the early poems, sequences, and collections of poems may provide fruitful approaches to later works whose structures defy analysis in terms of strictly discursive methods of organization—notably, *Hugh Selwyn Mauberley* and *The Cantos*.

The first chapter will examine in detail a number of Pound's early poems, not as a survey but rather as a means of suggesting the course of his development as it is apparent in his handling of traditional forms and his innovation of new ones according to the emotive curve of each poem as a whole. I have avoided the convenience of a chronological progression through the poems considered here and have arranged them instead in terms of their progression toward more open and improvisatory structures; as we shall see, that progression did not take place according to any neatly delineated chronology. Pound made extensive use, for instance, of traditional, highly regular or repetitive forms (or "symmetrical forms," in his terminology), not only in the early poems through *Ripostes* (1912), but also in some of his later work. Only certain traditional forms—such as the sonnet, the roundel, the canzone, and the villanelle—were used, however, and almost never without some adaptation. On the other hand, Pound also experimented with some open and fairly extended structures from the beginning of his poetic efforts, though usually without great success. In the aesthetic choices he made, even in the earliest poems, are to be found the seeds of the methods he was able to refine and to formulate precisely only at a later point in his development. A poem such as "Cino," for example, illustrates Pound's characteristic rehandling of inherited forms—in this case the dramatic monologue—and anticipates the organizational strategies of later, more elaborate achievements. Some of Pound's better-known structuring devices, such as the ideogrammic method, the use of subject rhyme, progression through alternating contrasts, and other modes of establishing rhythms of recurrence can also be observed in this and other early poems, including "Ver Novum," "Canzon: The Vision," "Δώρια," and "The Garden."

There are also experiments in the early works with groupings of poems as sequences, concurrent with the writing of the individual poems discussed in chapter 1; ultimately, the technique of the sequence is that of the single poem, though its demands are more rigorous and far more complex. Chapters 2 and 3 will discuss most of Pound's early sequences, and chapters 4 and 5 will explore the organization of his successive volumes of poetry, each of them carefully arranged in order to attain the integral dynamics of a unified "book-as-a-whole." The final chapter will consider the ways in which the organizational strategies that emerge in earlier works, beginning "in 1904 or 1905," contribute to the intricate patterning of *Hugh Selwyn Mauberley* and *The Cantos*.

1

"Revolt"

"Symmetrical Forms"

In many respects, Pound's earliest works clearly prefigure later developments. Even the opening strains of "Hilda's Book" (1905–7) and *A Lume Spento* (1908) offer the allusiveness, the sudden leaps of thought and feeling, the often unconventional use of syntax, and the polylingualism that are characteristic of later work. Most important, even where the early poems make extensive use of conventional forms for their structural basis, they show the same tendency as the later poems and the fully developed sequences to conceive of the completed work as an accretion or succession of smaller, lyrical pattern-units fused into an integral whole, though of course on a smaller scale and less consistently. Pound's adaptations of conventions also effect an integration of the music of the form *per se* with that of the poem's progression of thought and feeling. He seems to have recognized at an early stage in his development what he offered as advice much later (1917):

> Unless a man can put some thematic invention into *vers libre*, he would perhaps do well to stick to "regular" metres, which have certain chances of being musical from their form, and certain other chances of being musical through his failure in fitting the form. In *vers libre* his musical chances are but in sensitivity and invention. (*LE* 422)

Among the first of the traditional forms Pound experimented with is the sonnet. William Carlos Williams recalled that as an undergraduate, in 1902 or 1903, Pound wrote a sonnet daily and destroyed his productions at the year's end (53). Although relatively few of these were published, he persisted with the form and included some of the more successful results in nearly all of his volumes from *A Lume Spento* (1908) through *Ripostes* (1912). At their very best, these show an absorption of the sonnet tradition and a modification of its formal conventions in ways that forecast later orientations.

For instance, one of the earliest sonnets, "Fratello Mio, Zephyrus," left in manuscript in the "San Trovaso Notebook," fails in its unconvincing archaisms, its superficial medieval trappings, and its awkward inversions. Nonetheless, the least of its successes is its use of the Italian rhyme scheme, no simple feat in itself and one that shows the germinating technique of the later canzoni. There is also a shift in thought and affect after the twelfth line worked in from the English pattern, an adaptation characteristic of nearly all of Pound's sonnets:

> My wandered brother wind wild bloweth now
> Driving his leaves upon a dust-smit air.
> September, "proud-pied gold," that sang him fair
> With green and rose tint on the maple bough
> Sulks into dullard brown and doth endow
> The wood-way with an tapis rich and rare,
> And where King-Oak his panoply did wear
> The dawn doth show him but an shorne stave now.
>
> Me-seem'th the wood stood in its pageantry
> A castle galliarded to greet its queen
> That now doth bear itself but ruefully.
> A grief whereof I get no bastard teen
> Sith one there is doth bear the spring to me
> Despite the blast that blow'th the autumn keen.[1]

The rhythm of the emotive movement in the first twelve lines prepares for the optimistic declaration of the last two: moving contrapuntally across the conventional divisions of octave and sestet, the poem shifts in alternating couplets between the present and the past up until the final four lines, a *functional* elaboration of its central contrast between past splendor and present decay. The focus on "now," however, is reinforced by the repetition in lines 1 and 8 and by the poem's beginning and ending in the present. It is this alternation, along with an alternation between images of resplendent growth and images of autumn's decline—between suggestions of a concomitant depressiveness and a resurgent exuberance—that support the assertion of well-being at the end. This progression through alternating contrasts is a pattern that we will find recurring frequently in Pound's later sequences and volumes. Even at this early stage of his poetic development, then, we find Pound recasting inherited forms and adapting their conventions in terms of an arrangement of emotive pattern-units.[2]

The formal limits of the sonnet proved too confining rather quickly, however, and Pound came to think of the form as a degradation of the more intricate and more musical canzone, from which he believed the sonnet had been derived:

> The prestige of the sonnet in English is a relic of insular ignorance. The sonnet was not a great poetic *invention*. The sonnet occurred automatically when some chap got stuck in the effort to make a canzone. His "genius" consisted in the recognition of the fact that he had come to the end of his subject matter. (*LE* 168)

After experimenting with the sonnet's potential for expansion by arranging groups of sonnets into sequences, Pound ultimately abandoned it; one of the last sonnets, "Silet" (in *Ripostes*), bids farewell to the form in a cynical dismissal of both Pound's own and his predecessors' applications of it: "When it is autumn do we get spring weather. . . ?"

Even to the most cursory glance, "Silet" presents a departure from Pound's earlier sonnets. It is the only one, first of all, that strictly follows the English pattern, and gone are the syntactic inversions and the archaisms.[3] It seems as if Pound's dismissal of the form came only with a certain mastery of it.

The poem opens with a self-mocking parody of a Shakespearean commonplace (as in Sonnet 55) and turns, with the burlesque exclamation of the second line, to a comic pose of artless spontaneity:

> When I behold how black, immortal ink
> Drips from my deathless pen—ah, well-away!
> Why should we stop at all for what I think?
> There is enough in what I chance to say.

But this playfulness is abruptly dissipated by the futility introduced in the second quatrain: rhyme cannot recover what is lost or infuse new life amid decay. Line five, echoing the previous line, implies a broken relationship that cannot be mended by commemorating what once took place:

> It is enough that we once came together;
> What is the use of setting it to rime?
> When it is autumn do we get spring weather,
> Or gather may of harsh northwindish time?[4]

This quatrain focuses on the futility of attempting to recapture a time of fruition that has passed, for the relationship and for the woman addressed as well; human affairs follow natural courses that no amount of eulogizing can reverse, and the poem declines to struggle with the inevitable.

Like "Fratello Mio, Zephyrus," this sonnet's emotive pattern is built up through a contrasting alternation of past and present, fruition and decay, with less formal regularity but greater force beneath its exclamations, interrogatives, and repetitions. The fifth line, "It is enough that we once came together," becomes a refrain repeated twice in the third quatrain, as if attempting through its reiteration to hold down an impulse to at least remember the past, if it cannot be restored. The elements of nature here, like the lovers, have turned against each other and will not turn back; the past *is* finally irretrievable:

> It is enough that we once came together;
> What if the wind have turned against the rain?

It is enough that we once came together;
Time has seen this, and will not turn again;

And who are we, who know that last intent,
To plague to-morrow with a testament!

The refrain expands in the final couplet's irritable insistence on the truth of the lovers' present—"we, who know that last intent"—and its refusal to embitter the future by casting memory in rhyme. It invokes the silence of the title ("Silet"—"he is silent"), spurns the idea of preserving the past in the "black, immortal ink" of the opening line, and rejects even "what I chance to say." This circularity, a return to the poem's beginning, is another pattern that Pound explored extensively at every stage of his development and exploited fully in later poems and sequences. Here, it provides a sense of formal closure, yet the poem resonates beyond its formal boundaries through the paradox of its ending: despite its refusal to commemorate, it is itself "a testament!" Placed at the very beginning of *Riposte*, it leaves an opening for the poems that follow.

Though Pound moved on to other forms that provide a greater emotive range and flexibility and allow for further compression and a more predominantly organic mode of organization, the influence of his experiments with the sonnet is evident in some other poems that do not use a conventionally structured framework. "Occidit" and "In the Old Age of the Soul," for instance, in *Personae* (1909), and "Phasellus Ille" in *Riposte* can scarcely be construed as sonnets, yet their fourteen-line structures strongly suggest an adaptation of the sonnet's formal parameters.

Pound's experiments with other conventional forms also contributed significantly to the less formally-contained structures of later poems. In the "San Trovaso Notebook," for instance, we find a number of roundels that follow a pattern that Pound apparently invented, adapting the basic materials of earlier models. The form consists of two six-line stanzas using only two rhymes, with the first line of stanza 1 repeated in the first and last lines of stanza 2: *a(R)babab RabbaR*. Though this pattern is even more confining than the sonnet's and seems never to have been used again after this collection (it appears in *A Lume Spento*), the demands of its rhyme scheme, like those of the Italian sonnet, probably helped to develop the technique needed for the more challenging canzone. The use of repetition may also have contributed to the method of the sestinas, the villanelles, and some later works; it figures prominently in "free-verse" poems of the same period, such as "The Tree," and evolves into the elaborately orchestrated motivic repetition and variation of *The Cantos*. And the symmetry of the roundel is an important pattern in some later sequences.

In degree of complexity, Pound's canzoni stand midway between the containment of the sonnets and roundels and the agility and range of more organically organized structures. Their formal demands are more exacting than the sonnet's, yet their sustained repetition of a stanzaic pattern allows for more intricate motivic development and an emotive progression of greater depth.

"Canzon: The Vision" is representative of Pound's technique in this form. As his note tells us, the poem uses the framework of Arnaut Daniel's canzone "Sols sui que sai lo sobrafan quem sortz," consisting of six seven-line stanzas and a three-line coda (*CEP* 305). In Daniel's poem, rhyme is used not among the lines within each stanza, but between corresponding lines of every stanza, so that, for instance, the first lines of all six stanzas end with the same rhyme. In Pound's adaptation, one rhyme is allowed between the fourth and seventh lines of each stanza to impart a greater sense of internal unity. The result is that the stanzas, joined musically, can be developed in a way that permits them to resonate with one another rather than being bound together by a rhetorical framework, as in the sonnet. As Pound noted, Daniel "was the first to realize fully that the music of rhymes depends upon their arrangement, not on their multiplicity. Out of this perception he elaborated a form of canzone where stanza answers to stanza not boisterously, but with a subtle persistent echo" (*SR* 38).

In Pound's handling of the form, the shifts in context and direction of address from stanza to stanza are often sufficiently distant and abrupt as to make them almost independent units, linked by their rhyme and by contextual and motivic continuities. The first two stanzas present the "vision" itself, the memory of an encounter with a much-desired woman who emerges as if known instinctively, or as if in answer to an unconsciously urgent longing. The poem begins by addressing her directly, in the past, then gains in immediacy by shifting to present tense in its appeal for a return of proffered devotion:

I

When first I saw thee 'neath the silver mist,
Ruling thy bark of painted sandal-wood,
Did any know thee? By the golden sails
That clasped the ribbands of that azure sea,
Did any know thee save my heart alone?
O ivory woman with thy bands of gold,
Answer the song my luth and I have brought thee!

II

Dream over golden dream that secret cist,
Thy heart, O heart of me, doth hold, and mood
On mood of silver, when the day's light fails,
Say who hath touched the secret heart of thee,
Or who hath known what my heart hath not known!

O slender pilot whom the mists enfold,
Answer the song my luth and I have wrought thee!

These stanzas are closely interwoven not only by their shared imagery of the sea, the woman, and the gold and silver, but also by a subtle repetition and variation of motifs among them: "the silver mist," for instance, becomes "mood / On mood of silver," and the question "Did any know thee save my heart alone?" is answered by the assertion "Or who hath known what my heart hath not known!" Such devices, though highly artificial and melodramatic by comparison to Pound's later technique, do help to project a sense of heightening rapture.

The third stanza echoes the question and response of the first two and, of course, carries over their rhyme. But the imagery shifts to the radically disparate context of falconry, to convey a sense of love felt as inescapable in the swift, direct force of the hawk, which is in fact the force of illumination: "Lo! With a hawk of light thy love hath caught me." The stanza begins with meditative questioning, then returns to a direct address with the recognition that "in this vision is our past unrolled"—the past, presumably, of souls before incarnation.

The next two stanzas shift first to a recognition of the ritual quality of the *fin' amor* (McDougal 83), beside which the conventions of religious practice become almost contemptible, then to the inevitability and fulfillment of this sort of love, arising from the apparently predestined encounter.[5]

The final stanza turns to address the poem's jongleur, whose presence is unanticipated but conventional in the Provençal canzone (*SR* 31). Its urgency bespeaks the lover's desire for his sincerity as a "servant of Amor" to be recognized and brings to the poem as a whole the framework of the *alba* (*SR* 91). The dawn's illumination of the sky is presented as parallel to the illumination of the lover by his vision of the woman: "a background to the action, an interpretation of the mood; an equation, in other terms, or a 'metaphor by sympathy' for the mood of the poem" (*SR* 31). And the shift in mood in the coda—disappointment at the fading of night's vision—is projected through a very different image of dawn as "the golden scythe":

VII

O ivory thou, the golden scythe hath mown
Night's stubble and my joy. Thou royal souled,
Favour the quest! Lo, Truth and I have sought thee!

This shift is probably modeled on the form Pound adapted for his canzone from Daniel, who "often ends a canzone with a verset in different tone from the rest" (*LE* 111). Generally, while the poem owes much to its Provençal models, Pound uses the form to construct an idiosyncratic vision and to project the feeling behind it through a succession of contexts, each contained within a stanza focused by its central image. The resulting structure, as Kenner has observed of another poem, is to some degree "a constellation intrinsically and inevitably related to the inherent mood. . . . allotropic components into which the mood, the initial poetic 'idea,' has been fragmented" (*Poetry* 67).

"Canzon: The Vision" falls short of many of Pound's later works precisely to the extent to which its "constellation," blurred by the demands of the rhyme scheme and by a vocabulary too dated to realize the poem's affective potential, is not "intrinsically and inevitably related to the inherent mood." The principle of organization in terms of units carefully related to the central affect they project, however, is that of all of Pound's fully developed longer poems and sequences. It is particularly analogous, for instance, to the first part of *Hugh Selwyn Mauberley,* consisting of twelve sections and a coda ("Envoi"). The sections of that poem are also arranged as a "constellation" and linked by their emotive continuity and motivic recurrence, but they are less impeded by formal constraints.

Of course, Pound recognized the limitations of the canzone, and particularly those that its technical demands impose when it is used in English; it requires a "sacrifice of values" of the present, a sacrifice, at the least, of modernity of diction and sensibility:

As to the use of canzoni in English, whether for composition or in translation: it is not that there aren't rhymes in English; or enough rhymes or even enough two-syllable rhymes, but that the English two-syllable rhymes are of the wrong timbre and weight. . . .

Even so, it is not that one "cannot" use them but that they demand at times, sacrifice of values that had not come into being and were therefore not missed in Limoges, A.D. 1200. . . .

It is not that one language cannot be made to do what another has done, but that it is not always expeditious to approach the same goal by the same alley. (*LE* 168–69)

The form was clearly unsuitable for further development and could not retain in English the scope and depth it had had in Provençal at another time, amid a different cultural milieu. Nonetheless, the elemental structure of the canzone and even its conventions certainly contributed to the method of the more successful sequences. As Kenner has noted, "From 15 years' work with Arnaut's *canzoni* Pound learned not only to prefer crisp sounds to sleek, but to invest elaborate forms with spoken diction, to make it new, quickening conventions while passing through their forms, and to let structural analogies, reinforced by rhythm, do the work of assertion" (*Era* 374–75).

But Pound had already begun to explore and adapt another traditional form that allows for still greater emotive agility and expansiveness: the dramatic monologue. As Pound probably discovered in Browning's work, this form is inherently receptive to the projection of a contemporary awareness, while recovering some aspects of the past. And Pound's transformation of the monologue into the "persona" extended its capacity for presenting multiple perspectives almost simultaneously.

If one of Pound's aims in using the canzone was to revivify the craft and sensibility of Provence in the present—as he did several years later for Propertius— then the dramatic monologue was intrinsically better suited to the task. Instead of adopting a Provençal verse form, these poems present a focusing image of one or more dimensions of Provençal culture as Pound viewed it and as he conceived of its contemporaneity. Thus, there is an omnipresent modern aware-ness, continually modifying and augmenting the twelfth or thirteenth century frame of mind that the poem brings to life: "Eccovi! Judge ye! Have I dug him up again?"[6]

Because these poems are modeled more on Browning's method for resusci-tating the past than on the imagery and the versification that the pre-Raphaelites and Swinburne had used to that end, their diction is conversational and less obfuscated by archaisms. And their dynamics, unrestrained by an externally-imposed formal pattern, have the scope and flexibility of conversational or, in some cases, meditative association.

One of the earliest of the "personae," "Cino" (*A Lume Spento*), is character-istic of Pound's handling of the monologue. The poem opens with a cavalier exuberance and pride beneath its forceful exclamation of disgust and its dis-missal of women who have been left behind:

> "Bah! I have sung women in three cities,
> But it is all the same;
> And I will sing of the sun.

These opening three lines proleptically encapsulize the rest of the poem's move-ment, from dismissal to forced indifference (the singer's and, perhaps, the women's) and finally to an exultant "song of the sun." Prolepsis is another recurrent pattern in Pound's work.

Abruptly at the start of the next section the poem turns and addresses the women directly, condemning their profanation of the singer's gifts, "strange spells of old deity," for which they return only "ravens, nights, allurement." The effect is as if the women momentarily emerge through memory into actual presence, then recede as the poem returns to a third-person reference and the women become "the souls of song":

> Lips, words, and you snare them,
> Dreams, words, and they are as jewels,
> Strange spells of old deity,
> Ravens, nights, allurement:
> And they are not;
> Having become the souls of song.

This passage uses images in series much as the later Imagist poems do, though without quite the same immediacy. But the first line of the next section— "Eyes, dreams, lips, and the night goes"—presents a compressed yet highly vivid recollection of a night's (or nights') lovemaking and its transient thrill. The technique is used here almost as effectively as in the Imagist poems, four years before the formulation of their principles:

> Eyes, dreams, lips, and the night goes.
> Being upon the road once more,
> They are not.
> Forgetful in their towers of our tuneing
> Once for Wind-runeing
> They dream us-toward and
> Sighing, say "Would Cino,
> "Passionate Cino, of the wrinkling eyes,
> "Gay Cino, of quick laughter,
> "Cino, of the dare, the jibe,
> "Frail Cino, strongest of his tribe
> "That tramp old ways beneath the sun-light,
> "Would Cino of the Luth were here!"

Despite its repetition of denial—"They are not"—the passage swells with longing. Ostensibly, it is the women's inner longing for their singer, but because their thoughts are only imagined by him as they once more break through memory into present awareness, their words convey his own denied and displaced longing; indeed, he imagines them thinking of him first as "passionate Cino." In fact, their speech consists of a series of complimentary epithets, returning, as the singer might wish they would, the praises he has presumably sung for them.

The modulation to the women's imagined thoughts in the passage above takes place more quickly in the following section—as if impassioned imagination were gaining momentum—where the women are envisioned as hypocritically playing into the hands of a more powerful lover:

> Once, twice, a year—
> Vaguely thus word they:
>
> "Cino?" "Oh, eh, Cino Polnesi
> "The singer is't you mean?"
> "Ah yes, passed once our way,
> "A saucy fellow, but. . . .
> "(Oh they are all one these vagabonds),
>   "Peste! 'tis his own songs?
> "Or some other's that he sings?
> "But *you*, My Lord, how with your city?"

The complimentary epithets of the earlier section are transformed to a few scornful and dismissive characterizations—"A saucy fellow," "these vagabonds," "Peste!" (plague!)—as the women insultingly imply that Cino is not what he seems, a mere jongleur and not a troubadour. Of course, this takes place within a single emotive framework, one consciousness imagining the accusation, then reciprocating with a similar accusation—that "My Lord," "O Sinistro," is also not what he seems but really a bastard—which focuses contempt and disgust upon the rival:

> But you "My Lord," God's pity!
> And all I knew were out, My Lord, you
> Were Lack-land Cino, e'en as I am,
> O Sinistro.

In the following passage the imagined scenario is interrupted by the refrain, reiterating dismissal with an undertone of disappointment. Immediately, though, reminiscence and longing resurface in a brief image of "grey eyes" elliptically juxtaposed with none of the logical continuity or dramatic justification characteristic of the dramatic monologue *per se:*

> I have sung women in three cities.
> But it is all one.
> I will sing of the sun.
> . . . . eh? . . . . they mostly had grey eyes,
> But it is all one, I will sing of the sun.

The second repetition of the refrain combines its two lines into one, giving it a reinforced insistence. And the variation here from the earlier "it is all the same" to "it is all one" echoes the women's imagined dismissal, "Oh they are all one these vagabonds."

The poem ends with its song of the sun (or "cantico del sole"), which is colloquial and familiar, but hardly "facetious."[7] It is a song of praise and prayer to the sun, rather than to women, and its martial imagery and images of brightness and growth contrast sharply with the night setting of futile love that has been left behind. In his criticism of this period, Pound remarks that "myths are explications of mood" (*SR* 92), and this is precisely the function that Apollo serves in the closing song: in his track across the earth, he is the harbinger of an exuberant wanderlust that the song attempts to invoke:

> "'Pollo Phoibee, old tin pan you
> Glory to Zeus' aegis-day
> Shield o' steel-blue, th' heaven o'er us
> Hath for boss thy lustre gay!"

In its final lines, the song breaks into rhapsodic delight, focusing on images of the sky's beauty rather than women's, and "white birds" rather than the "ravens" used to characterize the women earlier in the poem:

> "I have sung women in three cities
> But it is all one.
>
> I will sing of the white birds
> In the blue waters of heaven,
> The clouds that are spray to its sea."

The repetition, variation, and inversion of images and motifs throughout "Cino" anticipate, with remarkable clarity, some of the central structural devices of *The Cantos* and its musical form.

To what degree does the poem's construction follow that of Browning's dramatic monologues? Certainly there are superficial resemblances in the colloquial diction and offhand manner of "Cino," and "more or less distinct echoes of Browning's versification and in particular of the Browningesque conversational rhythms" (De Nagy, *Poetry* 109), but here these are means to somewhat different ends from Browning's; they supply a flexibility and compression that allow for a rapid succession of disparate tonalities, such as the desire that erupts in the image of the "grey eyes" between insistent reiterations of dismissal. This is very unlike the more controlled modulations in Browning's poems but characteristic of Pound's technique both in other poems of this period and in much later work.[8]

Unlike Browning's monologues, Pound's "personae" are not constrained by dramatic presentation. In "Cino," a dramatic situation is suggested as a sort of "backdrop," but what dramatic movement there is consists only of an internal, imagined conflict (more in Donne's manner than Browning's) and is not shaped at all by an unfolding action or the presence of an implied auditor. Rather, the poem stands on its own as an independent verbal construct, a series of lyrical complexes that are built up through an associative succession from the opening dismissive exclamation to the closing rhapsody.

This is also essentially true of the other "personae" using the outline of the dramatic monologue, and apparent exceptions fail to hold upon closer examination. In "Marvoil," for instance, which De Nagy considers most dependent on dramatic structure, the apparent setting shifts completely in mid-course, so that the poem would collapse if it depended on any resources other than the emotive force of the language itself. Another poet might have supplied a narrative framework to support this type of shift, but all of this poem's "narrative" is in fact retrospection.

Other poems from the early period in which the presence of an implied auditor or dramatic situation is stronger than in "Cino" and "Marvoil"—"Fifine Answers," "Villonaud: Ballad of the Gibbet," and "Scriptor Ignotus," for instance—never rely upon these externally-imposed elements in the way that Browning's monologues characteristically do: "My Last Duchess," "Fra Lippo Lippi," "Pictor Ignotus" and other poems from the *Men and Women* group are cases in point. Certainly it is not far along the "rast-way" of poetic development from here to the abrupt shifts in focus, time, setting, and persona, unsupported by either a narrative or a dramatic framework, among successive *Cantos* or among pattern-units within each canto.

Pound's own remarks, contemporary with "Cino" and other "personae," point clearly to a lack of interest in drama, and the dramatic element in these lyrics is strongly qualified as "so-called" dramatic in his commentary to Williams on *A Lume Spento:*

> To me the short so-called dramatic lyric—at any rate the sort of thing I do—is the poetic part of a drama the rest of which (to me the prose part) is left to the reader's imagination or implied or set in a short note. I catch the character I happen to be interested in at the moment he interests me, usually a moment of song, self-analysis, or sudden understanding or revelation. And the rest of the play would bore me and presumably the reader. I paint my man as I *conceive* him. (*Ltrs* 3–4)

All but the lyrical component is relegated to appended notes and left to the reader's imagination. This process of stripping away dramatic props is clearly visible in Pound's deletion of superfluous quotation marks in early drafts of "Cino" and in the excision of the stage directions originally supplied in line 4: "(((meditating on women, what things they are, he saith:)))" (YC). The problem with drama, Pound later explained, is that "it does not rely on the charge that can be put into the word, but calls on gesture and mimicry and 'impersonation' for assistance" (*LE* 29). And despite Pound's many tributes to Browning's art, he also recognized that "Browning included a certain amount of ratiocination and of purely intellectual comment, and in just that proportion he lost intensity" (*LE* 419–20). As he recalled in 1915, "In my own first book I tried to rid this sort of poem of all irrelevant discussion, of Browning's talk *about* this, that and the other, to confine my words strictly to what might have been the emotional speech of the character under such or such crisis" (YC).

As we have seen, the result of Pound's reshaping of Browning's monologue—"the most vital form of that period in English" (*LE* 419)—by subordinating its dramatic element, is precisely the compression and intensification of an essentially lyrical structure: a movement among a series of charged moments of self-declaration, reminiscence, and imagined enactment of inner conflict. Ultimately, the "persona" itself is an encompassing image, an "intellectual and emotional complex": less a dramatic structure than a loosely jointed frame of consciousness showing no real character development, through which observation, meditation, and reflection, and their concomitant emotions, are projected. The organization of the poem around a construct of this sort breaks away from Browning's *dramatis personae* and anticipates Pound's Imagist formulations and practice by several years.

"The Shock and Stroke of It"

By contrast with the success of "Cino" and other short poems of this period, it is not difficult to locate the problems encountered in Pound's earliest attempts to adapt or abandon traditional models in order to "get a form" for a more extended work. Several poems have surfaced recently, dating from 1905–1907, that suggest the direction of these efforts. Although they are generally unsuccessful, some of them do use surprisingly ambitious, improvisatory structures that anticipate the solutions Pound discovered later. One of them, addressed to Robert Browning ("To R. B."), attempts a sort of tribute to the earlier poet combined with something like a formulation of poetics in quasi-mystical terms, in a manner that emulates Browning's monologues much more closely than the "personae" poems.[9] Another, "Ver Novum," is the lengthiest and most complex of the poems in "Hilda's Book."[10] Though it scarcely approaches the level of some of the poems discussed so far, its apparent significance among the earliest poems justifies a brief, attentive glance.

"Ver Novum" is certainly marred, as its sole commentator has noted, by "the rambling vagueness, the imprecise use of archaic or florid diction, the pseudo-Swinburnian syntax . . . and the abuse or absence of punctuation" (King 357), yet its failures suggest the direction of its ordering and provide an index for gauging the success of later sustained efforts. On the surface, the poem is a song of tribute (to Hilda Doolittle, presumably), yet from its outset it reveals a complex of interacting tonalities of which an appreciative and admiring affection is only one, perhaps subordinate strain:

> Thou that art sweeter than all orchards' breath
> And clearer than the sun gleam after rain
> Thou that savest my soul's self from death
> As scorpion's is, of self-inflicted pain
> Thou that dost ever make demand for the best I have to give
> Gentle to utmost courteousy bidding only my pure-purged spirits live:
> Thou that spellest ever gold from out my dross
> Mage powerful and subtly sweet
> Gathering fragments that there be no loss
> Behold the brighter gains lie at thy feet.

The woman addressed here represents a "Ver Novum" (or "new spring") not for the ebullient sense of rebirth that comes of a shared love, but as a sort of saviour from self destructive impulses—"from death / As scorpion's is, of self-inflicted pain"—who reveals the "gold from out my dross" and restores a sense of self-worth. Gratitude and praise are thus intertwined with a more prominent, self-deprecating pose, enforced by the anaphoric repetition "Thou that."

The following two strophes develop these central tonalities more elaborately, shifting from images of autumnal decay, "Mnemonic of spring's bloom and parody of powers / That make the spring the mistress of our earth," to a more lively series of sea images, which then veer off into abstract meditations on a realm

> Where all desire's harmony
>
> Tendeth and endeth in sea monotone
> Blendeth wave and wind and rocks most drear
> Into dull sub-harmonies of light; out grown
> From man's compass of intelligence,
> Where love and fear meet
> Having ceased to be.

This passage is notable not only for its use of the abstract diction Pound later eschewed ("dull sub-harmonies of light") and its imagery of light, which, better handled, becomes an important motif in the later poems, but also for its sudden juxtaposition of contexts—earth, sea, and a realm beyond human awareness—within two enjambed strophes. While the attempt is thwarted by obtrusive diction and abstractions, it does forecast later successes and distinguishes this poem from others in "Hilda's Book."

The poem regains its focus, somewhat, between the two final strophes, in a mystically abstract yet exuberant recollection of desire's fulfillment:

> By subtily incanted raed
> Every unfavorable and ill-happed hour
> Turneth blind and potently is stayed
> Before the threshold of thy dwelling place
>
> Holy, as beneath all-holy wings
> Some sacred covenant had passed thereby
> Wondrous as wind murmurings
> That night thy fingers laid on mine their benediction
> When thru the interfoliate strings
> Joy sang among God's earthly trees.

The muted yet poignant note of present longing introduced by this reminiscence is distanced once again in the final lines, which return to the laudatory and self-deprecatory strains of the beginning. But the current of feeling gains support here from the remembered contact that has momentarily been given voice:

> Yea in this house of thine that I have found at last
> Meseemeth a high heaven's antepast
> And thou thyself art unto me
> Both as the glory head and sun
> Casting thine own anthelion
> Thru this dull mist
> My soul was wont to be.
>
>   ("HB" 71–72)

The poem's irregular strophic pattern emulates the canzone form or, conceivably, the irregular choral movements of Greek drama. The lengths of lines and strophes and the positions of the rhymes are varied freely to suit the poem's "inner form," at times more successfully than in the poem's movement as a whole.[11]

"Ver Novum," despite a failure to sustain its central curve of feeling with directness and intensity, nonetheless represents, in its interweaving of tonalities, its abrupt shifts in imagery, its length, and its freedom of movement, a starting point for the methods Pound developed more fully and more successfully in his later extended poems. Though the work is not as finished as the sonnets and the "personae" of this period, it attempts a greater expansiveness and flexibility than the more conventional forms allow. But the technique needed for their attainment seems not to have been there yet: that awaited developments in diction and rhythm as well as structure.

As the poems so far discussed and their anticipation of later work seem to demonstrate, the development of Pound's technique and his formulated poetics does not follow the critically convenient notion of a directly linear progression: not only do we find rigorous quatrains in *Hugh Selwyn Mauberley,* a use of Provençal verse forms in "Langue d'Oc," and occasionally intact formal patterns, or traces of them, in *The Cantos,* but as we have seen, the technique of the "persona" and the agility and compression of later poems had already begun to emerge by 1908.[12] Even the principles of Imagism, as Kenner has shown, were not a new innovation in 1912 (*Poetry* 194). What, then, are the gradual but unmistakable differences and the apparent maturation (as Eliot observed [in "Metric"]) that we find between, say, "Hilda's Book" and *Lustra* (1916)?

The changes in Pound's technique during this period help considerably to explain the strategies he eventually adopted for structuring his more extended works. Among the first of these changes was a remaking of poetic diction:

What obfuscated me [in translating Cavalcanti] was not the Italian but the crust of dead English, the sediment present in my own available vocabulary—which I, let us hope, got rid of a few years later. You can't go round this sort of thing. It takes six or eight years to get educated in one's art, and another ten to get rid of that education.

Neither can anyone learn English, one can only learn a series of Englishes. Rossetti made his own language. I hadn't in 1910 made a language, I don't mean a language to use, but even a language to think in. (*LE* 193–94)

But this was more a matter of exorcising those elements unsuited to present purposes—"'good style' is 'language which renders its object accurately'"—than of replacing one set of vocabulary with another.[13] Analogously, Wordsworth's practice in *Lyrical Ballads* consisted of a shift in emphasis and proportion, rather than the replacement of one vocabulary with another. And his credo in the "Preface" also called for the "real language of men in a state of vivid sensation" (16), just as Pound insisted on "nothing that you couldn't, in some circumstance, in the stress of some emotion, actually say" (*Ltrs* 49).[14] To some degree, as we have seen in "Cino," for instance, the language and much of the craft of the later poems *were* available at an early date, if not the logopoeia and the lexical virtuosity. What was needed was a set of instruments that would allow an exploitation of available language to the fullest, without sacrificing either modernity or intensity (just as Wordsworth's principles could have gained no momentum had they been applied to the heroic couplets of his predecessors).

Indeed, poetic diction, meter, and form imply one another and function symbiotically in any given poem. When the relationship is organic, these dimensions of the poem are determined by their suitability to the emotive progression it embodies—its *inner* form; "alway the spirit within, shaping the form without" (YC):

You wish to communicate an idea and its concomitant emotions, or an emotion and its concomitant ideas, or a sensation and its derivative emotions, or an impression that is emotive, etc., etc., etc. You begin with the yeowl and the bark, and you develop into the dance and into music, and into music with words, and finally into words with music, and finally into words with a vague adumbration of music, words suggestive of music, words measured, or words in a rhythm that preserves some accurate trait of the emotive impression, or of the sheer character of the fostering or parental emotion. . . .

Also the "prose," the words and their sense must be such as fit the emotion. Or, from the other side, ideas, or fragments of ideas, the emotion and concomitant emotions of this "Intellectual and Emotional Complex" . . . must be in harmony, they must form an organism, they must be an oak sprung from an acorn. (*LE* 51)

And, as Pound was well aware, the connection between rhythm and diction is inextricable: "WHEN the metre is bad, the language is apt to be poor" (qtd. in Powell 7). The metrical refinements apparent even in some of the very first poems Pound eventually labeled "absolute rhythm": "to compose in the sequence of the musical phrase, not in sequence of a metronome" (*LE* 3); "a rhythm, that is, in poetry which corresponds exactly to the emotion or shade of emotion to be expressed" (*LE* 9).[15] Pound's effort "to get a form" beginning "in 1904 or 1905," then, was concomitantly a search for new ways of exploring language and shaping rhythms. It was, perhaps, a coordination of his discoveries in the use of language, rhythm and form, amid a number of often-noted influences between 1910 and 1912, that opened the way for the subtlety, depth, and range; the increased compression; and even the typographical nuances developed in poems from *Ripostes* through *The Cantos*.

What the change so often noted in *Ripostes* essentially consists of is a simplification and greater directness in diction and syntax in the volume as a whole; of course, these qualities are present in individual poems in earlier volumes. There is also an important shift in focus to the present, to contemporary dispositions, contemporary experience and contemporary *moeurs*, which, along with a more observational perspective, results in an objectified mode of presentation. But this, too, is not the product of any substantially new aesthetic reorientation, and its principles are in fact already anticipated in *The Spirit of Romance*. Pound there observes that "the preciseness of the description denotes . . . a clarity of imaginative vision" (105), and he commends Dante's insight in his "descriptions of the actions and conditions of the shades as descriptions of men's mental states in life, in which they are, after death, compelled to continue" (128). Even more crucial in terms of what lay ahead for Pound is the observation that "an epic cannot be written against the grain of its time: the prophet or the satirist may hold himself aloof from his time, or run counter to it, but the writer of epos must voice the general heart" (216).

We may conclude with Hugh Witemeyer, then, that "*Ripostes* is transitional, a volume of recapitulations and innovations, a conjunction rather than a caesura. There is no radical break in the line of Pound's development" (104–5). We have already seen how "Silet," at the start of the volume, retains connections with earlier works yet seems to open out toward new priorities, both in its playful use of the sonnet form and in its ironic refusal to commemorate the past. A close look at a few other poems in this volume and *Lustra* will help to locate Pound's subtle reorientations and their continuities with both earlier and later works.

"Δώρια" is a case in point, a poem that has received surprisingly little critical attention. From the first, this poem suggests the extent of Pound's refinement of absolute rhythm; a careful ear, assisted by the typographical arrangement, picks up the approximately equivalent but subtly varied lengths of time occupied by each of the shorter lines, and the approximate equivalence among the longer lines—"rhythm is a form cut into time" (*ABCR* 198):

> Be in me as the eternal moods
> of the bleak wind, and not
> As transient things are—
> gaiety of flowers.

> Have me in the strong loneliness
>   of sunless cliffs
> And of grey waters.
>   Let the gods speak softly of us
> In days hereafter,
>   The shadowy flowers of Orcus
> Remember Thee.

The affective movement of the poem is shaped by its climactic series of three prayerlike exhortations, each one launched by a long line and developed or modified in one or more shorter lines. The first projects a desire for the strength and intensity of feeling between lovers that will give their love the permanence of natural forces of decay, "the eternal moods / of the bleak wind." This is parenthetically contrasted in two short lines with the exuberance of a more delicate love that, like spring's growth, is also more fleeting. In this and the following unit, the poem invokes a completeness of interpenetration of lovers' spirits that will bind them even after death, among the "shadowy flowers of Orcus."

The final unit is hortatory, invoking the consideration of the gods, and, with increasing tenderness, it ends on a note of appreciative awe through which the poem is drawn into focus. The strains of appreciation and desire for continuity at its center beat back an underlying sense of helplessness against death's power. The urgency of this affect is conveyed through the successive exhortations, which build up an insistence like the patterns of repetition we have observed in other poems. It is carefully modulated, however, by the rhythms and by the "classicized values" that "tend to objectify the otherwise private feelings" (Alexander 79). The poem's construction in three main affective units and correspondingly, three sentences, prefigures the importance of triadic patterning in later sequences and volumes.

Thus the arrangement of pattern-units in "Δώρια," as well as their rhythmic definition, anticipate Pound's later method, especially that of *The Cantos*. A major difference, however, is the contextual containment of the poem's images, built into a vision very much like that of "The Coming of War: Actaeon." It also resembles that poem in the way it presents its starkly-cut otherworld through a paratactic crescendo of images that mount toward a central moment of charged awareness, then recede again toward a diminished conclusion: in "Δώρια" this begins with the line "In days hereafter," which removes the poem's vision from the present. In both poems the vision is extremely fleeting and there is no attempt to sustain it through abstract analysis, elaboration, or repetition, in the way a somewhat different vision is prolonged in "Canzon: The Vision." The later poems present the experience of the vision itself, with its immediacy and its transience, and without comment. The aesthetic involved here reflects, in part, a trend that is commonly traced back to Pater; more important are the ways in which these poems validate Pound's concurrent aesthetic formulations and the implications they have for his later practice.[16]

"Δώρια" was first published a few months before the formulation of the Imagist manifesto, "A Few Don'ts," in "the spring or early summer of 1912" (*LE* 12) and forecasts its precepts rather fully. First, it involves "direct treatment of the thing" and uses "absolutely no word that does not contribute to the presentation": all of its components participate in the experience that attains its virtual life and its affective force in the poem. And, as observed earlier, its rhythms are composed "in the sequence of the musical phrase" (*LE* 3).

"Δώρια" is also strongly visual, although, as Schneidau notes, Imagism does not involve a predominantly visual aesthetic (*Image* 8); the poem illustrates, rather, a practice Pound later formulated as "phanopoeia, which is a casting of images upon the visual imagination" (*LE* 25). The implication, of course, is that the image, "an intellectual and emotional complex in an instant of time," is not itself visual but *can be* cast "upon the visual imagination." "The image is itself the speech" (*GB* 88): the pattern-unit of thought and feeling, implicit in Pound's method from the beginning and central to the organization of his organically structured poems. All other dimensions of the poem grow inevitably out of its arrangement of images: "rhythm, sense-effect and structure must correspond to their guiding insight and emotion."[17] As Bornstein also notes, the Imagist poem uses "natural detail to capture and evoke emotion without talking directly about the emotion itself" (*Consciousness* 34). Imagism, then, entails an integrity and discipline of form, and not merely an adherence to a set of visual formulae. The result, ideally, is an organically conceived and structured work whose development, if any, must correspond to a progression of thought and feeling, of *inner* form, cannot be effected through rhetorical—or even visual—elaboration, and cannot be in response to the demands of an externally imposed, conventional framework. Hence Pound was careful to distinguish between poems whose inner form can be embodied in a "symmetrical" pattern, and those whose structure must be entirely self-determined:

> *Form.*—I think there is a "fluid" as well as a "solid" content, that some poems may have form as a tree has form, some as water poured into a vase. That most symmetrical forms have certain uses. That a vast number of subjects cannot be precisely, and therefore not properly rendered in symmetrical forms. (*LE* 9)

It is not difficult to see how poetic structures determined by "an intellectual and emotional complex" can be capable of tremendous compression and resonance, or how a succession of such complexes can supply a structure for an extended poetic work without sacrificing the mobility and intensity of thought and feeling traditionally associated with the shorter lyric.

To employ these pattern-units in an extended work, however, requires some mode of establishing connections among them. The imposition of a conventional narrative or dramatic framework would entail the violation of the image's organic integrity and the compromise of precisely those values of mobility and intensity that it is designed to preserve. The alternative that Pound rediscovered, a juxtapositional succession, was already available in the English tradition, as Pound knew (e.g., *SR* 157–62) and as others have demonstrated; but Pound went elsewhere and even further back in time and recognized it, for instance, in "Ibycus and Liu Ch'e" and Dante (*GB* 83).[18] In Pound's hands, this results in the extraordinary compression of poems using what he called "a form of super-position" (*GB* 89), which he came upon while trying to "get a form" for "In a Station of the Metro":

In a Station of the Metro

The apparition of   these faces   in a crowd;
Petals   on a wet, black bough.[19]

Two discrete units are superposed, one against the other; the emotive intensity and resonance attained through this procedure are striking. But what is most new about "In a Station of the Metro" is Pound's recognition that it is a complete poem and that its technique could be used as the *basis* of poetic structure. We have already encountered similar structures in earlier poems: in "Eyes, dreams, lips, and the night goes," for instance, the paratactic halves of the line function in much the same way as the two lines of "In a Station of the Metro." The effect is somewhat weaker, however, because "and the night goes" is not as sharply defined (visually or emotively), and because this complex is modified by all that precedes and follows it in "Cino."

The corollary of superposition, the ideogrammic method, has also been encountered before—in the women's series of complimentary epithets for Cino, for instance, through which their imagined desire and admiration are projected. This consists, as Pound has defined it, "of presenting one facet and then another until at some point one gets off the dead and desensitized surface of the reader's mind, onto a part that will register" (*GK* 51). The principle of this technique is essentially that of superposition *en large;* it allows for greater expansiveness because it presents not merely two structural "planes in relation" but a series of them, "one facet and then another," joined and clarified through their juxtaposition. As Kenner notes, "things explain themselves by the company they keep. Individual opacities reach upward towards an intelligible point of union" (*Poetry* 220). This method can be viewed in operation in another poem, "The Garden," from *Lustra*. The poem presents an encounter with a contemporary woman, and its approach to her is both pointedly satirical and more than compassionate. The first section focuses on her movement through a perspective at once fascinated and revolted:

Like a skein of loose silk blown against a wall
She walks by the railing of a path in Kensington Gardens,
And she is dying piece-meal
    of a sort of emotional anaemia.

With a flexibility that the formal patterns and archaisms of much of Pound's
earlier verse did not quite allow, each of these four lines presents another facet
of the woman's character. In the first half of line 1, the delicate interplay of *s, k,*
and *l* sounds projects the lilting elegance of her appearance, then is violently
ruptured by the perception of her helplessness, "blown against a wall."

The second line projects the compulsive quality of her movement, keeping
in line "by the railing of a path"—not the majestic movement of "Kung walked"
(Canto XIII) but a diminutive step, without vitality or self-direction. The next
two lines reveal two more facets: she is not simply dying, but dying "piece-
meal," since she can do nothing fully, and her malaise is a hybrid, cultivated
deficiency, "a *sort of* emotional anaemia."

The next section enters decisively, yet unobtrusively, into her point of
view, without the stage directions and the quotation marks that announce a
similar shift in "Cino." Another poet might have written "And round about *her*
is a rabble," but we are given the scene through her eyes:

And round about there is a rabble
Of the filthy, sturdy, unkillable infants of the very poor.
They shall inherit the earth.

All that she sees is in contrast with herself: "a rabble" lacking her social correct-
ness, "filthy, sturdy" and "unkillable," not, like her, delicate and "anaemic."
Ironically—from the point of view of the meek—these, rooted in the earth
("filthy"), shall inherit it.

With the barbed pun of the next line (the "end of breeding"), the poem
returns to an observer's perspective, still sharply analytical yet with a mounting
sense of the woman's desperation and a response that moves beyond empathy,
toward action:

In her is the end of breeding.
Her boredom is exquisite and excessive.
She would like some one to speak to her,
And is almost afraid that I
    will commit that indiscretion.

                                                      (*P*)

The break in the final line, "I / will commit," pivoting with its emphasis on
"will," supplies a contrast between the observer's responsiveness and the woman's

anaemia, and suggests a desire to help which she is equipped to perceive only as an "indiscretion." Like another in *Hugh Selwyn Mauberley,* "No instinct has survived in her / Older than her grandmother / Told her would fit her station."

The ideogrammic method is at work not only in the portrayal of the woman through juxtaposed facets of her character as observed in her movement, but also in the poem's presentation of an encounter between two people through the juxtaposition of their perspectives. This serves both to clarify those perspectives and to introduce the poem's central current of empathy. As the full sentence from which the epigraph was taken implies—*"Mon âme est une enfante en robe de parade"*—there is a moment of identification with the woman suggested at the center of the poem. If "The Garden" dismisses her, it does not do so lightly, for she represents an aesthetic of refinement out of existence, as it were, into exclusion, with which some of Pound's early works have an affinity, and with which we find "Mauberley" still struggling in 1920.

The precision of characterization and feeling in this poem and the completeness, depth and complexity of its presentation testify to a strength of vision that, as Pound said of Dante's, "comes from the attempt to reproduce exactly the thing which has been clearly seen" (*SR* 126). This and Pound's evolving ability, at his best, to suit the structure of the poem to the inner form of its vision are what bring "Cino" and "En Bertrans" to life, recapture departed "souls of blood" in "The Return" and "The Coming of War: Actaeon," and recreate in the present the mind and world of Niccolò d'Este and the lotus-eaters, among many, in the early *Cantos*—they are, in short, what give

> For shadows—shapes of power
> For dreams—men.

2

"Toward the Long Poem": Pound's First Sequences

"To Get a Form"

Though Pound's early adaptations and innovations of forms for single poems were often successful, none of them yielded an encompassing structure with the expansiveness, inclusiveness, and flexibility needed for an extended work. There were certainly attempts to devise a suitable form, as we have seen in "Ver Novum"; and the personae poems, along with various tributes to Browning, suggest an inclination to use Browning's monologue form as the basis for a long poem. Pound began with this mode again in the Ur-Cantos, but it proved untenable then as earlier. Other attempts at a unified longer poem in a satiric vein, in "Redondillas" (1911) and "L'Homme Moyen Sensuel" (1917), also failed to provide a suitable starting point.

Nor was there, "in 1904 or 1905," any current model of a single, integral structure adaptable to Pound's purposes, no form "elastic enough to take the necessary material." There was, however, a long-standing practice of building up extended works from smaller units, which seems to have arisen alongside of, or perhaps in reaction to, the conventions of classical epic. This procedure can be traced back at least as far as the Alexandrians, as Neil Fraistat suggests (*Book* 6), perhaps including Theocritus' *Idylls*.[1] It became rather common in Roman poetry: Virgil's *Eclogues*, Horace's *Satires, Odes,* and *Epodes*, Propertius's *Elegies*, and Ovid's *Amores, Heroides*, and *Metamorphoses* are major examples of obvious interest to Pound.[2] He would also have been attentive to later European developments, notably Dante's *La vita nuova* and Petrarch's *Canzoniere*, which Fraistat describes as "a strikingly flexible structural model in which—through a series of heterogeneous short poems written at different times—a poet could maintain shifting, even contradictory, perspectives and, above all, an openness before experience" (*Book* 9).

The individual units of which the larger work in this tradition is composed are usually lyrical, and, in early instances at least, while aspiring to epic scope they often explicitly oppose lyrical priorities to those of the epic:

> Yet you ask on what account I write so many love-lyrics
> And whence this soft book comes into my mouth.
> Neither Calliope nor Apollo sung these things into my ear,
> My genius is no more than a girl.[3]

The first major exemplar of this method of constructing a long poem in English is perhaps Chaucer, and continuing debates over the unity, and hence the success, of the *Canterbury Tales* (e.g., Baldwin) are remarkably similar to discussions of the same issues in Pound's *Cantos*. While the *Tales* are generally considered to be primarily dramatic, it could be argued that, like Ovid's *Metamorphoses*, they are quasi- or mock-epic with a strong lyrical component. Later English poets, drawing on classical and continental precedents, built on predominantly lyrical foundations, often employing contextual, philosophical or narrative frameworks, or else achieving a surface unity by using a stanzaic or other formal pattern throughout, to support the structure of the whole; the sixteenth-century sonnet sequence is an obvious example. Notable successors in this practice include Spenser's *The Shepherd's Calendar* and *Complaints*, Jonson's *The Forest* and *Under-wood*, Herrick's *Hesperides*, Herbert's *The Temple*, Smart's *Rejoice in the Lamb*, Dryden's *Fables*, and Blake's *Songs of Innocence and of Experience*.[4] In *The Poem and the Book*, Fraistat has comprehensively demonstrated that the English Romantics were also acutely conscious of the arrangement of their poems in published volumes, and he has examined in detail the thematic coherence of *Lyrical Ballads,* Keats's *Lamia* volume, and Shelley's *Prometheus Unbound, with Other Poems.*

Indeed, a growing disdain for the conventional epic's narrative, dramatic, and rational modes of progression during the nineteenth century helped to launch a proliferation of long poems built from lyrical units or components of varied genre and organized increasingly in terms of lyrical structure. As early as 1817, for instance, Coleridge concluded in the *Biographia Literaria* that "a poem of any length neither can be, nor ought to be, all poetry." He resolved the issue, without exploring its implications very far, by proposing that the remaining parts of the poem "must be preserved *in keeping* with the poetry." These parts must sustain "a more continuous and equal attention than the language of prose aims at" (173). In the 1830s, while recognizing the "ballad delineations" of the *Iliad* and consequently questioning its unity, Carlyle championed the poem as a model of organicism:

> This all-producing earth knows not the symmetry of the oak which springs from it. It is all beautiful, not a branch is out of its place, all is symmetry there; but the earth has itself no conception of it, and produced it solely by the virtue that was in itself. So is the case with Homer.[5]

It is precisely this conception of the long poem, built up from smaller units yet functioning as an organic whole, that heralds the emergence of the modern lyric sequence, a genre well established even before the close of the nineteenth century.

In America, the organic nature of poetry was propounded first by Emerson in "The Poet" (1844), and Poe, confronting the intractable consequences of lapses in poetic intensity that he considered inevitable in the conventional long poem, concluded that

> a long poem does not exist. I maintain that the phrase, "a long poem" is simply a flat contradiction in terms.
>
> I need scarcely observe that a poem deserves its title only inasmuch as it excites, by elevating the soul. The value of the poem is in the ratio of this elevating excitement. But all excitements are, through a psychal necessity, transient. That degree of excitement which would entitle a poem to be so called at all, cannot be sustained throughout a composition of any great length. ("The Poetic Principle" 91; cf. Rosenthal and Gall 7–8)

In England again, picking up from Poe's observation of the transience of all excitements, Pater asked, in 1873, "How shall we pass most swiftly from point to point, and be present always at the focus where the greatest number of vital forces unite in their purest energy?" (158).

For the modern writer of an extended poetic work, then, the problem was "to get a form" that could sustain the intensity of the transient moment of excitement in the poem by passing "most swiftly from point to point" of charged awareness. While the problem may have a specific fascination for American poets—certainly an American, Whitman, offered the first major example of a practical solution—it is not specifically an American problem, as some recent studies have implied.[6] Indeed, the first *critical* solutions seem to have come from the French, who took note of Poe's ideas more quickly than the Americans and the English. Mallarmé's "Crisis in Verse," for instance, seems almost to answer Poe and Pater directly while setting forth principles of structure now considered characteristic of the modern long poem:

> From each theme, itself predestined, a given harmony will be born somewhere in the parts of the total poem and take its proper place within the volume; because, for every sound, there is an echo. Motifs of like pattern will move in balance from point to point. . . . Everything will be hesitation, disposition of parts, their alternations and relationships—all this contributing to the rhythmic totality. . . . (41)[7]

These critical conclusions, from Coleridge to Mallarmé, demonstrate a growing modern aversion to epic conventions, but there is no universal critical agreement about the reasons for it. Certainly, reorientations in response to technological and scientific developments, shifting spiritual and cultural attitudes, and the consequences of these for the individual psyche were all contributing factors.[8] It is not surprising, in any case, that modern writers of the long poem would find recourse in the lyric, with the private sensibility at its focus rather than an idealized hero (parallel, in some respects, to Romantic reactions against eighteenth-century trends). The alternate tradition of the long poem built up from smaller units was also available as a suitable means of avoiding epic discursiveness; from the mid-nineteenth century onward, this became the dominant form of the long poem and was developed increasingly in terms of lyrical principles of organization. It is now generally agreed that "the most distinctive feature of the modernist long poem is the desire to achieve epic breadth by relying on structural principles inherent in lyric rather than narrative modes" (Altieri 653), and consequently in present criticism "the theory of the lyric, rather than being antithetical to any notion of the long poem, indeed is the only theory of the long poem" (Riddel 466).

It is not quite that simple, however. The lyric obviously does not become a long poem through elaboration or extension alone, yet despite critical concurrence over the lyrical basis of the long poem during the last 140 years, very few theories have been offered to account for the evolution and structure of the modern form. Perhaps the most comprehensive of these is the conception of the poetic sequence:

> Intrinsically—since it is made up of short and independent, yet interacting, units—the sequence solves the problem of writing a successful long poem by meeting the objections so cogently raised by Poe. For one thing, the form militates against that loss of sustained intensity which Poe deplored as inherent in long continuous works. For another, its surface fragmentation prevents our reading poetry as primarily narrative, discursive or self-expressive. Ideally, the changes of tonal key, perspective, formal surface, and context from unit to unit commit a sequence to lyrical rather than extraneous structure. (Rosenthal and Gall 173)

This view of the modern long poem's organization helps considerably to locate the precedents available to Pound "in 1904 or 1905" and corresponds precisely both to his conclusions about the structure of traditional models and to the principles underlying his critical formulations and his practice.

One of the most important exemplars of the modern long poem for Pound was Whitman, whose "Song of Myself" directly answers both Emerson's call for organicism and Poe's insistence on sustained intensity as the primary requisite of poetry. It also provided a model of an extended poem whose language, rhythm, and structure worked together in directions Pound's own poems were ultimately moving in. Though Whitman suffered by comparison with Villon in *The Spirit of Romance,* Pound had already acknowledged him as a "spiritual father" and recognized that "like Dante he wrote in the 'vulgar tongue', in a new metric. The first great man to write in the language of his people" (*SP* 145–46).[9]

The structure of "Song of Myself" is essentially determined by "the interaction among its major fields of affect (affirmation, confrontation of the negative, ecstatic experience)." From the outset, the poem establishes emotive patterns and motifs whose repetition, variation, and interplay help to attain its final balance and to reinforce its unity. There are strong parallels here with Pound's technique in *The Cantos* and, as Rosenthal and Gall conclude, "Pound's method is indeed a proliferation of Whitman's" (29–30). Of course, this is not an advancement of Whitman as a primary influence on Pound or of "Song of Myself" as another model for *The Cantos,* but it is clear that Whitman indeed "broke the new wood" and began to demonstrate the possibilities that lay open for the sculpting of the modern long poem.

Other precedents for long poem construction through the grouping of shorter poems and passages were also available before the turn of the century. These include, to name but a few, Tennyson's *In Memoriam* (1850) and *Maud* (1855), Meredith's *Modern Love* (1862), Rossetti's *House of Life* (1870), W. E. Henley's "In Hospital" (1888), Housman's *A Shropshire Lad* (1896),[10] and, among the nineties poets, Lionel Johnson's "In Memory" (1892), Dowson's "After Verlaine" (1899), and Symons's "Amoris Victima" and "Studies in Strange Sins." Yeats's *The Wind Among the Reeds* (1899), a volume whose influence Pound frequently acknowledged, may also have suggested ways of building a number of discrete, shorter pieces into an integral collection. Browning also produced several extended works of this type, including *Sordello* (1840), *Men and Women* (1855), *Dramatis Personae* (1864), and *The Ring and the Book* (1869). As Bornstein has convincingly shown, even "Browning's earliest collection of mature verse, *Dramatic Lyrics* [1842], displays considerable architectonic skill in its deployment of paired poems punctuated by individual, free-standing ones" ("Arrangement" 273). Not all of these works are successful as sequences, and most are restrained in some way from reaching their full potential as integrated works, whether by brevity, formal regularity, philosophical, contextual, narrative or dramatic frameworks, or by a failure to find a language for the poem that is "charged with meaning to the utmost possible degree" (*LE* 23). Along with *Sordello, The Ring and the Book* seems to have been among the most important of these works for Pound in some respects, considering especially its attempt, parallel to that of *The Cantos,* to locate truth through a juxtaposed series of perspectives (cf. Schneidau, "Cross-Cuts" 509).

But Pound looked back much further and found important precedents for long poem structure in two works often considered paradigms of the classical epic and its European progeny: the *Odyssey* and *La Divina Commedia.* His commentary offers a somewhat idiosyncratic conception of them, however, and places them firmly in the other tradition that has just been described—of long poems built on essentially lyrical principles. In *The Spirit of Romance,* for instance, he concludes that "the *Divina Commedia* must not be considered as an epic; to compare it with epic poems is usually unprofitable. It is in a sense lyric, the tremendous lyric of the subjective Dante" (153). And writing much later to W. H. D. Rouse, he remarks that he cannot translate the *Odyssey* because

> . . . when I do sink into the Greek, what I dig up is too concentrative; I don't see how to get unity of the *whole*.
> I suspect neither Dante nor Homer *had* the kind of boring "unity" of surface that we take to be characteristic of Pope, Racine, Corneille. (*Ltrs* 274)

Though later in this letter he advises Rouse to focus on the *movement* of the narrative in his prose translation, what he extols most in the poem is its lyric quality, its "raw cut of concrete reality combined with the tremendous energy, the contact with the natural force" (273) and "the indication of tone of voice and varying speeds of utterance. In that, Homer is never excelled by Flaubert or James or any of 'em" (298). A narrative framework was not only superfluous for Pound, but perhaps obstructive as well:

> I would almost move . . . to the generalization that plot, major form, or outline should be left to authors who feel some inner need for the same; even let us say a very strong, unusual, unescapable need for these things; and to books where the said form, plot, etc., springs naturally from the matter treated. When put on ab exteriore, they probably lead only to dullness, confusion or remplissage or the "falling between two stools." (*LE* 397–98)

Finally, Pound's editing of *The Waste Land* clearly demonstrates his adeptness at achieving intensity and immediacy in a unified, extended work partly through the *removal* of its narrative links. It was no doubt with reference to Poe's dictum that poetic intensity "cannot be sustained throughout a composition of any length," and to the modern tradition of the long poem which followed, that Pound told Eliot *The Waste Land* is "let us say the longest poem in the English langwidge" (*Ltrs* 169).

The Cantos is a still more far-reaching achievement in many respects, length the least of them; but the technique which made that work possible began developing at a very early date. As observed in chapter 1, Pound's early poems show a tendency even when using traditional forms to conceive of the work in terms of emotive pattern-units brought together in an arrangement of forms determined by the initial or controlling emotion of the poem or passage. By 1913, Pound's method was formulated clearly enough for him to affirm in a letter to Amy Lowell, after censuring her use of narrative, that "*my unity is an emotional unity.*"[11] This was restated in Vorticist terms in 1915: "An organisation of forms expresses a confluence of forces. These forces may be the 'love of God,' the 'life-force,' emotions, passions, what you will" (*EPVA* 7). The corresponding mode of poetic organization, based on a succession of emotive qualities rather than logical sequence, comports with a particular kind of mental process:

> My mind, such as I have, works by a sort of fusion, and sudden crystalization, and the effort to tie that kind of action to the dray work of prose is very exhausting. One should have a

vegetable sort of mind for prose. I mean the thought formation should go on consecutively and gradually, with order rather than epigrams. (YC)

Working by "fusion, and sudden crystalization," the result is an inherently fragmented structure proceeding through a sense of felt rightness in the succession of parts and their relations. This is implicit in Pound's method of arranging poems and sequences in terms of an emotional unity according to principles of lyrical structure, as Rosenthal and Gall have fully demonstrated. Hence in *The Cantos*—and much earlier—we are presented with a kind of structure that "maintains the separateness of its fragments at the same time that it suggests their relationship" (Malkoff 52). The resulting technique corresponds to what Kenneth Burke later called "qualitative progression," an alternative to proceeding by syllogistic or chronological means: "Instead of one incident in the plot preparing us for some other possible incident of plot . . . the presence of one quality prepares us for the introduction of another. . . . We are prepared less to demand a certain qualitative progression than to recognize its rightness after the event" (*Counter-Statement* 124–25). This can involve a structure based on "bold juxtaposition of one quality created by another, an association in ideas which, if not logical, is nevertheless emotionally natural" (39).

We have already had a glimpse of some of the structuring devices and the patterns of arrangement Pound developed for establishing relations among the parts of individual poems. These same devices are used to reinforce the emotional unity among the poems gathered into sequences and volumes. To briefly recapitulate: first, the juxtaposition or superposition of units, obviously the dominant organizational principle of "In a Station of the Metro," was also present earlier in the discontinuous emotive eruptions of "Cino" and elsewhere. This becomes, in an extended work, the ideogrammic method, noted in "Cino," "Canzon: The Vision," and "The Garden," and, less clearly, even in "Ver Novum." Several poems examined illustrate the principle of movement through alternating contrasts, resulting in a hierarchy or balance, most notably "Fratello Mio, Zephyrus." The later sonnet "Silet" uses both the principle of recurrence, or repetition, and circularity in its highly charged reference, in the closing lines, to its beginning. The establishment of motifs whose echoes, repetitions, inversions, and variations can impart both unity and musicality to an extended work is a prominent technique in "Cino," and the related device of antiphonal call and response is used in that poem and more clearly in "Canzon: The Vision."

Finally, "Cino," "Δώρια," and "The Garden" all use, in different ways, the technique Pound labeled "Unity of Image" (*Tr* 237), which he discovered in the Japanese Noh plays and incorporated into his conception of Vorticism, though he had employed it extensively before then. This consists primarily of the construction of a central, elaborate, emotional and intellectual complex that gathers the rest of the poem's materials around it. It can take the form of a loosely defined frame of consciousness labeled "Cino," for instance, or a particularly intense though understated projection of tenderness at a key moment in a poem that draws much of its strength from austerity; or the revelation of character of a woman encountered in Kensington Gardens.[12] As Miner notes, if the image is repeated in an extended work it can function as an "organizing archetype," where similar instances of the same image are brought together, the basis of Pound's subject-rhymes: "we may name a dominant mountain, for example, what we will—Fujiyama, Vesuvius, or Taishan" (*Japanese* 144).

Of course, all of these organizational strategies are dependent upon selection and emphasis, for "it is only by selection and emphasis that any work of art becomes sufficiently interesting to bear long scrutiny" (*EPVA* 79). Only certain key details are presented, for instance, in "The Garden"; they are what Pound called "luminous details." "Any fact is, in a sense, 'significant.' Any fact may be 'symptomatic,' but certain facts give one a sudden insight into circumjacent conditions, into their causes, their effects, into sequence, and law. . . . The artist seeks out the luminous detail and presents it. He does not comment" (*SP* 22–23). This principle is applied extensively to the materials of *The Cantos,* but its function is primarily poetic even where ideas and facts are involved; selection and accentuation help to transform document and belief into "a verbal statement of emotional values." "Poetry is the statement of overwhelming emotional values" (*LRA* 132, 269).

Clearly, the organizational principles developed in these individual early poems are precisely those needed for constructing an extended work, an "arrangement of forms," out of shorter poems and passages without sacrificing intensity, mobility or elasticity. As the following discussion in this chapter and in chapter 3 will show, these techniques figure prominently in Pound's sequences from the first and least successful groupings through the virtuoso arrangements of *The Cantos.* The balance of the present chapter will examine the structures of the shorter, early sequences written from 1908 through 1911.

"An Emotional Unity":
From the "San Trovaso Notebook" through *Canzoni*

While Pound's first sequences often fail to realize their full potential for the same reasons many of the early poems do—obtrusive archaisms, clotted rhythms, and the constraints of imposed conventional frameworks, for instance—and rarely achieve anything like the scope and flexibility of later works, they nonetheless show greater emotive breadth than most of the individual poems of the same period.

There are actually several sequences in Pound's early collections that have been relatively neglected and, understandably, overshadowed by later achievements. The "San Trovaso Notebook" (1908), for instance, includes three sequences, none of them outstanding but none without its particular advancement. "Piazza San Marco" is perhaps the most successful of these, partly as the result of a flexibility gained through variations of form, diction, tone, and perspective among its three distinct but interconnected poems. In its direct address to Shakespeare ("Master Will"), the first poem combines spirited tribute with an easy, colloquial comaraderie, carried rather buoyantly by the trochaic rhythms:

[I]

> Master Will, so cussed human,
> Careless-clouted god o' speech,
> Is there twist o' man or woman
> Too well-hidden for thy reach?
>
> Diadems and broken roses,
> Wind and Tritons loud at horn,
> Sack-stains half thy screed discloses,
> Th'other half doth hold the morn.

The opening two lines introduce the sequence's first paired opposition, one of Pound's most common structuring devices: "Master Will" is both "cussed human" and a "god o' speech," human in his works' sympathies and flaws yet superhuman in their verbal power and insight. His comprehension of "twist o' man or woman" evolves into the almost Imagist pairings of the second stanza, "diadems and broken roses," triumph and despair, human forces and the forces of nature.[13]

The second poem shifts immediately and dramatically: the admiration of poem I is dropped in the first line with a turn from second-person to third-person address, and a switch to iambic pentameter provides a sense of diminished tension and serves as a transition to the still more regular movement of the third section. This is characteristic of Pound's sequences: their juxtapositions are often quite sharp, yet each unit is prepared for in some way by preceding units and resonates with what precedes and follows it.

[II]

> Some comfort 'tis to catch Will Shaxpeer stealing.
> All bards are thieves save Villon, master thief,
> Who pilfered naught but wine and then, wide reeling,
> Lilted his heart out, Ballad-Lord in chief.
> (True to his song's good, spit the fate hands dealing,
> With lips the bolder for a soul-hid grief.)

The central contrast that emerges here is between Shakespeare's "stealing"

elements of the life around him and Villon, who sang his *inner* life and especially his "soul-hid grief." The poem responds with a hardier sort of admiration
for Villon's defiance of fate and his capacity to turn inner grief into song,
somewhat like "Cino."[14]

The urgency of the two parenthetical lines, with their jagged rhythms and
staccato movement, places them at the emotive center of the sequence and
suggests an oblique reference to some motivating "soul-hid grief." These lines
help to draw the sequence together and to unite the focus on song in the first
poem with the focus on a woman in the third.[15]

The stylistic juxtaposition of poem III is even more dramatic than that of
the first two. Both diction and imagery shift from colloquial contemporaneity to
a regulated formality. The apparent emulation of Shakespeare's Sonnet 98 draws
an element of self-irony from the earlier "all bards are thieves":

[III—AFTER SHAKESPEARE'S SONNET]
XCVIII

> When proud-pied April leadeth in his train
> And yellow crocus quick'neth to the breath
> Of Zephyr fleeting from the sun-shot rain,
> Then seek I her whom mine heart honoureth.
> She is a woodland sprite and suzerain
> Of every power that flouteth wintry death.
>
> When proud-pied April leadeth in his train
> And freeth all the earth from cold's mort-main,
> Then with her fairness mine heart journeyeth
> Thru bourgeon wood-ways wherein tourneyeth
> Earth's might of laughter 'gainst all laughter slain
> Ere proud-pied April led in feat his train.

But this is not strictly an emulation of Shakespeare. First of all, it gathers
up a whole current of traditional English love poetry that includes not only
Shakespeare but Spenser as well, in its diction, and Chaucer in the imagery that
echoes both the "General Prologue" to the *Canterbury Tales* and the prologue to
the *Legend of Good Women*. Second, the poem is not Shakespearean in form;
rather, it is one of the several roundels in the "San Trovaso Notebook" whose
form is Pound's own innovation. More important, the woman at the poem's
center embodies nature's forces of renewal, as the women in Pound's poetry
often do, and, like many of his early sonnets, this poem expresses an optimistic
faith in continuity. Pound's own method, then, is brought together with elements borrowed from tradition and makes this section more of an appreciation,
like the later homages, than a serious emulation.

Like the first two poems, the roundel develops partly through an opposition between "Earth's might of laughter" in spring's growth and "all laughter slain," the force of "wintry death" and despair. This returns the poem to the beginning of the sequence, and Shakespeare's "diadems and broken roses" are both personalized in their application to "her whom mine heart honoureth" and distanced by the traditional context and seasonal imagery through which they are presented. Finally, along with this circular pattern and the development through contrast, both common techniques in Pound's sequences, repetition and variation are also used, characteristically, in the refrain of lines 1, 7, and 12.

The three major emotive pattern-units of the sequence, then, along with the more subtle gradations and variations of feeling within them, set out from the jaunty admiration of the opening, through the ironic and self-ironic comparison in the middle unit, to an appreciation that both uses and moves beyond a sense of the past.

"Piazza San Marco" demonstrates that Pound's archaism in the early poems was not necessarily the result of inattention to diction, an incapacity to use common speech, or a mirroring of influences. The mixture of levels follows the sequence's movement from comaraderie to homage, and the archaism of the roundel, however stilted, is adjusted to its traditional orientation. While the range and agility of "Piazza San Marco" seem rather limited in relation to later works, its success within its confines is partly the result of this stylistic variation and Pound's recognition that the rapidity and clarity of the tonal shifts among its three sections would be compromised by a repetitive formal structure or unity of surface. The consequent fragmentation serves to emphasize the approximate balance attained between the beginning and end, to reinforce the interaction among the three tonal centers, and to define precisely the qualities and gradations of feeling they project. "Some comfort 'tis to catch Will Shaxpeer stealing," for instance, clarifies and partially resolves the tension between comaraderie and awe in "Master Will, so cussed human"; similarly, the self-irony in "All bards are thieves" and the muted implications beneath the "soul-hid grief" in poem II are illuminated by the echoes of tradition and the amatory focus in the closing unit.

Another, less successful sequence in this collection, "For Ysolt. The Triad of Dawn," consists of three sonnets. In many respects an extension of the poems in "Hilda's Book," it works its way through self-conscious meditation, built over a splintered narrative framework, from darkness to light both in imagery and in mood. And "For the Triumph of the Arts," a "persona" poem in two sections, presents the martyrdom of "Jacques Chardinel—Of the Albigenses" for the arts, gathering its assertion of their ultimate survival from its unusually melodramatic effusions of suffering.[16]

Pound's other early sequences are often similarly compromised by formal restraints. "To La Contessa Bianzafior (Defense at Parting)," for instance, in *A Quinzaine for This Yule*, is a sequence of four sonnets held together within the framework of the "persona" form. Like many of the other "personae," it presents the unfolding of an inner conflict, here over the value and effect of the lover's song of tribute and its calling forth of other lovers. Its moments of urgency strain against formal boundaries but eventually attain something of a balance in the closing, self-ironic pose: "Ye mock the lines. Pardon a poor fool's whim."

The currents of self-irony and satire that become keynotes in Pound's work, especially in *Lustra,* seem to emerge first in the longer poems and sequences, partly as a result of the expanded perspective that they make possible and indeed require. Irony is again the central force of the last of the sonnet sequences, "Leviora."[17] This work's central concerns are the conflicts between poetic verity and formal polish, popular recognition and artistic integrity, and poetic emulation and innovation. The self-irony of "Piazza San Marco" and "To La Contessa Bianzafior" becomes biting but humorous mockery here:

> Decorous dance steps ape simplicity,
> The well-groomed sonnet is to truth preferred;
> Let us be all things so we're not absurd,
> Dabble with forms and damn the verity.
> Bardlets and bardkins, I do bite my thumb.
> Corset the muse and "directoire" her grace,
> Marcel the elf-looks of *sa chevelure,*
> Enamel Melpomene's too sun-kissed face
> And then to have your fame forged doubly sure
> Let taste rule all and bid the heart be dumb.

The sequence as a whole anticipates Pound's farewell to the sonnet in *Ripostes,* and its resolution in the final section rejects conventionality for "Priapus . . . 'neath Jehovah's coat."

Pound's early sequences are indeed at their best when not constrained by conventional patterns. "An Idyl for Glaucus," for instance, in *Personae,* despite its "nineties diction" (Thomas 66), especially its frequent inversions, moves through the speech rhythms of its broken narrative, its numerous shifts of attention, and its choral interjections toward an acute intensification of its central note of longing for release from the mocking world of the senses, for transformation, and for communion with the sea-spirit Glaucus.

Exultations, from the same year (1909), contains the longer, more controlled, and more concentrated sequence "Laudantes Decem Pulchritudinis Johannae Templae." Its range, depth, and complexity help to make this one of Pound's more satisfying early sequences, and the sparsity of critical attention it has received is somewhat surprising in view of its handling of some of the major structural devices of *The Cantos.* Eliot, at least, must have recognized its importance when he suggested its inclusion in the 1928 *Selected Poems.*[18] The few subsequent critics who have mentioned the sequence (De Nagy and Jackson, for instance) are no doubt correct in their estimation of its debt to Yeats's stylistic nuances, and it seems likely that the occult allusions (to use De Nagy's term) in the sixth poem have a similar derivation. But the movement of the work is for the most part characteristically Pound's and both reflects the techniques he had developed for building sequences up to this point and anticipates later refinements.

The first poem announces the sequence as "my poor words" and "these mad words" and introduces a sense of futility that courses through the sequence in its pursuit of an ideal and unattainable beauty, along with a confident pride in the song's prophetic truth and in its distinction from the sighs of a "hopeless throng" of followers:

> When your beauty is grown old in all men's songs,
> And my poor words are lost amid that throng,
> Then you will know the truth of my poor words,
> And mayhap dreaming of the wistful throng
> That hopeless sigh your praises in their songs,
> You will think kindly then of these mad words.

This poem functions proleptically, and its prediction of the twilight that will come upon the woman's beauty is fulfilled when "the twilight comes upon the roses" and "these mad words" are replaced by the silence of "the thoughts of my heart" in the final section. In the first four poems, a flexible and unconstraining "unity of surface" is attained through the use of repetition, especially at line endings, and the repetition of "poor words" and "mad words" in poem I both serves this function and enforces the initial sense of futility.[19]

The low-pitched urgency of this poem shifts to a more demonstrative outpouring in poem II, and the initial undercurrent of futility is heightened into anguished exclamation and questioning, reinforced by an increased density of repetition. This unit introduces two of the sequence's central motifs, the rose and the "heart within me":

> I am torn, torn with thy beauty,
> O Rose of the sharpest thorn!
> O Rose of the crimson beauty,
> Why hast thou awakened the sleeper?
> Why hast thou awakened the heart within me,
> O Rose of the crimson thorn?

The rose in its numerous recurrences both remains specifically a rose and acquires a series of associations—faces, thoughts, a gentleness of mind—consistently projecting the desire for a vivid but ungraspable beauty that is focused in the woman but mirrored everywhere. It becomes, in other words, the verbal equivalent for a particular emotion defined by the contexts in which it emerges in the course of the sequence. By this means the image is partially freed from its status as a Symbolist and nineties cliché.

The more reflective third poem confronts the fruitlessness of desire born of a sort of enchantment—the woman's name "written upon the ivory doors" of false dreams—and recognizes that it can give rise only to delusion like that of the lotus. This threatens the dismissal of passion altogether, but instead launches its displacement into a more distant, visionary context where communion with elements of nature substitutes for love's consummation. From the fourth poem on, the woman, so far addressed directly, is relegated to a third-person reference, though she remains the focus of attention and feeling. This transition in perspective and immediacy is effected motivically between the third and fourth poems through a transformation of the fecund "green wave" of the heart into "the dark breast of the sea."

The fifth poem shifts to a mystic or pre-natural landscape and introduces, not very convincingly, the song of "*Voices speaking to the sun.*" The periphrasis of the sun as a "red leaf that art blown" is less effective than the sequence's more fully developed images, though it does project a sense of the lover's helplessness and thus unites him with the hopeless "wistful throng" of singers in I. This unit is the sequence's weakest link as well as its emotive nadir.

Poem VI is more successful in its construction of a paradisal setting and in its heightening rapture, evocative of the *Song of Songs*. Again in twilight, "the hour of purple," the poem builds through a counterpoint of vision and physicality (rooted in the repetition of "peach-trees" and "peach gardens") toward the outpouring of its last two lines:

I stood on the hill of Yrma
        when the winds were a-hurrying,
With the grasses a-bending
        I followed them,
Through the brown grasses of Ahva
        unto the green of Asedon.
I have rested with the voices
        in the gardens of Ahthor,
I have lain beneath the peach-trees
        in the hour of the purple:

Because I had awaited in
        the garden of the peach-trees,
Because I had feared not
        in the forest of my mind,
Mine eyes beheld the vision of the blossom
There in the peach-gardens past Asedon.
O winds of Yrma, let her again come unto me,
Whose hair ye held unbound in the gardens of Ahthor!

But the moment of most intense physicality follows in poem VII, emerging suddenly through memory and then reflected, again at twilight, in elements of nature, "all the loveliness in the world." The perception of a frail beauty that persists through decay, "the rose-colour in the grey oak-leaf's fold," harkens back to the first poem's prediction that the sincerity and passion of "these mad words" will become meaningful to the unattainable woman in her old age:

> Because of the beautiful white shoulders and the rounded breasts
> I can in no wise forget my beloved of the peach-trees,
> And the little winds that speak when the dawn is unfurled
> And the rose-colour in the grey oak-leaf's fold
>
> When it first comes, and the glamour that rests
> On the little streams in the evening; all of these
> Call me to her, and all the loveliness in the world
> Binds me to my beloved with strong chains of gold.

This poem opens out toward the lyrical focus of the sequence in the following unit, its moment of deepest introspection and most concentrated tenderness, where imagined and remembered faces, frail "like petals of roses," become refractions of a single face to which the lover is drawn until his thoughts take on their delicacy. Love persists through confused memory, like "the rose-colour in the grey oak-leaf's fold":

> VIII
>
> If the rose-petals which have fallen upon my eyes
> And if the perfect faces which I see at times
> When my eyes are closed—
> Faces fragile, pale, yet flushed a little, like petals of roses:
> If these things have confused my memories of her
> So that I could not draw her face
> Even if I had skill and the colours,
> Yet because her face is so like these things
> They but draw me nearer unto her in my thought
> And thoughts of her come upon my mind gently,
> As dew upon the petals of roses.

This image is a recurrent one in Pound's work, not only in "Piccadilly" and "In a Station of the Metro," where it is most obvious, but often in *The Cantos,* notably in the fleeting appearances of women's and goddesses' eyes in the *Pisan Cantos.* These moments are characterized by a sudden clearing of perspective and the mingling of profound admiration with a sense of pathos in the perception of beauty's fragility and transience. Pound's arrangements often build, as here, toward this sort of climactic or transitional moment.

Poem IX ("*He speaks to the rain*") is linked in motif and mode with poem IV ("*He speaks to the moonlight*"), reinforcing the sequence's continuity and symmetry. The woman's recollected "soft and eager speech" unlocks in memory the "crimson and white flowers"—herself embodied in the rose and her "beautiful white shoulders"—just as the "beauty of the rains" unbinds the life-force of the earth.

In the final poem, although the "mad words" of poem I are replaced by the silent "thoughts of my heart," there is again a movement "Toward my beloved, / Toward the crimson rose, the fairest," a less distanced and abstract perspective than that of the visionary realm punctuated by memory in poems IV through IX. The pace is quieter than in the forceful rhythms and repetitions of the opening poems and suggests a tentative resolution; the urgent passion of the "heart's green wave" will find place after all in the "thoughts of my heart" rather than being entirely cast off:

> The glamour of the soul hath come upon me,
> And as the twilight comes upon the roses,
> Walking silently among them,
> So have the thoughts of my heart
> Gone out slowly in the twilight
> Toward my beloved,
> Toward the crimson rose, the fairest.

What "Laudantes Decem" presents, in sum, is a struggle to come to terms with an unfulfilled but persistent passion. Its various poems project a series of dispositions, exploring the qualities and degrees of its controlling emotions, desire and futility, as they color the entire perceptual and experiential world of the thwarted lover. The central movement is from an initial urgency to disillusionment and a consequent distancing, approaching the woman through memory and vision only in poems IV through IX, to a subdued acceptance of this internalization at the end. This final balance becomes less common in later sequences, especially in the more open and volatile movement within sections of *The Cantos*. But within the framework of the whole, the two poles of the later work—the strident, willful movement of the opening canto and the *serenitas* of Canto CXX,

> Do not move
> Let the wind speak
> that is paradise

—do effect a similar, though infinitely more resonant and broader containment, and there is a similar inevitability in the succession of emotive patterns; the initial stridency prepares for a later sense of stillness. The earlier sequence anticipates the method of *The Cantos* even more definitely in its shifts among different settings and perspectives, modes of utterance, and nuances of feeling; in its complex patterns of motivic echo, repetition, and variation; and in its relative fluidity of form. Its proleptic opening and its pivotal transition through the physicality of poem VII are both important strategies in later works.

A unity among the sections of "Laudantes Decem" is attained not only through repetitive motivic means, but also through a rather intricate development and interplay of color patterns, moving through much of the spectrum from rose and crimson in poem II back to rose and crimson in poem X. The effect is not unlike Whistler's distribution of color motifs through his canvases, a technique that he considered musical. For Pound, this is an elaborate development of "phanopoeia—a casting of images upon the visual imagination." But a color, or the name of a color, does not in itself constitute an image, which is "an intellectual and emotional *complex*"; rather, color is a visual means of projecting an image. The images themselves are "emotional states of mind": "It would be vain to deny that certain kinds and tones of colour have real correspondence with emotional states of mind" (*GB* 135). The disposition of color motifs through the sequence serves to impart unity to the whole and to define the emotive center of each poem.[20] For instance, the green of the "heart's green wave" in III is linked with the "green sheaf of the world" in V and the "green of Asedon" in VI, in contrast to the "brown grasses of Ahva," and in each case the color, drawing its initial force from its first occurrence, suggests a surging, irrepressible fecundity. Similarly, the soft but voluptuous sheen of the "white foam" in II is picked up again with its sexual connotations in the "white shoulders" of VII and "white flowers" of IX.

It is certainly arguable that the still more complex use of this technique in *The Cantos* serves primarily the same emotive end, as do the prolific contrasts between light and darkness throughout Pound's poems and the insistence on light as the embodiment of intelligence, sincerity, and life-force.[21]

What locates "Laudantes Decem" among Pound's first sequences and links it with Yeats's early manner is its concentrated introspection, its dominant concern with psychic events almost to the point of excluding the external. This helps to block narrative control, though later sequences manage to circumvent narrative effectively while presenting a more dynamic interaction between psychic and external developments.

"Victorian Eclogues," in *Canzoni,* also focuses on the experience of love, but its presentation of emotion through three very different perspectives, three juxtaposed "personae," precludes a sense of internal confinement. This reflects a direction Pound was consciously working toward: "The 'Eclogues' are I think over-strained & morbid but part of my criticism of emotion, the whole book is in sort that—to the working out from emotion into the open" (*EP/DS* 38). This progression is apparent among the three eclogues in their modulation from the

stanzaic patterns of the first to the more fluid, irregular, yet controlled movement of the third. Perspective and mode progress, in tandem with modulations
in rhythm, from the rejection of one lover for another in the first poem, through
yearning for a past lover in the second, to the remorse, pride, and tenderness of
Abelard's prayer for protection and comfort of his beloved (Héloise) in the last.

But this working out "into the open" is achieved still more clearly through
the enlarged exploration of personal circumstance and feeling in "Translations
from Heine," first published in *Canzoni*.[22] Here the irony introduced in earlier
poems and sequences, such as "Piazza San Marco," evolves through a wit and
urbanity partly derived from the "logopoeia" (or "dance of the intellect among
words") that Pound located in Heine's poems, and in this as well as in its
concern with contemporary moeurs and the current critical temper it strongly
anticipates the *Homage to Sextus Propertius*.[23] The modes of construction of
the two sequences are also similar: like the assemblage of the *Homage* from
different sections of Propertius's *Elegies*, "Translations from Heine" consists of
translations or adaptations of various poems and passages in Heine's oeuvre,
given an idiosyncratic continuity through Pound's selection, ordering and juxtaposition of them. This method of gathering adapted passages into integral
sequences is also employed successfully in "Cathay," "Impressions of François-
Marie Arouet (de Voltaire)," "Homage to Quintus Septimius Florentis Christianus" and "Langue d'Oc."

While aesthetic issues enter prominently into "Translations from Heine,"
the sequence does not, as Demetz insists, speak of "poetry, and nothing but
poetry"; from the outset it too, like Heine's poems, addresses the "sorrows of
experience" (288). The first section reacts with shocked bewilderment at the
inconstancy of love, now turned to hatred. But a controlling distance is imparted
by the irony of the rhetorical questions and exaggerated emphasis, and of the
address, in the second stanza, not to the woman but to her treacherous lips:

> Is your hate, then, of such measure?
> Do you, truly, so detest me?
> Through all the world will I complain
> Of *how* you have addressed me.

> O ye lips that are ungrateful,
> Hath it never once distressed you,
> That you can say such *awful* things
> Of *any* one who ever kissed you?

The second poem is a song of deprecation and dejection, mixed with
continuing desire—the key set of conflicting affects which the sequence sets out
to reconcile. Aesthetic concerns are expressed in the singer's pride, in the
second stanza, but in relation to a sense of betrayal and not as a separate issue;

pride builds toward the dismissal in the last line of this unit as a means of assuaging dejection:

> So thou hast forgotten fully
> That I so long held thy heart wholly,
> Thy little heart, so sweet and false and small
> That there's no thing more sweet or false at all.
>
> Love and lay thou hast forgotten fully,
> And my heart worked at them unduly.
> I know not if the love or if the lay were better stuff,
> But I know now, they both were good enough.

Though "lay" may be an inadvertent mistranslation of *Leid* or "sorrow" (Demetz 288), it is poetically felicitous and the musicality of a "lay" is effected through repetition and alliteration. Particularly notable is the playing out of the conflict between "thy heart" in the first stanza and "my heart" in the second through the contrasting repetitions "sweet and false" and "love and lay."

In the third poem the singer addresses and answers himself with a mixture of self-irony and desolation. Pride in his song reaches an apex in an attempt to displace sorrow and achieve an emotive equilibrium: "Behold this book, the urn of ashes, / 'Tis my true love's sepulchre." But taken to hyperbolic extremes of self-inflation, this gives rise in IV to a self-mocking treatment of grandiose poetic aspirations:

> I dreamt that I was God Himself
> Whom heavenly joy immerses,
> And all the angels sat about
> And praised my verses.

Pride, or rather a sort of tongue-in-cheek haughtiness, reemerges in the next section by contrast to critics and poetic eunuchs, "mutilated choir boys," who, lacking virile impediments, rise to heights of glittering abstraction. The contempt here is, of course, also a self-consoling stratagem; the lover's rejection is the result of his superiority:

> The mutilated choir boys
> When I begin to sing
> Complain about the awful noise
> And call my voice too thick a thing.
> When light their voices lift them up,
> Bright notes against the ear,
> Through trills and runs like crystal,
> Ring delicate and clear.

> They sing of Love that's grown desirous,
> Of Love, and joy that is Love's inmost part,
> And all the ladies swim through tears
> Toward such a work of art.

Poem VI focuses on an obsequious disciple, a poetic poseur at once contemptible and useful, but in the closing stanza an unrestrained and penetrating lament over age's debilities and satisfaction's transience momentarily breaks down all the sequence's ironic defenses:

> O what comfort is it for me
> To find him such, when the days bring
> No comfort, at my time of life when
> All good things go vanishing.

This opens out to a pivotal interlude, *"Translator to Translated,"* that draws the sequence into focus and answers its central conflicts in art and love by offering Heine—or the personal and aesthetic values he represents—as a standard of integrity, polished but unrhetorical, and as a genuine though unattainable source of consolation for the pain of lovers' and critics' pretenses and treacheries:

> *O Harry Heine, curses be,*
> *I live too late to sup with thee!*
> *Who can demolish at such polished ease*
> *Philistia's pomp and Art's pomposities!*

This detachment of a poem from its context in order to use it as a pivot in a sequence is an important strategy for attaining emotive coherence in Pound's works (as in the "Envoi" of *Hugh Selwyn Mauberley*). From here the sequence returns to the comforts and disconsolations of love, though a concern with aesthetic values remains connectedly in the background.

In its initial configuration in *Canzoni,* the sequence was roughly symmetrical, ending with the song of poem VII. This poem at first appears to offer some comfort in Ilza's "white arms" and her pity, in answer to the betrayal of love in the opening; but in her empty, platitudinous coaxing and her yoking of a pompous dance of life with death's solemn music, she ultimately promises a repetition of that betrayal:

> If my heart stay below there,
> My crystal halls ring clear
> To the dance of lords and ladies
> In all their splendid gear.

The silken trains go rustling,
The spur-clinks sound between,
The dark dwarfs blow and bow there
Small horn and violin.

Yet shall my white arms hold thee,
That bound King Harry about.
Ah, I covered his ears with them
When the trumpet rang out.

In its original form, then, the sequence moved through a cycle from betrayal to solace-seeking to betrayal, confronting the almost irresistible seductiveness of passions that ultimately prove destructive, all the more so for the sincerity and intensity of the singer who follows them. A jocund balance is managed through the wry, distancing irony, but the devastating potential of passionate extremes is a recurrent emotive pattern in Pound's poems, usually unallayed by irony: this was already present in the very early "Ver Novum," "La Fraisne," and "Marvoil," and it later attains concentrated force in the conflation of Actaeon and Vidal in Canto IV, the hallucinations of Niccolò d'Este in Canto XX, and elsewhere.

However, in this sequence's final form in *Lustra* (1917), with the addition of poem VIII, it ends by embracing life's offer of "joy breathless at heart" with its urgent desire, whatever the consequences. This is indeed a voluptuous *carpe noctem,* but it maintains an ironic qualification through its exaggerated epithet, "Heart's-all-belovèd-my-own," and through the implication that its loving spirit extends through a single night and reaches as far as its kisses, with no promise of anything beyond them; the sequence's earlier betrayals are momentarily put aside but not entirely forgotten. In fact, the closing song echoes the opening poem motivically, in its repeated focus on lips, and formally, in its similar stanzaic pattern, its use of repetition, and its alternation of questioning and assertion:

NIGHT SONG

And have you thoroughly kissed my lips?
    There was no particular haste,
And are you not ready when evening's come?
    There's no *particular* haste.
You've got the whole night before you,
    Heart's-all-belovèd-my-own;
In an uninterrupted night one can
    Get a good deal of kissing done.

(*P*)

"Translations from Heine," then, demonstrates Pound's characteristic method of sequence construction, an arrangement of poems and passages selected and ordered not according to a succession in Heine's works or any other externally-imposed framework, but in terms of the emotive curve of the whole. While its technique shows more of a continuity with earlier sequences than a departure from them, certainly its urbane refusal to idealize the lover's experience or the beloved strongly anticipates the central disposition of later poems and sequences, especially in *Lustra,* as much as does its ridicule of critics, poseurs, and aesthetic pomposities. The combination of aesthetic and private concerns that helps to achieve an objectifying distance, a breadth of vision, and a universality in this sequence is also a crucial dimension in the most important of the later sequences, including "Cathay," *Homage to Sextus Propertius, Hugh Selwyn Mauberley,* and *The Cantos;* further development between this period and *The Cantos* is primarily a matter of scope, depth, and agility.

"Und Drang," the final work in *Canzoni,* is situated directly after "Translations from Heine" and functions in many ways as an expansion of it, addressing the same key concerns and tones of mind, though with somewhat greater breadth and a wider range of stylistic variation. Nearly all the critics who have recognized "Und Drang" as a sequence have focused on its dichotomy between the problems of modernity and the richer values of the medieval or Provençal world, dividing the sequence neatly in half, into six modern poems and six medieval.[24] While this opposition is clearly operant in the sequence (though not so simply defined), its central current of thought and feeling is again located within the private realm of love and disappointment and, as in "Translations from Heine," aesthetic values are implicated but peripheral.

Though there is hardly room here for as extensive an examination as "Und Drang" merits, its major contours may be outlined briefly. The sequence begins with a sense of weariness and oppression, stemming not from anything specifically modern but rather from a concentrated effort to transcend human boundaries and reestablish contact with universal truths, "winds of good and evil," and primal energies:

> The great oblivions and the labouring night,
> Inchoate truth and the sepulchral forces.

Poem III locates this sense of depressiveness and tedium in the betrayal and transience of affection:

> The will to live goes from me.
> I have lain
> Dull and out-worn
> with some strange, subtle sickness.
> Who shall say
> That love is not the very root of this,
> O thou afar?

And poem IV initiates an effort to come to terms with this central feeling of loss and futility:

> All things in season and no thing o'er long!
> Love and desire and gain and good forgetting,
> Thou canst not stay the wheel, hold none too long!

Poem V views the problem against a backdrop of "modernity, / Nerve-wracked and broken"; VI tries to locate "O thou afar" amid a modern setting, unsuccessfully; and poems VII ("The House of Splendour") and VIII ("The Flame") move toward a visionary realm and spiritual detachment:

> Search not my lips, O Love, let go my hands,
> This thing that moves as man is no more mortal.

Poems IX ("Horae Beatae Inscriptio") and X ("The Altar") strike a tentative balance, affirming continuities of perception and affection against the dispersions lamented in poems III and IV. "Au Salon" (XI) extends this balance through an aesthetic context:

> I suppose, when poetry comes down to facts,
> When our souls are returned to the gods
>   and the spheres they belong in,
> Here in the every-day where our acts
> Rise up and judge us;
>
> I suppose there are a few dozen verities
> That no shift of mood can shake from us.

The final poem, "Au Jardin," offers a partial resolution, rejecting, in its riposte to Yeats's "The Cap and Bells," a love that entails devotion unto death, adopting instead a more cavalier attitude reminiscent of "Cino"—"I am set wide upon the world's ways / To say that life is, some way, a gay thing"—and reaching toward a reconciliation with the brevity of love's fulfillment that does not preclude an intense and deeply appreciative involvement. This final orientation is focused in the vivaciousness and poise of the "pink moth in the shrubbery," a unifying image for the sequence as a whole:

>   And I loved a love once,
>   Over beyond the moon there,
>   I loved a love once,
>   And, may be, more times,
>
>   But she danced like a pink moth in the shrubbery.

"Und Drang," then, explores the cycle from betrayal to betrayal traced in "Translations from Heine" through a wider range of contexts and attitudes, directed toward its closing balance by the tentative acceptance of transience in poem IV. Its final point of equilibrium supplies a cadence not only for its twelve poems and for "Translations from Heine," but also for *Canzoni* as a whole, which begins, in "Canzon: The Yearly Slain," with a lament over "Love that is born of Time and comes and goes!" The balance attained here is similar to that of "Laudantes Decem," but more complex and with a less definite sense of closure. Pound's later, more expansive sequences build on the volatility, range, and depth that this more open mode of constructing an "arrangement of forms" accommodates.

3

"Arrangements of Forms": From *Ripostes* through *Quia Pauper Amavi*

From *Ripostes* through *Lustra*

The increased flexibility and openness of Pound's later sequences begin to emerge most clearly about the time of *Ripostes* (1912)—for instance, in "Effects of Music Upon a Company of People," a short sequence placed at the end of that volume. This work traces the movement of souls that take on form and color from patterns of music, much as "The Return," which directly precedes it, projects the momentarily palpable emergence of "souls of blood." Both establish a visionary context whose experiential immediacy and fluidity are partly conveyed through the use of juxtapositional rather than syntactic containment. The first of the sequence's two sections is developed in "Deux Mouvements," "*Temple qui fut,*" and "*Poissons d'or.*" In "Mouvement" I, music evokes an increasingly excited effluence of spirit shaped through a succession of similes, pattern-units of color, suggestions of movement, and exclamations—"O Flower animate! / O calyx!"—abruptly halted by contrast with the immovable: "O crowd of foolish people!"

The second "Mouvement" focuses on the interweaving flux of enraptured souls as they follow the course of the music to its final cadence:

> The petals!
> On the tip of each the figure
> Delicate.
> See, they dance, step to step.
> Flora to festival,
> Twine, bend, bow,
> Frolic involve ye.
> Woven the step,
> Woven the tread, the moving.
> Ribands they move,

> Wave, bow to the centre,
> Pause, rise, deepen in colour,
> And fold in drowsily.

Part II, "From a Thing by Schumann," repeats the progression of the "Deux Mouvements" at a lower pitch, with the souls collectively straining against their physical confines, and ends with greater finality on the tonic of the crowd:

> And then across the white silken,
> Bellied up, as a sail bellies to the wind,
> Over the fluid tenuous, diaphanous,
> Over this curled a wave, greenish,
> Mounted and overwhelmed it.
> This membrane floating above,
> And bellied out by the up-pressing soul.

> Then came a mer-host,
> And after them legion of Romans,
> The usual, dull, theatrical!

The construction of the poems in this sequence through a paratactic disposition of verbal units—words and phrases charged by their isolation and juxtaposition, set together with minimal syntactic hierarchy—is an important precursor to the style of *The Cantos* and reflects the continuing drive in Pound's aesthetics toward a concentration on primary forms and the reordering of elemental units into vital arrangements. As we have seen, this was already implicit in the structure of the earliest poems, and the primary form was later formulated in Imagist terms as the pattern-unit or image. The potential for expansiveness, flexibility, and sustained intensity through nonrepresentational arrangements of these units was explored more fully through Vorticist theory and practice.

Pound's Vorticism began from the premise that "every conception, every emotion presents itself to the vivid consciousness in some primary form," and "the primary pigment of poetry is the IMAGE" ("Vortex. Pound," *Blast* I 153–54). Primary forms, for the sculptor, the painter, and the poet as much as the musician, become expressive through their patterned arrangement: "It is no more ridiculous that a person should receive or convey an emotion by means of an arrangement of shapes, or planes, or colours, than that they should receive or convey such emotion by an arrangement of musical notes" (*GB* 81). Through this conception, the discursive component of language is suppressed and its emotive force is emphasized; consequently, discursive connections among verbal units, the logical procedure of syntax, become superfluous and inexpressive:

> We no longer think or need to think in terms of monolinear logic, the sentence structure, subject, predicate, object, etc.

We are as capable or almost as capable as the biologist of thinking thoughts that join like spokes in a wheel-hub and that fuse in hypergeometric amalgams. (*EPVA* 166)

And the subordination of syntactic coherence naturally results in the dissolution of narrative progression; as Dasenbrock has noted, "the discontinuities . . . in *The Waste Land, The Cantos,* and *Finnegans Wake* are discontinuities in narration as well as in syntax. Just as syntactic continuity always breaks down, so too does narrative continuity, and these are really aspects of the same thing" (138). As Pound put it later, "vorticism from my angle was a renewal of the sense of construction" ("Int" Hall 30).

Of the numerous and widely varied claims made and retracted by Pound and his Vorticist colleagues and later by critics of the movement, two, at least, are substantiated by Pound's use of the aesthetic in his poems and sequences. First, the combination of primary forms in nonrepresentational, nondiscursive arrangements achieves heightened emotive precision:

When Mr. Epstein says "Night" is the subject he means rather more. Everybody knows what "Night" is, but Mr. Epstein or Mr. Phidias or whoever, is presumably intent on expressing a *particular* and definite complex (ideas, emotions, etc.,) generally oriented by a rather vague concept already mapped out. The difference is as great as that between firing a bullet in a generally easterly direction and hitting a particular bird. (*EPVA* 163)

And second, the Vorticist conception of form allows for greater compression and intensification, especially in an extended work:

Vorticism is an intensive art. I mean by this, that one is concerned with the relative intensity, or relative significance of different sorts of expression. One desires the most intense, for certain forms of expression *are* "more intense" than others. They are more dynamic. I do not mean they are more emphatic, or that they are yelled louder. (*GB* 90)

In Pound's work, a departure from inherited conventions and an increasing reliance, even before the Vorticist formulations, on the arrangement of primary forms into nondiscursive patterns results in a rapidity, variety, and intensity of dynamics that open new possibilities for the long poem, in the form of the lyric sequence.

It is ultimately through this Vorticist focus on primary form that Pound's discontinuous, juxtapositional technique attains its full development in *The Cantos*. The particular combination of epigrammatic compression and asyntactic patterning that Pound uses to effect an emotive coherence among sections of his long poem begins to emerge into full view in some of the short sequences published in *Poetry* and other periodicals between 1913 and 1916. Pound's additions, deletions, and rearrangements of constituent poems and his comments on them, particularly to Harriet Monroe, demonstrate the insistence and deliberateness with which these sequences were shaped.

The first of these, the "Contemporania" series published in *Poetry* in April, 1913, went through at least three radically different configurations. In its original version, the sequence began with the rhapsodic "Dance Figure" and ended with the declamatory "Epilogue."[1]

1 Dance Figure
2 Contemporania
   I Tea-Shop
   II Courtesy (bathtub)
   III The Garden
3 A Pact
4 An Epilogue (UCL)

It is clear that Pound's subsequent revisions were directed toward attaining a particular emotive progression and balance among the constituent poems. In what is probably the second phase, Pound submitted a number of new poems, marked according to their importance to the sequence and their desired placement, and he specified the basis for his selection and arrangement of them:

> I've marked the following poems . . . in accordance as they are necessary to the integrity of the series—there's got to be a certain amount of pictures to ballance the orations, and there's got to be enough actual print to establish the tonality, or whatever you want to call it. (UCL)

Thus of one poem, ultimately deleted, he wrote: "I rather want this to follow 'The Garret' for the sake of the 3d & 4th lines, which uphold the effect 16 [line six] in The Garret & give contrast in colour. The series needs these few touches of beauty" (UCL).[2] From Pound's markings, Monroe inferred the arrangement of the next phase, and Pound responded by suggesting possible deletions.

The Garden
The Garret—come, let us pity
Dance Figure
In a Station of the Metro
Ortus
Reflection & Advice
Commission
O my fellow sufferers
Tenzone
Salutation ~~the Second~~
A Pact
~~Epilogue~~ (UCL)

Finally, Pound wrote that "in the present order of the versicles I seem to jaw too much to myself. It's the deevil to arrange fragments of one design into anything like another. However. Please shift the order to the following," and he went on to specify the final arrangement as published:

1   Tenzone
2   The Condolence
3   The Garret
4   The Gardens
5   Ortus
6   Dance Figure
7   Salutation (O generation of the thoroughly smug)
8   Salutation II.
9   Reflection . change title to "PAX SATURNI"
10 Commission
11 Pact
12 The station of the METRO (UCL)

This reverses the tonal progression of the first phase, moving from the confrontative tenor of "Tenzone" to the more delicate and plangent focus of "In a Station of the Metro." The sequence courses through an alternation of these tonalities, and the two ends of the original grouping are represented at the center of the final arrangement by "Dance Figure" and "Salutation."

"Contemporania" was probably the seed of *Lustra* and was incorporated, in slightly altered and opened form, at the head of that volume; the tonal contour of the published sequence is in miniature that of *Lustra* (1917) as a whole. Pound's next *Poetry* sequence, published in November 1913, also played a seminal role in the formation of *Lustra* and was positioned almost intact near the center of the volume. Beginning with "Ancora" and ending with "Dum Capitolium Scandet," it courses through essentially the same polarities as "Contemporania," from the reemergence of the gods amid an atmosphere of playful exuberance to a declamatory address to the poems' future progeny, modeled on Whitman's "Crossing Brooklyn Ferry" and affirming the immortality of the poet's effort.[3] The focus of the group is split between "pictures" tracing a sense of loss and the wastage of life-force (in the key pairing "April" and "Gentildonna"), on the one hand, and "orations" on the other, caricaturing social misdirection and confrontatively offering up the poems as correctives in a central triad of the group subtitled "Lustra." The printed version of this sequence retains much the same contours as an earlier draft, of which Pound wrote to Harriet Monroe:

Mindful of your prayer for "pure homage to beauty" or whatever your phrase was, I have, after the opening frolic, dealt chiefly with gods and such like. And been, I dare say, fairly unintelligible. . . .

  For the rest, I want this group to appear as I have arranged it. I include none of the earlier verse that I have sent you, save the "O helpless few in my country."

  The tone of the whole is more serious than that of the other lot, and this is, I suppose, what you wanted. (UCL)[4]

Interestingly, a very different effect was attained in another sequence published in the *New Freewoman* in December 1913 by radically reorganizing almost all of the same poems. This sequence is roughly symmetrical, launched by the declamatory "Further Instructions" and closed by "The Rest" ("O helpless few"), but it is focused by the same poignant pair, "April" and "Gentildonna," as in the November *Poetry* group.[5] This placement of a key unit at the center of a sequence or volume, either to draw together its two ends or to provide a resonant contrast to what surrounds it, as here, is one of Pound's most characteristic and effective organizational strategies.

  In April of the following year, in the course of explaining his insistence on the order of the poems in his next *Poetry* sequence (published in August), Pound complained of the ineffectiveness of both the November *Poetry* group and the sequence "Zenia" published in the *Smart Set* in December 1913:

I must ask you to keep the *order* of this lot, the poems in last Nov. and in the S.S. created less interest than Contemporania partly because they had no coherence as a group, no cohesion. The S.S. arrangement was hopeless. The arrangement in Poetry was I suppose inevitable but there was no drive to the lot.

  "Blast" has got the most effective lot, I think, but you wouldn't have wanted them. . . .

  As for my scrawny lot. I think, if you print 'em just as they are you'll get some sort of result. And I think if you try to remove even the ones I've marked optional, the energy will leak out and you'll get no more friction than you got out of the last lot. (UCL)

"Zenia," the "hopeless" arrangement, attempts a curious mixture of satiric epigrams and epigrammatic elegies, in the manner of *Lustra*. The sequence is organized proleptically, so that the mode of the whole is apparent in the first two poems, juxtaposing the ironic contrast in "To Dives" with the appreciative awe and frail simplicity of "Alba."[6] But it lacks both focus and variation in intensity: its key oppositions are not drawn together by any central grouping, and the constituent poems succeed one another at approximately the same emotive pitch. Most of them were reprinted in *Lustra* but positioned very differently there.

  The poems in *Blast* I (June 1914) certainly have more "drive," framed by the irritating impetuousness of "Salutation the Third" at the opening and the wry encounter of "Pastoral" at the close. Its overall curve is in fact remarkably similar to that of "Zenia," but is held together by the visionary movement of

"Before Sleep" at its center, followed by a succession of pungent epigrams and the softer cadence of "Pastoral."[7]

In May 1914, apparently having met with some resistance from Harriet Monroe over the poems submitted for his August sequence, Pound wrote instructing her to "Cut out any of my poems that would be likely to get you suppressed but don't make it into a flabby little Sunday School lot like the bunch in the November number. . . . Any way I haven't any new things that will mix with the lot I've sent in" (*Ltrs* 37). But two days later he wrote again, enclosing additional poems which "may add that gaiety to the group, the lack of which you so much deplored" (UCL), though none of these was actually included. As published, this sequence moves from the subtle, self-ironic "Tò Καλόν" and "The Study in Aesthetics," to the bombastic, anti-imperial satire "Abu Salammamm, A Song of Empire," a direction almost the reverse of the November *Poetry* group. Pound achieved the coherence he felt lacking in the other sequences by building this one out of a succession of shorter groupings: "Tò Καλόν," "The Study in Aesthetics," and "The Bellaires" work together, bound by strains of self-irony, and this triad is followed by three more short groups, "Salvationists," "Amitiés," and "Ladies." These clusters of epigrams are wittily urbane but sometimes disclose slightly more vulnerable undercurrents, as in the forced indifference at the end of "Ladies": "The faint odour of your patchouli, / Faint, almost, as the lines of cruelty about your chin, / Assails me, and concerns me almost as little."[8]

Pound's next *Poetry* sequence, in March 1915, is shorter but still more effective, and handles many of the same key tonalities and central oppositions as the first version of *Cathay,* published the following month. The *Poetry* group begins with the wandering and the attempt to imaginatively reconstruct a vital past out of its ruins in "Provincia Deserta" and closes with continued wandering in "The Gypsy" and a dynamic study of movement in "The Game of Chess."[9] The sequence is focused and unified by the pairing of "The Spring" and "The Coming of War: Actaeon" at its center, sharing a vulnerability and visionary power that resonate through the other poems.

The last of the periodical sequences to concern us here was published in *Poetry* in September 1916 and was originally supposed to be focused at its beginning by "To a Friend Writing on Cabaret Dancers," then "cooled" by the short pieces to follow: "I hope the first of this lot (damn it all it *has* Cabaret Dancers) has a little firmness and sap. . . . On the other hand I think it rather needs the calm marble of the short things that follow it. Cool after stuffiness. And on the whole I would rather wait until there is room for the lot together" (UCL).[10] But after Monroe refused to risk the "Cabaret Dancers," the original arrangement was almost reversed, and the now very different *ubi sunt* focus was built into the end of the group in the short sequences "Impressions of Voltaire" and "Homage to Quintus Septimius Florens Christianus."[11]

Before moving on to a closer view of these two sequences and "Near Perigord" (*Poetry*, December 1915), it will be useful to summarize the directions of Pound's efforts in arranging constituent poems in order to effect a particular emotive progression and a sense of coherence in the periodical sequences. Most of them are developed through dynamic oppositions: mordant satire set against a sense of loss, vulnerability offset by visionary immediacy, "pictures" balanced by "orations," celebrations of resurgent life-force juxtaposed with caricatures of sterile social types, and so on. Emotive currents are developed through subtle variations and tend to invoke their opposites, so that the sequences arranged in this way, when most effective, unfold with a sense of felt inevitability. Many of them make their central oppositions explicit by placing them at different ends, and Pound seems also to have paid special attention to the center of each group, where the oppositions are sometimes juxtaposed, as in "Contemporania," or else the sequence is focused by a key grouping or pair, such as "April" and "Gentildonna," placed together at the center of the November 1913 *Poetry* group and the *New Freewoman* sequence of December 1913. These are strategies exploited increasingly in the most successful of the sequences to follow, beginning with "Cathay."[12]

Three Short Sequences

"Near Perigord" is often considered one of the most important antecedents to *The Cantos*. Its questioning of historical and geographic circumstances surrounding Bertrans de Born's poetry indeed suggests an attempt to locate objective truths that parallels the treatment of historical materials in *The Cantos*. Yet the variation of mode among the three sections of the earlier sequence has given rise to elaborate critical deliberations over "the indeterminate identity of the speaker";[13] considered as a whole, however, it becomes apparent that these units, despite their discontinuities, are ranged coherently within an encompassing overview and reflect a fluidity of movement through related states of consciousness, much as in *The Cantos*.

The first section opens with a self-interrogating challenge: in order to revivify the hearts and reveal the secrets of men of the past, documents must be interpreted and transformed, not used as "evidence." The injunction is at once playful and posed with the utter seriousness of the sphinx:

> You'd have men's hearts up from the dust
> And tell their secrets, Messire Cino,
> Right enough? Then read between the lines of Uc St. Circ,
> Solve me the riddle, for you know the tale.

> Bertrans, En Bertrans, left a fine canzone:
> "Maent, I love you, you have turned me out.

The voice at Montfort, Lady Agnes' hair,
Bel Miral's stature, the viscountess' throat,
Set all together, are not worthy of you. . . . "

As the section proceeds, it follows precisely the pattern established in this first passage, alternating between interrogation and imaginative reconstruction in order to penetrate the motives of the figure at its focus, de Born. No decisions about the "real" de Born are made or can be made within the framework of the poem, however; it is the *process* of thinking about him intensely that brings him to life again. The concentrated deliberation of this section opens out to the more presentative mode of the next:

En fact. Try fiction. Let us say we see
En Bertrans, a tower-room at Hautefort,
Sunset, the ribbon-like road lies, in red cross-light,
Southward toward Montagnac, and he bends at a table
Scribbling, swearing between his teeth; by his left hand
Lie little strips of parchment covered over,
Scratched and erased with *al* and *ochaisos*.
Testing his list of rhymes, a lean man? Bilious?
With a red straggling beard?
And the green cat's-eye lifts toward Montagnac.

The tonal center of this section is admiration for the character it brings to life, who, placed in a range of envisioned circumstances, acquires heroic stature and receives the poem's homage. The section closes by juxtaposing Dante's recreation of de Born, which it uses as a means of penetrating further into the character's psyche; for Pound regarded "Dante's descriptions of the actions and conditions of the shades as descriptions of men's mental states in life, in which they are, after death, compelled to continue: that is to say, men's inner selves stand visibly before the eyes of Dante's intellect. . . . " (*SR* 128).

The final section presents de Born's rapture, inner conflict, and thwarted love from within his resurrected psyche, and closes with an imagined vision of Maent as she is reflected through the canzone by de Born that Pound's sequence sets out to penetrate:

There shut up in his castle, Tairiran's,
She who had nor ears nor tongue save in her hands,
Gone—ah, gone—untouched, unreachable!
She who could never live save through one person,
She who could never speak save to one person,
And all the rest of her a shifting change,
A broken bundle of mirrors . . . !

Hence Kenner's conclusion that de Born's canzone, as imaged here, is "an arrangement of words and images corresponding to the mode of being possessed by the subject" ("Mirrors" 9) seems accurate, though naturally the correspondence is to a particular vision of the woman that "*is*" her mode of being as far as we are concerned" (Witemeyer 158), and not to any woman outside of de Born's canzone and Pound's sequence.

The sweep of the sequence, then, moves from deliberation, through vivid reenvisionment, to imaginative penetration of the figure at its focus. What it finally presents is neither de Born nor Maent but the movement of a consciousness through various states in its consideration of them. The sequence's movement and the relations among its parts prevent us from viewing it as either historical research or as a strictly subjective response to imagined circumstances; rather, we are given something of both and, more than that, the vital process of a mind moving freely between them. In this respect, more than in its historicism, the technique of this short sequence anticipates that of *The Cantos*.

Among the sequences following "Near Perigord," "Homage to Quintus Septimius Florens Christianus" (*Poetry,* September 1916) is concerned with forces of death and desire, a combination that links it to other works of this period. These affective centers are treated through momentary, predominantly ironic glimpses and are kept undeveloped, emulating the classical austerity and impersonality of the epigrams in the *Greek Anthology* from which the constituent poems are adapted. An ironic distance from both women and death is kept constant, with one exception. In the fourth poem, the *ubi sunt* motif introduces a straightforward, though mildly ironic ("barbecues") lament over lost glories, which focuses and informs the poems constellated about it:

Troy

Whither, O city, are your profits and your gilded shrines,
And your barbecues of great oxen,
And the tall women walking your streets, in gilt clothes,
With their perfumes in little alabaster boxes?
Where is the work of your home-born sculptors?

Time's tooth is into the lot, and war's and fate's too.
Envy has taken your all,
Save your douth and your story.

Both the emotive pattern of this sequence, an array of ironies refracted from a deeper affective focus, in this case loss, and its design—a series of poems whose interwoven emotive currents are drawn together at approximately their center—are familiar from other sequences of this period and are used again in later efforts such as the *Homage to Sextus Propertius*.

"Impressions of François-Marie Arouet (de Voltaire)," published together with the "Homage," extends and deepens its sense of loss, here not specifically as a consequence of death but of change and aging and their erosion of youthful passion; as Harmon notes, this sequence draws together a range of dispositions toward time's ravages from the early poems (64).

Like a number of sequences already examined, "Impressions of Voltaire" is constructed triadically. The first poem laments and derides change induced by wealth, momentarily picking up and reapplying the *ubi sunt* motif of "Homage." Gone are the days of simplicity and their rapport, given over to the haughtiness and superficial glitter of the present:

> Where, Lady, are the days
> When you could go out in a hired hansom
> Without footmen and equipments?
> And dine in a soggy, cheap restaurant?

Gone too are the unadorned beauty and desire of another time.[14]

In the second poem, age has brought exile "from the fine plaisaunces" of passion but not from the memory of them. Ripeness and fecundity are recollected in a series of brilliant, sensuous details, evoking the vitality of love before confronting age's dissipation:[15]

> If you'd have me go on loving you
> Give me back the time of the thing.
>
> Will you give me dawn light at evening?
> Time has driven me out from the fine plaisaunces,
> The parks with the swards all over dew,
> And grass going glassy with the light on it,
> The green stretches where love is and the grapes
> Hang in yellow-white and dark clusters ready for pressing.
>
> And if now we can't fit with our time of life,
> There is not much but its evil left us.

The imaginative force of the desire momentarily recaptured in this passage is all that these first two poems offer in anticipation of the sequence's reversal in the third. Though the vitality of youth is gone, its passion finds continuity through memory and devotion:

> You'll wonder that an old man of eighty
> Can go on writing you verses. . . .
>
> Grass showing under the snow,
> Birds singing late in the year!

> And Tibullus could say of his death, in his Latin:
> "Delia, I would look on you, dying."
>
> And Delia herself fading out,
> Forgetting even her beauty.

This final poem is climactic and the transition is swift and positive, drawing the rest of the sequence into focus and striking a final, affirmative balance.

When the sequences discussed so far in this chapter are viewed as a continuum, it becomes clear that their sometimes eruptive ironies and mirthful ejaculations are alternate facets of their "aesthetic of glimpses" and are rooted in their more plangent dimensions, the informing undercurrents of pathos, loss, and exile for which they help to provide an objectifying framework and a tentative balance. As Kenner has noted, this is a period in Pound's development "of looking back a little wistfully, a period of laments for departed experience, the period inaugurated by *Cathay*" (*Era* 71).

"Cathay"

The most important sequence of the *Lustra* period, "Cathay," began as a booklet of poems adapted and selected from Ernest Fenollosa's notes on over 150 poems by Rihaku (or Li Po) and other Chinese poets (Kenner, *Era* 198). To attain the balance of the nearly final, 1917 version, the anomalously interjected "Seafarer" was removed and the four poems that now close the sequence were added.[16] Although "Cathay" has often been referred to by critics as a sequence or a suite—especially after Kenner observed that "in the method of *Cathay* we have that of the *Cantos* in pencil-sketch" (*Era* 356)—its structure has received little critical attention; most commentaries have focused on its technique of translation and on the differences between the original Chinese and the English adaptations.[17] However, since Pound worked from Fenollosa's notes *in English,* and not strictly from the Chinese, this approach is limited in its capacity to explain either the construction of the individual poems or the unity and the lyrical progression of the sequence as a whole. As Eliot noted, as early as 1917, in the individual poems "it matters very little how much is due to Rihaku and how much to Pound" ("Metric" 180).

Nonetheless, we may certainly attribute the shape of the sequence as a whole not to Rihaku or Fenollosa, but to Pound's selection and arrangement of constituent poems. In its final form, the contents of "Cathay" are as follows:

Song of the Bowmen of Shu
The Beautiful Toilet
The River Song

The River-Merchant's Wife: A Letter
Poem by the Bridge at Ten-Shin
The Jewel Stairs' Grievance
Lament of the Frontier Guard
Exile's Letter
Four Poems of Departure:
   Epigraph
   Separation on the River Kiang
   Taking Leave of a Friend
   Leave-Taking Near Shoku
   The City of Chōan
South-Folk in Cold Country
Sennin Poem by Kakuhaku
A Ballad of the Mulberry Road
Old Idea of Chōan by Roshōrin
To-Em-Mei's "The Unmoving Cloud"[18]

Like some other poems and sequences examined so far, "Cathay" is arranged proleptically; the organizational key to the sequence as a whole surfaces through a close examination of the movement of its first poem, "Song of the Bowmen of Shu." The first part of the poem is developed in three clearly defined segments, each of them characterized by a stage in the cycle of growth and decay of fern shoots picked for food. The progression is from spring's promise of fertility to autumn's decay, and the poem's initial tones of longing and desolation are concomitantly intensified and mingled with bitterness and despair:

> We grub the old fern-stalks.
> We say: Will we be let to go back in October?
> There is no ease in royal affairs, we have no comfort.[19]

In the second part of the poem, the splendor of the general's entourage provides a source of aesthetic relief and introduces notes of heroic endurance and a sense of common purpose—

> Our sorrow is bitter, but we would not return to our country.
> What flower has come into blossom?
> Whose chariot? The General's.

—but this too ultimately collapses. In the final lines, weariness and sorrow return in the image of willows that droop with the weight of new leaves in spring and snow in winter, and the tired, despondent movement of "we go slowly." The anguish of the bowmen's campaign is voiced through the dense and varied repetition of *o* sounds in their closing question:

> When we set out, the willows were drooping with spring,
> We come back in the snow,
> We go slowly, we are hungry and thirsty,
> Our mind is full of sorrow, who will know of our grief?

The structure of "Song of the Bowmen of Shu" serves as the matrix upon which the rest of the sequence is built. In the next six poems, the three-part movement of "Song of the Bowmen" is intensified and elaborated in three units of paired poems:

"The Beautiful Toilet"—"The River Song"

"The River-Merchant's Wife: A Letter"—"Poem by the Bridge at Ten-Shin"

"The Jewel Stairs' Grievance"—"Lament of the Frontier Guard"

The first poem in each pair traces the abandonment and decay of female beauty and fertility, parallel to the growth and wastage of the fern shoots in "Song of the Bowmen of Shu"; and the second focuses on the thwarting of masculine creative potential in first aesthetic ("The River Song"), then aristocratic ("Poem by the Bridge at Ten-Shin"), and finally martial contexts ("Lament of the Frontier Guard"). Like the three-part movement in "Song of the Bowmen of Shu," these three pairs of poems evolve from a promise of fulfillment in "The River Song" to desolation and the sequence's climax of despair in "Lament of the Frontier Guard."

The juxtaposition of poems within each pair, emotive "planes in relation," clearly serves to heighten the poignancy with which the females' isolation and the ravaging of the land and depredation of male creative potential by war are experienced. One cogent analogue for this alternation of context and sensibility, female and male, is the yin/yang pairing that Wai-Lim Yip has located as operative in "Lament of the Frontier Guard":

> The word *yang* originally meant sunshine, or what pertains to sunshine and light; that of *yin* meant the absence of sunshine, i.e. shadow or darkness. In later development, the *yang* and *yin* came to be regarded as two cosmic principles or forces, respectively representing masculinity, activity, heat, brightness, dryness, hardness, etc. for the *yang*, and feminity [sic], passivity, cold, darkness, wetness, softness, etc., for the *yin*. Through the interaction of these two primary principles, all phenomena of the universe are produced.[20]

Looking more closely at the three units outlined above, we find within the poems, as well as within their grouping, a series of repetitions and variations of the three-part movement of "Song of the Bowmen of Shu" and its progression from spring to autumn. In "The Beautiful Toilet" and "The River Song" the setting is spring and our attention is directed in each poem through a triadic series of images: in "The Beautiful Toilet" from the garden to the mistress within to her isolation, and within the garden from the grass to the willows to the mistress herself. In "The River Song" the movement proceeds from the boat on the river to the Emperor's garden to the Emperor himself.

"The River-Merchant's Wife: A Letter" begins in spring, with the fertile promise of a youthful relationship:

> I played about the front gate, pulling flowers.
> You came by on bamboo stilts, playing horse,
> You walked about my seat, playing with blue plums.

The ensuing marriage is traced in three stages:

> At fourteen I married My Lord you. . . .
>
> At fifteen I stopped scowling. . . .
>
> At sixteen you departed. . . .

and the poem closes in autumn with a three-part view of past, present, and future (a contrast implicit in nearly all the poems of "Cathay"), drawing to its focus of delicately underspoken yet powerful yearning:

> You dragged your feet when you went out.
> By the gate now, the moss is grown, the different mosses,
> Too deep to clear them away!
> The leaves fall early this autumn, in wind. . . .
>
> If you are coming down through the narrows of the river Kiang,
> Please let me know beforehand,
> And I will come out to meet you
>   As far as Chō-fū-Sa.

Again it is spring at the opening of "Poem by the Bridge at Ten-Shin"— "March has come to the bridge head"—and autumn at its close:

> Night and day are given over to pleasure
> And they think it will last a thousand autumns,
>   Unwearying autumns.

And within this movement the inevitable progression from growth to decay is governed by natural cycles that the dissolute aristocracy ignore:

> At morning there are flowers to cut the heart,
> And evening drives them on the eastward-flowing waters.

The climactic third pair of poems remain in autumn, passing from the pure, condensed, oblique lamentation of "The Jewel Stairs' Grievance" to "Lament of the Frontier Guard." The very compression of the first poem intensifies by contrast the desolation at the height of the second, in its summation of the sequence's movement up to this point and its overview of war's consequences: "A gracious spring, turned to blood-ravenous autumn." This precise echo of the central curve of the sequence—the disappointment of spring's promise and the wastage of life and creative energy—emerges through a series of images linked predominantly in groups of three. It is worth quoting this poem in full in order to observe the repetition, "ply over ply," of this structural motif:

[1]

> By the North Gate, the wind blows full of sand,
> Lonely from the beginning of time until now!
> [2]   [3]
> Trees fall, the grass goes yellow with autumn.
> I climb the towers and towers
>   to watch out the barbarous land:
>   [1]   [2]   [3]
> Desolate castle, the sky, the wide desert.
> [1]   There is no wall left to this village.
> [2]   Bones white with a thousand frosts,
> [3]   High heaps, covered with trees and grass;
> [1]   Who brought this to pass?
> [2]   Who has brought the flaming imperial anger?
> [3]   Who has brought the army with drums and with kettle-drums?
> Barbarous kings.
> A gracious spring, turned to blood-ravenous autumn,
> A turmoil of wars-men, spread over the middle kingdom,
> Three hundred and sixty thousand,
>   [1]
> And sorrow, sorrow like rain.
>   [2]   [3]
> Sorrow to go, and sorrow, sorrow returning.
> [1]   Desolate, desolate fields,
> [2]   And no children of warfare upon them,
> [3]   No longer the men for offence and defence.
> Ah, how shall you know the dreary sorrow at the North Gate,
> With Riboku's name forgotten,
> And we guardsmen fed to the tigers.

Much of the force of the poem's expression of tragic, senseless destruction is derived from its use of repetition, its climactic arrangement of triadic units, and its shift in perspective from the timeless, universal scope with which it opens to the more immediate focus of its closing lament.

Like the second part of "Song of the Bowmen of Shu," the remainder of the sequence breaks away from a strictly triadic pattern of development, though the triad is recapitulated briefly and recurs frequently as a unifying motif in all of the remaining poems. The progression toward winter at the end of "Song of the Bowmen" is also repeated in the following poems, culminating in "South Folk in Cold Country." And the aesthetic relief discovered momentarily in the general's accoutrements in "Song of the Bowmen" becomes predominant in the last poems of the sequence, where moments of sorrow and intense longing for a distant time or place, or for severed companionship, alternate with moments of excited engagement in memory, vision, and keenly-attuned perception. The overall movement of the last part and its conclusion in spring strongly suggest a resolution through aesthetic reenvisioning.

"Exile's Letter" unfolds through the heightened recollection of three gatherings in youth, their festivities and their companionship, in contrast to the isolation and old age of the present. While the season of the first gathering is unspecified, the second and third certainly take place in spring:

> We met, and travelled into Sen-jō,
> Through all the thirty-six folds of the turning and twisting waters
> Into a valley of the thousand bright flowers. . . .
>
> And one May he had you send for me,
> despite the long distance.

A fourth meeting is briefly alluded to, and the final parting is

> like the flowers falling at Spring's end,
> Confused, whirled in a tangle.

While "Lament of the Frontier Guard" is the climax of the sequence in its desolation, bitterness, and outrage, "Exile's Letter" projects its most deeply personal sense of nostalgia, regretful yet tempered by the recreation of aesthetic delight through memory:

> Pleasure lasting, with courtezans, going and coming without hindrance,
> With the willow flakes falling like snow,
> And the vermilioned girls getting drunk about sunset,
> And the water, a hundred feet deep, reflecting green eyebrows
> —Eyebrows painted green are a fine sight in young moonlight,
> Gracefully painted—
> And the girls singing back at each other. . . .

"Four Poems of Departure" echo the central concern in "Exile's Letter" with the brevity of meaningful communion and the persistence of isolation. These are suggested by the thwarting of spring's fertility—

> Here we must make separation
> And go out through a thousand miles of dead grass

—and the decay of civilization:

> The bright cloths and bright caps of Shin
> Are now the base of old hills.

The next three poems briefly recapitulate and vary the movement of the opening three poems of the sequence. "South Folk in Cold Country" returns to the martial context, the deprivation, and the heroic overtones of "Song of the Bowmen of Shu"; "Sennin Poem by Kakuhaku" echoes the creative ecstasy of "The River Song"; and "A Ballad of the Mulberry Road" recalls the delicacy and isolation of the mistress in "The Beautiful Toilet," though here the aesthetic sensitivity of the heroine introduces an artistic order into her surroundings. Each of these poems is also built up through a triadic arrangement of images and motifs.

The winter landscape of "South Folk in Cold Country" brings the sequence to its seasonal nadir and functions as a pivot toward the partial resolution in spring at the end. The three statements at the opening of the poem reiterate the sense of dislocation that courses through "Cathay," and the staccato, triadic phrases at the poem's center understate its hardship, deprivation, and bitterness:

> Surprised. Desert turmoil. Sea sun.
> Flying snow bewilders the barbarian heaven.
> Lice swarm like ants over our accoutrements.
> Mind and spirit drive on the feathery banners.

While the images of nature in this poem tend to universalize the harshness of experience, in the following "Sennin Poem by Kakuhaku" the "high forest" provides a setting for spiritual communion. The interchange between spirit and mortal is presented triadically, and the poem closes with a denunciation of those impervious to such experience:

> He rides through the purple smoke to visit the sennin,
> He takes "Floating Hill" by the sleeve,
> He claps his hand on the back of the great water sennin.

> But you, you dam'd crowd of gnats,
> Can you even tell the age of a turtle?

The greatest concentration of triadic patterning in the sequence occurs in the aesthetic order that "Rafu" constructs about her from elements of her surroundings in "A Ballad of the Mulberry Road." The closing section of the poem presents an ideal of reciprocity between her and a world appreciative of her (the artist's) efforts:

> Her earrings are made of pearl,
> Her underskirt is of green pattern-silk,
> Her overskirt is the same silk dyed in purple,
> And when men going by look on Rafu,
>   They set down their burdens,
>   They stand and twirl their moustaches.

In "Old Idea of Chōan by Roshōrin," transitional toward the sequence's closing, the resplendent intricacy of the setting makes it "a place of felicitous meeting" and its ornamented structures become a form of imaginative companionship:

> Riō's house stands out on the sky,
>   with glitter of colour
> As Butei of Kan had made the high golden lotus
>   to gather his dews,
> Before it another house which I do not know:
> How shall we know all the friends
>   whom we meet on strange roadways?

This is temporary, however, and the final poem, "To-Em-Mei's 'The Unmoving Cloud,'" opens at a climactic pitch of nearly despondent isolation. In the first three sections the deepening gloom of the rain-filled landscape is punctuated only by a frustrated hope for visitors, embodied in an unshared cask of wine, and by the garden's futile offering of spring's renewed possibilities, in a world apart from that of the melancholy speaker.

The closing lines of the sequence introduce its first notes of self-ironic humor in the projection of human dislocation onto the sun and moon and a sense of intractable isolation into the voices of birds:

> And men say the sun and moon keep on moving
>   because they can't find a soft seat. . . .

> The birds flutter to rest in my tree,
>   and I think I have heard them saying,
> "It is not that there are no other men

> But we like this fellow the best,
> But however we long to speak
> He can not know of our sorrow."

By means of this objectification of intensely personal feeling, the central emotive streams of "Cathay"—displacement, longing, and isolation—are resolved through a partial and tentative acceptance of them as universal facets of experience. This instance of what Hugh Witemeyer discusses as "objective imagination" serves here, as often in Pound's poetry, to universalize the expression of strong emotion and to subordinate its confessional implications (29ff.).

Through a close examination of the construction of "Cathay" and its mode of unification as a sequence, the devices by which it forecasts the technique of *The Cantos* emerge into full view. First, its juxtaposition of poems with apparently disparate contexts and a range of settings and voices, joined loosely by their oriental reference, exemplifies the arrangement of emotive "planes in relation" central to Imagist and Vorticist poetics and crucial for the continuity of attention among the associatively related passages of *The Cantos*.

Second, as Pound told Yeats and others, *The Cantos* were intended "to display a structure like that of a Bach Fugue" (Yeats 4).[21] The analogy is equally applicable to "Cathay" thematically and tonally in the introduction, through the opening "Song of the Bowmen of Shu," of the subject—the hardship and deprivation of war—and the countersubject, the preservation of the individual sensibility under duress through an aesthetic reordering of perception, memory, and experience; and, as in a fugue, these two contexts are interwoven throughout the course of the sequence. Parallel to these is an alternation between the martial setting itself and contrasting scenes of festivity, companionship, and spiritual communion, and between a sense of heroic endurance and the fragility of the sequence's female personae. All of these motifs in "Cathay" are picked up and used extensively in *The Cantos,* as are its distant cultural setting and its presentation of models for positive action. Additionally, the longing for home with which "Cathay" opens and the setting at home, with no companions, that closes the sequence strongly suggest the Odyssean voyage that informs both the structure and the central concerns of *The Cantos*.

"Cathay" also follows the order of a fugue in its use of the initial poem as the matrix upon which the entire sequence is built; in the construction of its central framework using a pattern of triadic movement, echoed and varied in the poems' phrasing and interplay of motifs; and in its incorporation of seasonal cycles as a constant though shifting modal background, a sustained "metaphor by sympathy."

Both thematically and structurally, then, the proleptic order of this earlier sequence anticipates the broader, more loosely arranged introduction of essential materials and their basic modes of organization into *The Cantos* through the initial set of poems:

> The first 11 cantos are preparation of the palette. I *have* to get down all the colours or elements I want for the poem. Some perhaps too enigmatically and abbreviatedly. I hope, heaven help me, to bring them into some sort of design and architecture later. (*Ltrs* 180)

Another key principle of organization in *The Cantos* that Pound specified in conjunction with the fugue, the "repeat in history" (*Ltrs* 210), appears in "Cathay" in the three scenes of battle that direct the course of the poems (along with the implicit subject rhyme with the war in progress at the time of writing) and, relatedly, in the repeated abandonment and decay of female beauty.[22]

Beyond these schematic modes of organization just identified in "Cathay," its primary *modus operandi* as a sequence is its lyrical movement. Ultimately, all of the numerous voices of the poems and the experience, reminiscence, and reflection they project are refracted elements of a single, unified consciousness. In its abrupt shifts from a tragic awareness of war's destructive force and a sense of personal desolation to moments of aesthetically heightened perception and revery, and in its movement "through confusion and ambiguities toward a precarious balance" (Rosenthal, "Structuring" 4), an emotional unity is attained not unlike that achieved much later, in the *Pisan Cantos*. Of course, there is no initial pressure in "Cathay" comparable to the violent intensity of the personal and political turmoil beneath the later sequence, and consequently the movement is more controlled and distanced; the form, too, as this analysis has shown, exhibits a carefully planned containment very different from the volatile fluidity of *The Cantos* as a whole and especially of the *Pisan* sequence. Nonetheless, the central force that generates the emotive streams of the sequence, mobilizes their interaction, and gathers them toward a sense of resolution, however tenuous, can be characterized equally well in "Cathay" and in *The Cantos* as the effort "to pit personal, historical and artistic memory against anomie and alienation" (Rosenthal, "Structuring" 4).

In at least these respects, then, the method of "Cathay" is clearly a significant step toward that of *The Cantos*. And despite its obvious differences from the longer sequence—especially its more controlled movement and its greater sense of resolution and closure—the extended scope and complexity of "Cathay" and its successful organization of a varied range of emotive pattern-units into a sustained and unified whole must certainly have provided much of the technique and the impetus for the major work.

"Cathay" picks up the external focus of the periodical sequences preceding it and coordinates this quite successfully with underlying strains of a more vulnerable, personal awareness, which are presented more explicitly and emphatically. These key dimensions are interwoven in "Cathay" within an integral whole whose scope and structure tend to impart objectivity and universality to the most intimately personal currents of vision and emotion. This is not, of course, solely a matter of depersonalizing autobiographical materials, although this process is also involved: indeed, as Pound remarked to Ford, "'Homage to S. Propertius,' Seafarer, Exile's Letter, and Mauberley are all 'me' in one sense; my personality is certainly a great slag heap of stuff" transformed through poetic "crystalizations" into art, rather than simple self-expression (*P/F* 42).

More important is the sequence's mode of imparting resonance and intensity through an objectification of the personal focus of the language itself and its affective force. This is, for instance, the end attained through the placement of the muted complaint of "The Jewel Stairs' Grievance" and the more open lamentation of "Exile's Letter" in their respective positions within the larger framework of "Cathay," where they are set against the parallel or divergent emotive pattern-units of other poems.

This is also the technique of *The Cantos*. One notable instance in *A Draft of XXX Cantos* is the emergence of the heightened lyrical vision of Canto XVII out of the epic sweep of Canto I (linked by the phrase "So that," which ends I and begins XVII) and in juxtaposition with the scatological inferno of Cantos XIV–XVI immediately preceding it. The contrast in attention here between what Pound called the "cult of beauty" and the "cult of ugliness" (*LE* 45) is less dramatic, perhaps, than the way the epic and satiric distance of I and XIV–XVI impart a universal dimension to the lyric, personal immediacy of XVII.

This breadth of lyric scope is characteristic of the modern sequence, which is at once both intensely personal and impersonal—less paradoxically than this initially seems. It is personal to the degree to which the poem must provide a focusing and unifying consciousness to replace the heroic figure conventionally at the center of the epic, yet it achieves epic objectivity through the expansion or fragmentation of its controlling sensibility. If a single figure occupies the focus of the modern long poem, he does so as representative of a larger whole— Whitman as the type of the new-world man, for instance. But more commonly, as in "Cathay" and *The Cantos* or in *The Waste Land,* the central figure is replaced by an array of perspectives or a fluid succession of varied states of consciousness. These states and the sense they project of a protean but integral sensibility emerging from their juxtaposition provide at once a sense of personality and a broader, decentralized view of the poem's concerns—psychic, cultural, political, and so forth. In effect, the modern long poem presents almost simultaneously the perspectives of both the "scene" and the "panorama" whose alternation Thomas Greene has noted as characteristic of traditional epic.[23] We are given the materials of the poems directly—historical facts, anecdotes, reminiscences, reveries, visions, fragments of other poems—and although often from a distanced perspective, never entirely without their experiential impact on the unifying consciousness. This is, of course, closely related to the fragmented, improvisational structure of the modern sequence, since no formally repetitive pattern and no structure limited by narrative, dramatic, or discursive exigencies can allow for the necessary rapidity and range in shifts of focus between the distant and the immediate, the universal and the personal.

The process of expansion from the restricted introspection of individual lyrics toward the more impersonal overview of the long poem is apparent in the course of Pound's evolution from the framework of the early "personae" to the more complex and fragmented structures of the later sequences, where the "persona" is objectified partly through its ideogrammic juxtaposition with other personae. These disparate frames of consciousness become, through this procedure, Imagist backdrops for the interacting currents of affect in the sequence as a whole. Thus the frame of consciousness that barely allows her anguish to find voice in "The Jewel Stairs' Grievance" and the frame of consciousness that laments age, loss, and exile in "Exile's Letter" become objective facets of an encompassing sensibility within "Cathay" and acquire a scope and intensity on the same level as the broad vision at the opening of "Lament of the Frontier Guard."

This mode of expansion and transformation is exactly the process involved in the reworking of the Ur-Cantos toward their present form, where "the man talking gave place to rapidly dissolving images. . . . The Ur-Canto urge to be present and talking . . . reflected an anxiety about keeping control; but a structure incorporates its own controls" (Kenner, *Era* 360). Pound's own description of the stages in his poetic development, as a way of explaining Imagism, traces the course of this evolution in his poetics:

> In the "search for oneself," in the search for "sincere self-expression," one gropes, one finds some seeming verity. One says "I am" this, that, or the other, and with the words scarcely uttered one ceases to be that thing.
>
> I began this search for the real in a book called *Personae*, casting off, as it were, complete masks of the self in each poem. I continued in a long series of translations, which were but more elaborate masks.
>
> Secondly, I made poems like "The Return," which is an objective reality and has a complicated sort of significance, like Mr. Epstein's "Sun God," or Mr. Brzeska's "Boy with a Coney." Thirdly, I have written "Heather," which represents a state of consciousness, or "implies," or "implicates" it. (*GB* 85)

This is not strictly a matter of chronological progression, nor do these distinctions provide rigid categories into which Pound's poems, even those cited here as paradigms, can be readily classified. Rather, much of Pound's work can be viewed cogently in terms of all three categories; this evolution refers to a shift in focus and context from the limited scope of the early "personae" to the greater psychic depth and universality of other poems such as "Heather." Both sorts of poems present "states of consciousness," as it were, but differently, and the difference is that between the mode of the Ur-Cantos and the mode of *The Cantos*. Especially noteworthy in Pound's revisions is the retention of skeletal details and the more impersonal focus they are given through the removal of the Ur-Cantos' dramatic framework and the excision of the repeated "I":

> Hang it all, there can be but one *Sordello!*
> But say I want to, say I take your whole bag of tricks,
> Let in your quirks and tweeks, and say the thing's an art-form,
> Your *Sordello*, and that the modern world
> Needs such a rag-bag to stuff all its thought in;
> Say that I dump my catch, shiny and silvery
> As fresh sardines flapping and slipping on the marginal cobbles?
>
> ("Three Cantos" I 113)

> Hang it all, Robert Browning,
> there can be but the one "Sordello."
> But Sordello, and my Sordello?
> Lo Sordels si fo di Mantovana.
> So-shu churned in the sea.
>
> (Canto II)

In Pound's later formulation of the "persona," it is an ineffective means of attaining impersonality:

> When art fails to reach or does not seek the impersonal, when it fails to become the roving eye or the voice [of an impartial observer], one can use a persona, as Cervantes does, but the social position of Quixote or Sancho serves rather to render the ridiculous. (*P/F* 98)

The "persona" in Pound's work in fact obtains only in the use of a single figure, often only momentarily, to impart a local habitation and a name to a state of consciousness. While the centrality of states of consciousness rather than dramatic characterization is implicit even in the earliest "personae," such as "Cino" and "Marvoil," it becomes increasingly apparent in sequences that use composite figures—"Translations from Heine," "Impressions of Marie-François Arouet (de Voltaire)" and *Homage to Sextus Propertius*, for instance—and those that present a succession of them: notably "Cathay," "Near Perigord," *Hugh Selwyn Mauberley*, and *The Cantos*.

Quia Pauper Amavi

There is a strong continuity between the central affective currents of the sequences in *Lustra* and those in the subsequent collection, *Quia Pauper Amavi*, though ironic contrasts are often more prominent and more sharply defined in the latter, and they encompass a greater breadth of vision, especially in the *Homage to Sextus Propertius*.

Contrasts between the hollowness of the present age with its poseurs and the rich achievement of past and present figures, attained through sincerity of effort, are again central to *Quia Pauper Amavi* and are dramatically illuminated in the juxtaposition of "Moeurs Contemporaines" and "Langue d'Oc." These sequences are complementary, published together in the *Little Review* (May 1918) after Harriet Monroe objected to the frankness of some passages in "Moeurs Contemporaines."

The framework of "Langue d'Oc," first, is established by the albas of its epigraph, poem I and poem IV, which project a fulfillment of love, desire, and devotion despite the obstacles of time, the ubiquitous cuckold, and unnamed detractors: all, of course, elements drawn from Provençal convention. Fruition reaches its apex in the joyful reciprocality of satiate voices singing in poem IV (*"Vergier"*) and its final tribute:

> "My pretty boy, make we our play again
> Here in the orchard where the birds complain,
> 'Till the traist watcher his song unrein,
> Ah God! How swift the night
>   And day comes on."

> "Out of the wind that blows from her,
> That dancing and gentle is and thereby pleasanter,
> Have I drunk a draught, sweeter than scent of myrrh.
> Ah God! How swift the night.
>   And day comes on."

> *Venust the lady, and none lovelier,*
> *For her great beauty, many men look on her,*
> *Out of my love will her heart not stir.*
> *By God, how swift the night.*
>   *And day comes on.*[24]

Between the albas framing the sequence are a song of yearning in spring, in poem II (*"Avril"*), and a song of utter devotion despite the thwarting of desire, in poem III, where all experience is focused through that devotion on the beloved.

The contrasts between the Provençal world revivified in these poems and the world of "Moeurs Contemporaines" are readily apparent. The moment of dawn that pervades this sequence is, as often in Pound's poems, a moment of ecstasy, illumination, and renewal, even if also a moment of parting (cf. Witemeyer 56–58); and this is set against the aesthetic obtuseness of Styrax and his circle in "Moeurs Contemporaines." The plenitude of life-impulse and desire in

these poems answers the inadequacy of the figures in "Moeurs"; and the reciprocality of poem IV here is alive and vibrant with song between lovers, not the
relic of an irrecoverable past, frozen in a photograph, between a parent and child
in V,1 of "Moeurs." Finally, desire in "Langue d'Oc" is a natural force and an
expression of devotion, not a licentious drowning, "after years of continence,"
"in a sea of six women," as in "Moeurs" VI. All of these differences are
reflected in the sharpness of diction and flat, direct rhythms of "Moeurs" and the
ebullient sonorities of "Langue d'Oc." As McDougal observes of "Langue d'Oc,"

> Taken as a whole, this sequence affirms the transitory nature of the moment of bliss between
> lovers. In spite of the separation or loss that inevitably follows this, the lover remains perenni-
> ally optimistic, determined, and faithful to the memory of his beloved, whom he reveres above
> everything else. . . . Love has become debased [in the modern world] . . . and we have lost the
> mystical reverence for *Amor* that permeated the medieval world. Consequently, *Amor* cannot
> adequately be described in nineteenth or twentieth century English, and a new language must
> be created. The modern, ironic diction of "Moeurs Contemporains" [sic] and *Homage to Sextus
> Propertius* is simply not applicable to *fin' amors*. (138–39)

The poems of "Moeurs Contemporaines" can hardly make the same claims
on our attention as the *Homage to Sextus Propertius,* yet they have been so
overshadowed by the more accomplished sequence that they are almost univer-
sally neglected. Their greatest value may be as a preparatory effort for *Hugh
Selwyn Mauberley,* but Pound apparently thought them successful and significant enough to be recorded (Caedmon SWC 2088). In fact, the sequence brings
together many of the concerns of the earlier works and anticipates not only *Hugh
Selwyn Mauberley* but sections of *The Cantos* as well. The construction of
"Moeurs" also mirrors that of the *Homage to Sextus Propertius* in its essentially
symmetrical design.

"Moeurs Contemporaines" consists of a series of satirical sketches much in
the manner of the earlier periodical sequences. The first, *"Mr. Styrax,"* presents
the inadequacy of its subject—specifically, the sexual inadequacy—and its cor-
ollaries in his superficiality ("And even now Mr. Styrax / Does not believe in
aesthetics") and in the disposition of others around him. Out of its restrained
sarcasm emerges indignation at the continuity of morals and empire maintained
by so perverse a state of affairs:

> His brother has taken to gipsies,
> But the son-in-law of Mr. H. Styrax
> Objects to perfumed cigarettes.
>   In the parlance of Niccolo Machiavelli:
>   "Thus things proceed in their circle";
>   And thus the empire is maintained.

By contrast, the closing two poems lament the passing of "the old men with beautiful manners" and their circle, with Henry James at the focus of the elegy; the sincerity and aesthetic perspicuity of "gli occhi onesti e tardi" are set against the mountain-climbing and the "large muscles" that veil the hollowness of Mr. Styrax.

This key opposition between the passing of men with integrity and the continuity of the poseur is brought to a focus in the two parts of poem V, the central section of the sequence. Part 1 draws, from a scene of days past preserved in a photograph, a context of tenderness in an exchange between parent and child:

> It is a lady,
> She sits at a harp,
> Playing,
>
> And by her left foot, in a basket,
> Is an infant, aged about 14 months,
> The infant beams at the parent,
> The parent re-beams at its offspring.
> The basket is lined with satin,
> There is a satin-like bow on the harp.

Although the poem's perspective is distanced by the technical detail of its observations and by its ironic view of the frozen figures (*"It* is a lady"), it offers a contrast to the complete failure of sensibility derided in other sections. Significantly, the harp is played in this setting, while "in the house of the novelist" in part 2 it is untouched, the bric-a-brac of opulence accumulated through popular, hence economically successful prose. The emotional overtones of part 1 are also replaced by empty "symbolical" flowers, and by the concerns with empire and morality characteristic of Styrax and his circle:[25]

> And in the home of the novelist
> There is a satin-like bow on an harp.
> You enter and pass hall after hall,
> Conservatory follows conservatory,
> Lilies lift their white symbolical cups,
> Whence their symbolical pollen has been excerpted,
> Near them I noticed an harp
> And the blue satin ribbon,
> And the copy of "Hatha Yoga"
> And the neat piles of unopened, unopening books,
>
> And she spoke to me of the monarch,
> And of the purity of her soul.

Thus the key tonal centers of the sequence are established in I, V, and VII, and the remaining poems are ranged about them; as Pound wrote Harriet Monroe, "the old man, and the harp, and Mr. Styrax will hold the balance" (*Ltrs* 127). The sexual and aesthetic nullity of Styrax find their female counterpart in Clara, in poem II; the literary pretense of V is anticipated by the "darn'd clever bunch" of III; and Styrax is reproduced in the sexual neutrality and immaturity of the "it" caricatured in IV, "*Sketch 48b.11.*"[26] The sexual exhaustion joined with an evocation of Homer's richness in the epitaph of VI answers the vapidity of I and IV:

> *Stele*
> After years of continence
>   he hurled himself into a sea of six women.
> Now, quenched as the brand of Meleager,
>   he lies by the poluphloisboious sea-coast. . . .

The allusion to Meleager ironically evokes a heroic context—for Meleager's "brand" of life ended by consumption in flames, not by being "quenched"—which illuminates Mr. Hecatomb Styrax's empty nature as well.

The major oppositions of "Moeurs Contemporaines" and their concomitant affective currents—admiring approbation and nostalgia for the emotional and aesthetic vitality of the past, set against sardonic caricatures of empty, contemporary figures—are carried over into the *Homage to Sextus Propertius* and *Hugh Selwyn Mauberley*. The jeers and the caustic wit directed at the sterility of the present age in "Moeurs Contemporaines" are again a key note in *Mauberley*, although they receive a more strongly personal emphasis in the *apathein* of the controlling consciousness of part 2 of that sequence.

A contrast between past genius and present vapidity is also an implicit but subordinate concern in the *Homage to Sextus Propertius;* more central is the contemporaneity and vitality of the past, and particularly of past lyrical genius. Of course, the *Homage* also looks askance at current "distentions of Empire," parallel to Roman imperialism, but too much has sometimes been made of this, partly because of Pound's later political preoccupations and partly because of statements he made much later in defense of the sequence:[27]

I may perhaps avoid charges of further mystification and wilful obscurity by saying that it presents certain emotions as vital to me in 1917, faced with the infinite and ineffable imbecility of the British Empire, as they were to Propertius some centuries earlier, when faced with the infinite and ineffable imbecility of the Roman Empire. These emotions are defined largely, but not entirely, in Propertius' own terms. If the reader does not find relation to life defined in the poem, he may conclude that I have been unsuccessful in my endeavour. (*Ltrs* 231)

The emphasis on "certain emotions" should warn us away from viewing the sequence as a political statement or as programmatic in any other sense; surely it is no more an exposition of "an artistic credo" (Sullivan 27) than of a political one, though both concerns, among others, are woven through the fabric of the poems. The essential material of the sequence is not topical but emotional, as Pound reiterated elsewhere: "The tacit question of my 'Homage to Propertius' is simply: 'Have I portrayed more emotion than Bohn's literal version or any other extant or possible strict translation of Propertius does or could convey?'" (qtd. in Sullivan 8).

The dominant emotive current in the *Homage,* as in Propertius's *Elegies,* is exuberant eroticism and compelling devotion. This links it to the lyric tradition it invokes, to the other sequences in this volume, to Pound's earlier works and, in combination with a view of the underworld, to *The Cantos;* in both the *Homage* and *The Cantos,* love is an assertion of life-force and of creative powers against the forces of decay and death.[28]

As in *The Cantos,* the central concerns of the *Homage*—love, death, poetic effort and direction, social and political pressures and reactions to them, and the affect that surrounds each of these and gives it significance and force in the tonal flux of the poems—are fused into an integral, dynamic whole and unified by their containment within a broadly encompassing state of consciousness. As Turner notes, "the mental state of the love poet is like the main theme of a musical piece, passed from one instrument to another, while other, less dominant themes reinforce or tax the main theme, provide consonance and dissonance and highlight or mute it" (244), a process analogous to the fugue-like construction of *The Cantos* and the interplay of affective movements in "Cathay." Thus each of the key strains of thought and affect in the *Homage* emerges with its particular tensions and predominates at different moments and at varied levels of intensity.

To view the contour of the sequence as a whole, in brief: the amatory current is present to some degree throughout, but reaches its greatest erotic intensity in V,2, VI, and VII; similarly, a concern with death is a continuous undercurrent but surfaces with particular force in VI, where it plays off and intensifies the dominant amatory focus, and in IX; reactions to political and social pressures are centered in I and II; and a concern with the evolution and refinement of a poetic voice and its claims to a place within an established lyric tradition is most prominent in I, II, V, and XII. Like many sequences before and after it, the *Homage to Sextus Propertius* is constructed around the lyrical focus at its center: "Not only does the poem progress linearly from one section to the next, but also it proceeds symmetrically by pairs toward its center. The poem's end sections present its theme of love versus war poetry, while its two central sections [VI and VII] settle the issue by first theoretically and then practically exemplifying the love poetry Pound's Propertius writes" (Thomas 57).[29] This

construction thus has both thematic and tonal significance: the climactic eroticism of the central poems resonates throughout the sequence and extends its
vitality toward the two ends.

Of course, the method of proceeding among these concerns, between adja-
cent poems or even within a poem, is predominantly through juxtaposition. As
Sullivan observes, "The sort of poetry we find in the *Homage* makes violent use
of this emotional linkage, this abrupt juxtaposition of different feelings and
tones. All formal and grammatical connection may vanish in the interests of the
harder poetical impact. But the juxtaposition of apparently unrelated subjects is
a *significant* juxtaposition with its own logic. The new theme affects the preceding theme and modifies the feeling of the whole poem" (89). Nothing in poems
I and II, for instance, prepares logically for the sudden plunge into the turmoil
of lovers' private world in III, yet only by means of such a plunge, thematically
and affectively, can the public stance of the first two poems gain force. Or,
typically, a poem may leap from a panoramic view to a more intimate perspective, releasing a surge of poignancy, or irony, or both:

> Caesar plots against India,
> Tigris and Euphrates shall, from now on, flow at his bidding,
> Tibet shall be full of Roman policemen,
> The Parthians shall get used to our statuary
>   and acquire a Roman religion;
> One raft on the veiled flood of Acheron,
>   Marius and Jugurtha together.
>
> Nor at my funeral either will there be any long trail,
>   bearing ancestral lares and images;
> No trumpets filled with my emptiness,
> Nor shall it be on an Atalic bed. . . .

$$(VI)^{30}$$

While there is hardly space here for as comprehensively detailed an examination of this sequence as it merits, some of the key patterns of its design may
be touched on briefly. To begin, the proud note of triumphant procession sounded
at the opening of the first poem is echoed again in the confident assertion of lyric
immortality, tinged with a tragic awareness of mutability, in its closing lines:

> Shades of Callimachus, Coan ghosts of Philetas,
> It is in your grove I would walk,
> I who come first from the clear font
> Bringing the Grecian orgies into Italy,
>   and the dance into Italy.
> Who hath taught you so subtle a measure,
>   in what hall have you heard it;

> What foot beat out your time-bar,
>> what water has mellowed your whistles?
>
> . . . .
>
> Flame burns, rain sinks into the cracks,
> And they all go to rack ruin beneath the thud of the years.
> Stands genius a deathless adornment,
>> a name not to be worn out with the years.

As Rosenthal and Gall observe (193–94), this proleptically establishes the essential, symmetrical curve of the sequence, which ends with a similarly proud claim to lyric ascendancy in the face of death:

> Varro sang Jason's expedition,
>> Varro, of his great passion Leucadia,
> There is song in the parchment; Catullus the highly indecorous,
> Of Lesbia, known above Helen;
> And in the dyed pages of Calvus,
>> Calvus mourning Quintilia,
> And but now Gallus had sung of Lycoris.
>> Fair, fairest Lycoris—
> The waters of Styx poured over the wound:
> And now Propertius of Cynthia, taking his stand among these.

(XII)

These passages, representative of the orientation of the sequence as a whole, also offer a defiant challenge to the writers of official epic and the annalists scorned in the first poem and derisively parodied elsewhere. More than that, they offer to supplant both the epic poet and the hero he celebrates with the lyric poet's heroic labor of love. This emerges with magnificently strident clarity out of the juxtapositional leap from a burlesque of imperial bombast, with comic sexual entendres, in V,1, to the richly playful eroticism of the lyric poet's "matter" in V,2. Naturally, the lyric poet's achievement is of greater magnitude than the feats celebrated in epic, for he "shall construct many Iliads" and "spin long yarns out of nothing":

> Up, up my soul, from your lowly cantilation,
>> put on a timely vigour.
>
> Oh august Pierides! Now for a large-mouthed product.
> Thus:
> "The Euphrates denies its protection to the
>> Parthian and apologizes for Crassus,"
> And "It is, I think, India which now gives
>> necks to your triumph,"

And so forth, Augustus. "Virgin Arabia shakes
    in her inmost dwelling."
If any land shrink into a distant seacoast,
    it is a mere postponement of your domination.
And I shall follow the camp, I shall be duly celebrated for
    singing the affairs of your cavalry.
May the fates watch over my day.

2

Yet you ask on what account I write so many love-lyrics
And whence this soft book comes into my mouth.
Neither Calliope nor Apollo sung these things into my ear,
    My genius is no more than a girl.

If she with ivory fingers drive a tune through the lyre,
    We look at the process.
How easy the moving fingers; if hair is mussed on her forehead,
If she goes in a gleam of Cos, in a slither of dyed stuff,
There is a volume in the matter; if her eyelids sink into sleep,
There are new jobs for the author;
And if she plays with me with her shirt off,
    We shall construct many Iliads.
And whatever she does or says
    We shall spin long yarns out of nothing.

These passages are of central importance, since they draw together the two
halves of the sequence. At this point a concern with defining a poetic credo and
the key affective current of eroticism are virtually inseparable; the credo is a
dedication to love poetry and a refusal to celebrate empire, and the element of
love presented directly and excitedly is the basis of that credo as well as a
demonstration of it. Before this, in poem II, the opposition of lyric and epic is
figured in the contradictory injunctions of Apollo and Calliope and the conflicting images they sling at the helpless poet between them: "Orgies of vintages, an
earthen image of Silenus / . . . Night dogs, the marks of a drunken scurry, /
These are your images. . . . "[31] Poem III picks up the self-deflating image of the
poet from II and, in a compressed vignette, presents him mock-heroically braving the perils of the Roman night, compromised by both his fear and Cynthia's
imperious demands. Poem IV has him farcically guzzling "with outstretched
ears" at Lygdamus's magniloquent depiction of Cynthia's desolation because of
his absence and at an account of her venomous jealousy. Thus "whatever she
does or says / We shall spin long yarns out of nothing."

On the other side of the central focus in poems V,1 and V,2, poem V,3
momentarily reintroduces a concern with death—"It is noble to die of love"—
and this is expanded in poem VI in a vision of the underworld, a confrontation
with the inexorability of death, and a reaffirmation of the immortality of lyric.
This launches the sequence toward its most jubilant celebration of love and,

concomitantly, its most piercing recognition of love's transience. Poem VII mounts to the sequence's highest pitch of exuberant sensuality: the poem begins with a remembered moment of joyful, erotic play, then places that moment within a mythic context of immortal loves and lovers, giving it a timelessness beyond that of individual experience. Picking up the current of fatality from poem VI, it proceeds in a mixture of prayerful and prophetic strains to assert the power of love over change and death, and ends with a declaration of devotion and of the lover's elevation beyond mortal status:

> Nor can I shift my pains to other,
>> Hers will I be dead,
> If she confer such nights upon me,
>> long is my life, long in years,
> If she give me many,
>> God am I for the time.

Poems VIII and IX are built over a more distanced, fragmented narrative: Cynthia's life is in danger, and the teasing irony of poem VIII is directed first at Jove, to induce him to avert her fate, and then at Cynthia, to reconcile her with "the gentler hour of an ultimate day." The beginning of IX prophesies her death, but beneath its mock augury is a more poignant recognition of death's inescapability, which surfaces in a prayer for clemency in IX,2:

> Persephone and Dis, Dis, have mercy upon her,
> There are enough women in hell,
>> quite enough beautiful women,
> Iope, and Tyro, and Pasiphae, and the formal girls of Achaia,
> And out of Troad, and from the Campania,
> Death has his tooth in the lot,
>> Avernus lusts for the lot of them,
> Beauty is not eternal, no man has perennial fortune,
> Slow foot, or swift foot, death delays but for a season.

Upon Cynthia's recovery, IX,3 transfers this urgency to a more lighthearted injunction to reciprocate her lover's attention: "And unto me also pay debt: / The ten nights of your company you have / promised me."

Poem X is a self-ironic depiction of the poet as lover, a counterpart to his diminishment by the muse in II. Here, he is at the mercy of first a band of cupids and then of Cynthia's caustic wit: "'You are a very early inspector of mistresses. / Do you think I have adopted your habits?'"

Poem XI,1 presents a blatantly and comically self-mocking image of the poet as martyr:

> The harsh acts of your levity!
> Many and many.
> I am hung here, a scare-crow for lovers

—and this builds, through a catalogue of Eros' mythic conquests in XI,2, to an image of the heroic singer of amor as a conquered and "obviously crowned lover" in XII. Though he japes at his cuckolding, he converts his horns to laurels by ridiculing his rival's poetic "fashion" and the age's, the official work of "the ancient, / respected, Wordsworthian," and the closing passage conclusively restores his triumphant lyric poise.

The *Homage to Sextus Propertius* opens with an assertive entry, *in medias res,* into a lyric tradition, invoking Callimachus and Philetas, much as Canto I begins *in medias res*—"And then"—with an evocation of Homer. The *Homage* ends with a vision of futurity, of a continuing tradition to which "Propertius" can now lay claim, thus moving from the timeless past to the timeless future, as does *The Cantos* as a whole. While the sequence's state of consciousness is rooted in the realm of mortal love, it moves freely among that realm, the underworld and the world of the gods, and, as in *The Cantos,* establishes a personal relationship with otherworldly powers, addressing the gods with colloquial joviality, accepting or defying their injunctions lightheartedly, and caricaturing them freely. In its breadth of vision, its confrontation with cosmic forces, and its elevation of the poet/lover to heroic stature, the *Homage to Sextus Propertius* clearly exhibits epic aspirations and is the most important achievement in that direction between "Cathay" and *Hugh Selwyn Mauberley.*

In at least one other respect, the *Homage to Sextus Propertius* is an important step toward *The Cantos:* that is, in its use of a compound central figure. Not only is it, as Pound wrote to Hardy, "the super-position [?] the doubling of me and Propertius, England to-day and Rome under Augustus" (qtd. in Hutchins 99), but also the "composite character" he "wished to render . . . including something of Ovid, and making the portrayed figure not only Propertius but inclusive of the spirit of the young man of the Augustan age, hating rhetoric and undeceived by imperial hogwash" (*Ltrs* 150). This use of a composite figure or series of figures is, of course, a central principle of the construction of *Hugh Selwyn Mauberley* and *The Cantos* and, as we have observed, of "Cathay" as well. As chapters 4 and 5 will show, this integration of states of consciousness within a single framework is what all of Pound's volumes were also designed to achieve, each of them planned out as a unified "book-as-a-whole." Sequences such as the *Homage* accomplish that purpose with enormous compression, containing the scope of an entire volume within a smaller structure whose integrity can be more readily apprehended.

Many of Pound's statements from the time of the first Ur-Cantos onward suggest that he was striving for a form not only "elastic enough to take the necessary material" but also compressed enough to attain the "sense of proportion and balance" of a longer work: "when a novelist says by way of praise that a six-line poem has the 'form of a novel' or that it 'is like a good novel' or 'contains' a novel, he is making an interesting criticism of the poet's sense of proportion and balance and 'form'" (*EPVA* 221). Of the *Homage to Sextus Propertius,* he wrote that he was "making a portrait and condensing or eliminating from 80 pages to 12,"[32] and he later called *Hugh Selwyn Mauberley* "a study in form, an attempt to condense the James novel" (*Ltrs* 180). No doubt Pound was able to present, within so brief a space, complex nuances of sensibility comparable to those of James's characters partly because of his sustained efforts in the more expansive format of the "book-as-a-whole."

4

"The Book-As-a-Whole," 1905–1909

"A Definite Scheme for a Sequence"

Just as Pound was meticulous and insistent about the arrangement of his poems into sequences, so, too, from the very beginning of his development his volumes of verse evidence considerable care in the selection and organization of poems in order to attain the integral unity of what he came to refer to as a "book-as-a-whole." This was also part of his effort to "get a form" for a long poem, and the finished volumes, like the sequences, display a range of formal patterns that help to effect an emotional unity. In a letter to Marianne Moore in 1918, Pound urged her to pay attention to "the actual order of poems in a booklet" and offered the benefit of his own "ten or more years of practice, failure, success, etc." This suggests that his conception of the book of poems as an integral whole began to emerge soon after he started the experimentation that ultimately led to *The Cantos*, "in 1904 or 1905":

> For what it is worth, my ten or more years of practice, failure, success, etc. in arranging tables of contents, is à votre service. Or at any rate unless you have a definite scheme for a sequence, I would warn you of the very great importance of the actual order of poems in a booklet. (I have gone right and wrong in this at one time or another and know the results). (*Ltrs* 143)

Pound was also quick to recognize the integrity of others' volumes of verse. In 1913, for instance, he remarked in a letter to Harriet Monroe that "one of Fletcher's strongest claims to attention is his ability to make a *book,* as opposed to the common or garden faculty of making a 'Poem,' and if you don't print a fairish big gob of him, you don't do him justice or stir up the reader's ire and attention" (*Ltrs* 22). In his 1915 preface to an edition of Lionel Johnson's verse, he noted that the poems "are literary criticism in verse, for that is the impression which they leave, if one have laid them by for long enough to have an impression of the book as a whole, and not a confusion, not the many little contradictory impressions of individual poems" (*LE* 361). In 1918, while reworking his first drafts of *The Cantos*, Pound observed that Joyce's *Chamber Music* "comes to its end and climax in two profoundly emotional poems; quite different in tonality and in rhythm-quality from the lyrics in the first part of the book" (*LE* 414). And in 1926, after the first section of *The Cantos* had attained its final arrangement in *A Draft of XVI Cantos* (1925), Pound concluded from the typescript of Ralph Cheever Dunning's *The Four Winds* that it was "a whole book," though it was not published as a volume until 1929: "Dunning has written a whole book, not simply a few good poems, with a book trailing after them. The former is, I need hardly say, a much rarer phenomenon" ("Mr. Dunning's Poetry" 608).

Characteristically, the aesthetics demanding a consciousness of the relations among poems within a volume were also applicable to other media. Pound claimed, for instance, that his projected but unpublished *Collected Prose* "is no more a series of vols . . . than my cantos are a series of lyrics," since "the components need the other components in one piece with them" (*P/J* 244), and in *The Spirit of Romance, Pavannes and Divisions,* and *Instigations,* he called attention to "a fairly coherent and continuous process, underlying the whole, from 1901 to the present, for what 25 years may have been worth" (YC). One plan for this collection was to make it "a four or five vol. edtn. of my works (prose) properly sorted out into Mediaeval, French modern, yanko-British modern, frivelacious, traductions, etc." And the essay, "How to Read," he wrote in a letter to his mother, "is a sort of pivot, or whatchercall it";

> Any how, that gives the central idea, or ideas, and the until-now apparently random and scattered work all falls into shape, and one sees, or shd. see wot is related to wot, and why the stuff is not merely inconsequent notes. (YC)

Elsewhere, he wrote of his design in *The Spirit of Romance* as "a gallery of photographs," arranged so as to present the poets discussed there in terms of "a sort of chemical spectrum of their art" (*SP* 24). And in 1933, he complained that "No one has . . . ever noticed the ground-plan of my *Instigations*" (*SP* 391).[1]

The effectiveness of a journal, too, depended on the arrangement of its contents. Pound "admonished Margaret Anderson about pacing *The Little Review*'s contents so as to order and unify the eventual bound volume" (Kenner, *Era* 355–56), and when considering the possible inclusion of some letters by Yeats's father in *The Little Review* he wrote that

> even though I am trying to run the paper on "wholly different lines," I must recognize that the "magazine" is a form to itself having its own "laws" like all other forms. It is [the] same with a book of poems, many are ruined because [the] authors have thought only of individual poems and no[t] to the arrangement of the volume.[2]

And complimenting Harriet Monroe on the February 1931 issue of *Poetry,* Pound explained, "The point is that although most of the contents was average, the *mode* of presentation was good editing. The zoning of different states of mind, so that one can see what they are, is good editing" (*Ltrs* 231).

The organization of materials was also an important consideration in the visual arts and music. An exhibit of Wadsworth's and Lewis's Vorticist paintings in 1914, for instance, displayed a dialectic pattern of emotive forces: "One's differentiation of the two groups of pictures arranges itself almost as a series of antitheses. Turbulent energy: repose. Anger: placidity, and so on" (*EPVA* 192). And Pound later discerned a continuity in "the effect of Brancusi's work": "The effect of Brancusi's work is cumulative. He has created a whole universe of FORM. You've got to see it together. A system. An Anschauung. Not simply a pretty thing on the library table" (*EPVA* 308). In his music criticism in *The New Age,* we find a similar insistence on the importance of arranging the works performed in a concert, for "a concert is like a play; it consists usually of four groups of songs; of these, the third group must be the climax. The fourth can be farce after the drama, it can be a change of tone, it can be a curiosity, a bit of research; or simply a diminuendo" (*EPM* 196). As in the arrangement of a sequence or a volume of poems, the primary consideration in planning a concert is the attainment of an "aesthetic unity" and not adherence to a discursive framework. Pound called two of William Rosing's concerts, for instance,

> examples of perfect programme-construction, perfect from the point of view of combining a set of different pieces of music into an aesthetic unity. . . .
> The error . . . of the programme grouped about a topic is that it substitutes a metaphysical or intellectual unity for a strictly musical unity. (*EPM* 155)

Critical appreciation of Pound's arrangement of his volumes and of the crucial role this practice played in his development of a form for the long poem has been curiously sparse during the nearly seven decades since the publication of his last major volume of short poems, *Poems, 1918–1921.* Eliot, whom Pound helped with the selection and arrangement of the contents of *Prufrock and Other Observations* some years before his assistance in shaping *The Waste Land,*[3] and who therefore had a certain privileged insight into "The Method of Mr. Pound," first observed (in his essay of that name) that *Quia Pauper Amavi* is "probably the most significant book . . . [and] the most coherent extended work since 'Personae' and 'Exultations'" (1065). Kenner was the next to consider Pound's arrangements, noting that "Arrays comport with the aesthetic of that decade, part of the Symbolist legacy" (*Era* 355). And more recently, Alexander, Longenbach, and McKeown have begun to lay the foundation for an understanding of the importance of Pound's conception of the book-as-a-whole in the development of his strategy for a long poem.

The structures of individual volumes demonstrate the same principles and patterns of construction as the poems and sequences that have been examined in the preceding chapters, but on a larger and more complex scale. As Fraistat suggests in his seminal study of major Romantic collections of verse, opening and closing poems often supply a framework that helps to impart coherence to the "perceptual field" of a complexly structured volume, and he also calls attention to the importance of poems positioned at the center of such a volume (*Book* 39). Whether or not Pound consciously emulated these Romantic precedents, his own volumes, particularly the earliest of them, often use similar patterns. Later collections show a drive toward increasing compression and more open modes of organization, culminating in *The Cantos*, a "sequence of sequences" with a structure of enormous breadth and flexibility. The balance of this chapter will explore the designs of Pound's early "books-as-wholes," and chapter 5 will trace their evolution through the later volumes of short poems toward *The Cantos*.

"Hilda's Book" and *A Lume Spento*

Some of Pound's early volumes have, unfortunately, been lost or disbanded, and their constituent poems have been consigned to obscurity, integrated into other volumes, or left unpublished. From one of the first collections, which may have been sent to the publisher Thomas Mosher for consideration, a table of contents survives, and several of the poems were incorporated into *A Lume Spento*.[4] In a letter to his father in 1908, Pound referred to another, apparently completed volume, *The Dawn*, as "a sequence of prose and verse." Elkin Mathews later agreed to publish the book but ultimately never did, and the project was abandoned sometime in 1910 (*EP/DS* 361). Some of the poems in this volume were drawn from "Hilda's Book" and the "San Trovaso Notebook," others were published separately or in *A Quinzaine for This Yule,* and a selection has been printed in *Ezra Pound and Dorothy Shakespear* (362–68).

The earliest completed and published volume, "Hilda's Book," was written from 1905 through 1907 and compiled in 1907 ("HB" 67–68). Though published as an appendix to *End to Torment* in 1979, it received little attention until the recent resurgence of interest in Hilda Doolittle. Hugh Kenner has pointed out the volume's thematic continuity and its "sureness of array" (*Era* 355), and more recently Michael King has demonstrated its motivic coherence. In particular, he has traced the consistency of "the manner in which 'Hilda' is treated as an imagined figure and as the assumed catalyst of the poetic impulse," and has shown that "several of the poems identify Hilda with images of nature and natural imagery, and through these nature motifs, connect her to divinity" (354–55).

The structure of "Hilda's Book" actually displays a remarkably firm but complex balance, anticipating the designs of some later sequences such as "Laudantes Decem." An unpublished preface (in the Yale collection) sets forth the volume's spirit of tribute, describes its process of composition and the personal transformation it entailed, and characterizes its design as an integral whole in terms of "an arc of a larger circle I propose to disclose later." This provides strong support for Pound's claim to have begun planning his long poem "in 1904 or 1905," and his discovery that his material "fits no ready made commeasurement" suggests he was already working to get a form "that wouldn't exclude something merely because it didn't fit" and perhaps had already recognized that "you haven't got a nice little road map such as the middle ages possessed of Heaven" ("Int" Hall 23):

> Having at one time proposed to make of these stray petals a dear book of this "mine own youth" holding in bond recording of my new lives several and most of all that last novelty of light Ysolda. [B]ut this is life and no dramaticing, and vainly have I striven to make of it some form, set as of old, [m]erely this that truth here fits no ready made commeasurement. The thing assumes no nicely ballanced figure[,] is in short an arc of a larger circle I propose to disclose later in its fuller sweep with its equation and laws more patent.
> Ergo for what they are and not what some think they should be, among which some, a self of mine that was.
> Striving to bind them in the robes of form, [h]aving written oer a century of sonnets, I yet find there (these) high(est) truths too restless, nay un containable in the smoothe sway of metric, unable to be revived (???) Rimed with iambics[.]
> Wherefor as wind teareth thru man made artificialities
> I give them rein, they take the bit.

The contents of this first volume fall into four tonal groups, as follows:

Child of the grass
I strove a little book
Era Mea
And afterwards . . . [prose interlude]
La Donzella Beata
The Wings
Ver Novum

To One That Journeyeth With Me
Domina
The Lees
Per Saecula
Shadow
The Banners

"To draw back into the soul of things." PAX.
Green Harping
From another sonnet
Li Bel Chasteus
The Arches
Era Venuta
The Tree
Being before the vision of Li Bel Chasteus
Thu Ides Til

L'Envoi
The Wind
Sancta Patrona Domina Caelae
Rendez-vous

The opening poem, "Child of the grass . . . ," not only establishes themes developed in subsequent poems and echoed again in the closing sonnet, as Kenner has observed (*Era* 355), but also plots out the major directions for the volume, which traces an emotional journey, a quest for continuity between lovers. In this respect, "Hilda's Book" shows a consistency of focus absent from Pound's subsequent collections. This first poem commands the lovers' continuity, calling on forces of nature—"Shadows of air," "winds for our fellows," and autumn colors—and on the binding force of lovers' spirits for support. "Hilda" is addressed directly and affectionately, and an ongoing unity between lovers is assumed, though with an undertone of fear that this may not be so easy to sustain:

> . . . Be we well sworn
> Ne'er to grow older
> Our spirits be bolder At meeting
> Than e'er before All the old lore
> Of the forests & woodways
> Shall aid us: Keep we the bond & seal
> Ne'er shall we feel
> Aught of sorrow.[5]

The facile rhymes, the naïveté, and the monotone of this passage are representative of the poetic quality of much of the book but may be overlooked for now, since we are primarily interested in its structure.

The following poems test the lovers' unity and attempt to locate sources of reinforcement for it, drawing in part on moments of remembered physical contact, their ecstatic power, and their spiritual resonance, often projected through the image of "mystic wings," as the dedicatory second poem explains:

> . . . I speak of mystic wings that whirr
> Above me when within my soul do stir
> Strange holy longings
> That may not be told . . . .

This image surfaces again at the focus of "The Wings" and attains its sharpest contours in the strains of longing at the close of the sixth poem, "Ver Novum." These first poems also call on the splendor of autumn colors as a source of continuity (as the later "Δώρια" calls on the bleakness of forces of decay), though Hilda ultimately embodies a renewing impulse that transforms autumn into spring, particularly in "Ver Novum," "Per Saecula," "The Banners," and "Era Venuta." In the course of the sequence, she acquires powers of benediction and redemption, beginning in the litany of the third poem, "*Era Mea*," and especially in "Ver Novum," where she is "Thou that savest my soul's self from death / As scorpion's is, of self-inflicted pain." The sequence's balance is partly attained through a reiteration of this image of Hilda as redeemer in the penultimate poem, "*Sancta Patrona Domina Caelae*": "Out of thy purity / Saint Hilda pray for me."

Along with the attribution of these powers to Hilda and the search for sources of continuity in natural forces and the remembrance of physical contact, the opening group—"Child of the grass" through "Ver Novum"—introduces a self-deprecatory strain and confronts the problem of separation, especially through wandering and the physical distance it implies. We see this first in the brief prose interlude between "*Era Mea*" and "La Donzella Beata":

> And afterwards being come to a woodland place where the sun was warm amid the autumn, my lips, striving to speak for my heart, formed those words which here follow.

"His" wandering is at issue here, but later it is Hilda's wandering in spirit that must be dealt with. In "Green Harping," she is implored not to stray—"Hold thou thy heart for my heart's right"—and in "The Wind" she is helplessly drawn away by a "little lonely wind" and he is compelled to await her return.

But separation is prepared for early in the sequence, in the sonnet that follows "Ver Novum" and launches the second group of poems, "To One That Journeyeth With Me." This is the book's most forceful declaration of devotion, resolving to withstand separation by internalizing an image of Hilda and keeping her "all day long as one not wholly seen / Nor ever wholly lost unto my sight."

The following poems attempt to come to terms with separation through a range of strategies. In "Domina," Hilda is addressed in the third person as "My Lady," and the ensuing ballad catalogues her virtues, laments her distance— "My Lady's smile is changed of late"—and projects the force of longing for her: "With my lady far, the days be long / For her homing I'd clasp the song / That the wind bloweth merrily." "The Lees" tries to reestablish contact through "song wine that the master bards of old / Have left for me to drink thy glory in," and the next poem, "Per Saecula," seeks a substance for that song and a medium of reunion in recollection of the past:

> . . . But speak that spring
> Whisper in the murmurous twilight where
> I met thee mid the roses of the past
> Where you gave your first kiss in the last,
> Whisper the name thine eyes were wont to bear
> The mystic name whereof my heart shall sing.

The book reaches its nadir in "Shadow," which laments continued separation from Hilda and the pain of seeing her without making contact, and rejects the advances of another. Loss and anguish are embodied in the sun's absence, and the poem closes with a prayer for the sun's reemergence and hers: "Oh that the sun steeds were wise / Arising to seek her! / The sun sleepeth in Orcus." Images of darkness in this poem are in sharp contrast to the bright autumnal colors and spring imagery that course through most of the volume. These colors reappear in "The Banners," which effects a transition into the medieval setting of the third section, "To draw back into the soul of things. PAX" through "Thu Ides Til." This group offers a concrete (though facile) grounding, in an imagined castle and its surroundings, for the more intangible strains of mystic devotion in the opening section, and it provides a stronghold for the lovers' continuity. By giving them an escape from the world's forces of separation, this vision allows them "to draw back into the soul of things," to experience a restorative peace, and to glimpse "Unto that shadow land where ages' feet / Have wandered, and where life's dreaming done / Love may dream on unto eternity." From this vantage point, the forces that threaten to spirit Hilda off become an "elfin horn," "elfin knights," and "the elf-old queen," and the lovers' stronghold is a "wind-swept castle."

Yet Hilda is of that elfin world—"I know thy thought doth pass as elfin 'Hail' / That beareth thee as doth the wind a rose"—and transformation that leads to understanding and that comes about through spiritual and emotional receptiveness, in "The Tree," is a further stay against separation and a protection against becoming "one of them that fail / Denying that God doth God's self disclose / In every beauty that they will not see" ("Era Venuta"):

> I stood still and was a tree amid the wood
> Knowing the truth of things unseen before
> Of Daphne and the laurel bow
> And that god-feasting couple old
> That grew elm-oak amid the wold

'Twas not until the gods had been
Kindly entreated and been brought within
Unto the hearth of their hearts' home
That they might do this wonder thing.
Naethless I have been a tree amid the wood
And many new things understood
That were rank folly to my head before.

This poem presents a remarkably rich empathetic extension of imagination that distinguishes it from the rest of the volume. It is a node of origin for later developments in the projection of visionary immediacy, as in "The Return" and "The Coming of War: Actaeon," and the centrality of this element in Pound's work may readily be grasped through a brief glance forward to the treatment of a similar motif in Canto XLVII:

By prong have I entered these hills:
That the grass grow from my body,
That I hear the roots speaking together,
The air is new on my leaf,
The forked boughs shake with the wind.

Because of the union established through empathy in "The Tree," when Hilda is spirited away in "The Wind" separation lacks finality and the poem expresses a stronger continuity, built on kinship of spirit and understanding (however melodramatically stated), than the opening of the sequence could claim:

And I await her here for I have understood.
Yet held I not this very wind—bound fast
Within the castle of my soul I would
For very faintness at her parting, die.

This, in effect, resolves the sequence by establishing the strongest basis of the continuity it sets out to locate, but the two preceding poems, "Thu Ides Til" and "L'Envoi," and the two final poems, "*Sancta Patrona*" and "Rendezvous," help to attain the balance and provide the sense of closure of the book-as-a-whole. "Thu Ides Til" offers a Chaucerian vintage of the "song wine that the master bards of old / Have left for me to drink thy glory in," in "The Lees," and reiterates that poem's plea to "Grant that the kiss upon the cup be thine." "L'Envoi" answers the dedicatory second poem, "I strove a little book to make for her," promising that although "My flower's outworn, the later rhyme runs cold / Naethless I loving cease me not to sing." "*Sancta Patrona*" recapitulates the litany of poem III with a final prayer for Hilda's benediction, and the closing sonnet, "Rendez-vous," echoes the opening poem's exhortation for continuity, but without its optimistic command. Rather, this poem acknowledges the inevitability of Hilda's separation, or at least her independence of spirit; addressing her in third person with some of the opening poem's tenderness and a muted strain of its hope, the sequence closes with a challenge to "meet my dream" and answer it:

> She hath some tree-born spirit of the wood
> About her, and the wind is in her hair
> Meseems he whisp'reth and awaiteth there
> As if somewise he also understood.
> The moss-grown kindly trees, meseems, she could
> As kindred claim, for tho to some they wear
> A harsh dumb semblance, unto us that care
> They guard a marvelous sweet brotherhood
> And thus she dreams unto the soul of things
> Forgetting me, and that she hath it not
> Of dull man-wrought philosophies I wot,
> She dreameth thus, so when the woodland sings
> I challenge her to meet my dream at Astalot
> And give him greeting for the song he brings.

The book-as-a-whole, then, sets out in the opening dedicatory poems with a strong note of tribute to Hilda, accompanied by a forced assertion of the lovers' stability. It moves through a series of confrontations with the physical, emotional, and spiritual distance that will inevitably separate them, and works toward the construction of an imaginative stronghold for their continuity. The lover ultimately attains an understanding of the spiritual world Hilda moves in, by means of his own transforming empathy, and he concludes by challenging her to match his devotion and to preserve the bond between them. This key progression is the basis of the book's emotional unity, although its movement is not as fully and clearly developed as the arrangement itself promises, because of the puerility of the poems and the obstructive archaism in diction and syntax of most of them.

There is also a uniformity in the volume grounded in its focus on Hilda, its dedication to her, and its conception of her as muse and redeemer. Its imagery supplies a further binding force—in particular, the wings, the autumn colors, and the medieval setting of the castle and its surrounding clouds and fields. As Michael King points out, "Hilda's Book" shares some of the motifs that characterize the imaginative world of Pound's other, early volumes (356–57). Of the several that Hugh Witemeyer has catalogued, the "magical wind" and "dreams" are most prominent here:

Its main elements are (1) disembodied spirits seeking incarnation in an earthly form or union with the divine essence; (2) a magical wind conveying sometimes death but more often a transcendental inspiration; (3) dawn, and especially the false dawn, the strange illusory harbinger of day, real and unreal; and (4) dreams, symbolizing rare psychic states of contemplation and insight. In addition, fire is a ubiquitous symbol of inspired spirituality, and the literary tradition of the past is a vague but potent influence in the form of runes, legends, druidings, and old songs. (51)

The three others—fire, disembodied spirits, and especially dawn—enter Pound's poetry through his next volume, *A Lume Spento*. To this catalogue may be added the imagery of lips, eyes, and hands as media for physical and spiritual contact, and the more prominent imagery in this next volume of trees and flowers as embodiments of the life-force, its transformation, and its renewal—in "La Fraisne," "The Tree," and "La Regina Avrillouse," for instance.[6] These clusters of imagery are an important means of imparting coherence to a volume, but their greatest value, poetically, is their usefulness in defining and directing emotive patterns in individual poems and groups. The difference between the imaginative world of the early poems and that of *The Cantos* can be located not so much in the imagery used—most of which is retained, except for dreams—as in the way it is used.

The same may be said of the poems' themes, which, as Pound succinctly pointed out, are inherently limited. In a letter to Williams concerning *A Lume Spento,* he lists eight "facts on which I and 9,000,000 other poets have spieled endlessly," which break down into nature, love, war, and voyages. There is also a concern "with the creative problem as such (what the poet is, what he does, and why it matters)," which Jackson considers the dominant theme of the early volumes (63). "Beyond this," Pound's letter goes on, "men think and feel certain things and see certain things not with the bodily vision. About this time I begin to get interested and the general too ruthlessly goes to sleep?" The themes, in other words, are subordinate to the imaginative vision they help to project and the thought and feeling that inform it. As the letter continues, it becomes clear that the basis of Pound's selection and arrangement of poems in *A Lume Spento* is its mood:

> If you mean to say that *A.L.S.* is a rather gloomy and disagreeable book, I agree with you. I thought that in Venice. Kept out of it one tremendously gloomy series of ten sonnets—à la Thompson of the *City of Dreadful Night*—which are poetically rather fine in spots. Wrote or attempted to write a bit of sunshine, some of which—too much for my critical sense—got printed. However, the bulk of the work (say 30 of the poems) is the most finished work I have yet done. (*Ltrs* 4–6)

Though *A Lume Spento* follows "Hilda's Book" by less than a year, it presents a greater emotive range and a much more complex structure.[7] It abandons the latent narrative dimension of the first volume and more fully embraces the principle of *varietas* that informs the organization of a great many classical verse collections.[8] Accordingly, in carrying over some of the poems from "Hilda's Book," Pound regrouped them with other poems, sometimes revising them and giving them new titles, in order to fit them into a very different arrangement, as a glance at the table of contents reveals:

Grace Before Song
La Fraisne
Cino
In Epitaphium Eius
Na Audiart
Villonaud for This Yule
A Villonaud: Ballad of the Gibbet
Mesmerism
Fifine Answers

Anima Sola
In Tempore Senectutis
Famam Librosque Cano
The Cry of the Eyes

Scriptor Ignotus. To K. R. H.
Donzella Beata
Vana
Li Bel Chasteus
That Pass Between the False Dawn and the True
In Morte De
Threnos
Comraderie

Ballad Rosalind
Malrin

Masks
On His Own Face in a Glass
The Tree
Invern
Plotinus
Prometheus
Aegupton

Ballad for Gloom
For E. McC.

Salve O Pontifex! To Swinburne; An Hemichaunt
To the Dawn: Defiance
The Decadence

Redivivus
Fistulae
Song
Motif
La Regina Avrillouse
A Rouse
Nicotine: A Hymn to the Dope
In Tempore Senectutis: (An Anti-stave for Dowson)
Oltre la Torre: Rolando
Make Strong Old Dreams Lest This Our World Lose Heart

Read in terms of the book-as-a-whole, the poems in the volume fall into fairly well-defined tonal groups, each of which contains its own particular emotive movement and contributes to the larger patterns of the whole. Unlike many of the later volumes and sequences, beneath its juxtapositions of poems and groups *A Lume Spento* uses carefully modulated transitions in tone, theme, context, and imagery. In the gradations of emphasis, the interplay, the exchanges and recapitulations of these elements, the book displays a musical mode of arrangement much in anticipation of *The Cantos;* in fact, song and harmony provide another significant current of imagery in this volume.

The opening poem, "Grace Before Song," is an invocation that, along with the closing envoi, "Make-strong old dreams," provides the framework of the sequence. Both poems call for inspiration from the world of permanence—God's world in the first poem and the world of "old dreams" in the last—in contrast to the transient world of the poet ("Our days as rain drops in the sea surge fall") and the brief flash of the poetic moment. Hence, the poems contained within this framework are passing reflections of the permanent world, "evan'scent mirrors every opal one," a gleam of divine light and strength that will enliven and illumine "this grey folk," "lest this our world lose heart." The inspiring and invigorating focus of these two poems sets the tone for the volume and especially for its first and last sections.

The first section consists of eight poems, "La Fraisne" through "Fifine Answers," roughly unified by their setting in the past and their use of artists as personae. They are drawn together through the interaction of a strain of nostalgia and regret and a strain of cavalier exuberance that ascends to a bold, virile pride, specifically the pride of the artist, toward the end of the group. Transformation of spirit, and correspondingly of feeling, is another recurrent theme: the *"Note Precedent to La Fraisne"* tells us that transformation takes place as an expression of being "in such a mood, feeling myself divided between myself corporal and a self aetherial."

"La Fraisne" introduces the first note of nostalgia; memory and regret for past love, welling up into consciousness at a maddened pitch, are incompletely transformed into contentment through communion with the genii of the woods:

> . . . I do not remember. . . .
> I think she hurt me once but. . . .
> That was very long ago.
>
> I do not like to remember things any more.
>
> I like one little band of winds that blow
> In the ash trees here:
> For we are quite alone
> Here mid the ash trees.

"Cino" picks up this note of regret and tosses it off with an abrupt, cavalier dismissal—"Bah! I have sung women in three cities / But it is all the same"—although this too is not without recurring nostalgia and persistent desire: "eh? . . . . they mostly had grey eyes."

The devotion to one woman (or one tree) in "La Fraisne" and the dismissal of "women in three cities" in "Cino" are both multiplied in the troubadour's ardor for "half an hundred eyes" (or twenty-five different women) in "In Epitaphium Eius." The nostalgic potential of this poem's elegiac form is transmuted by its tongue-in-cheek hyperbole and its loosely handled couplets into a lightly ironic eulogy. "Na Audiart" picks up that irony in its playful, teasing assemblage of one woman out of many women's separate features and shifts, near the end, to the regret that the singer already experiences and that Maent will feel in her next incarnation, transformed from her present beauty into a hag:

> And being bent and wrinkled, in a form
> That hath no perfect limning, when the warm
> Youth dew is cold
> Upon thy hands, and thy old soul
> Scorning a new, wry'd casement
> Churlish at seemed misplacement
> Finds the earth as bitter
> As now seems it sweet. . . .

This sense of loss reaches its climax in the *ubi sunt* lament of the following poem, "Villonaud for this Yule," whose strident rhythms and boisterous revelry effectively redirect the group toward a resurgence of life-force:

> Aye! where are the glances feat and clear
> That bade my heart his valor don?
> I skoal to the eyes as grey-blown mere
> (Who knows whose was that paragon?)
> Wineing the ghosts of yester-year.

Much of this spirit of proud defiance is carried over, along with the persona (Villon) and some of the imagery, into "A Villonaud. Ballad of the Gibbet":

> Skoal!! to the Gallows! and then pray we:
> God damn his hell out speedily
> And bring their souls to his "Haulte Citee."

This group moves toward its close with the similarly jaunty colloquialism of a tribute in "Mesmerism" to another poet, Browning, and to his virile stylistic bravado: "Aye you're a man that!"

The transitions among the poems juxtaposed within this group are also characteristic of the junctures between groups. The second group, like the first, is concerned with poets or creative spirits, and a modulation is effected by picking up one of Browning's personae, the artist (and perhaps prostitute, according to Jackson [7]) Fifine, a social outcast who in some ways embodies an ideal of Christian and artistic self-sacrifice. Thus a concern with the artist provides a thematic transition, while above this the perspective shifts and we are given not the poet's proud, exuberant and defiant spirit but his isolation and sacrifice. Concomitantly, the key tones of the second section—"Anima Sola" through "The Cry of the Eyes"—verge on desolation and depressiveness, and the poems' rhythms are gentler and more subdued than those of the first group. This section moves through age ("In Tempore Senectutis"), transience and disorder ("Famam Librosque Cano"), and weariness ("The Cry of the Eyes"), but the playful self-irony of this last poem introduces a more invigorating note at its close:

> Free us, for there is one
> Whose smile more availeth
> Than all the age-old knowledge of thy books:
> And we would look thereon.

The first poem of the third section, "Scriptor Ignotus," presents, as a natural sequitur, a woman, along with another poet, intent on writing an epic in her tribute. Hope and devotion struggle against doubt and the epic is left unwritten, as Pound's note tells us, although the tribute is clear. This sets the direction for the group, containing most of the poems carried over from "Hilda's Book"; the focus is a lover's tribute, and it briefly echoes the contour of "Hilda's Book" as a whole. At its center is the imaginative stronghold of continuity, "Li Bel Chasteus," but in the two roundels that follow, "That Pass Between the False Dawn and the True" and "In Morte De," the lovers are disembodied and ultimately separated spirits. "In Morte De" recapitulates the lamentative climax of "Villonaud for this Yule" ("Wineing the ghosts of yester-year") in its farewell—"O wine-sweet ghost how we are borne apart"—and "Threnos" establishes the finality of separation and the dissolution of desire:

> No more do I burn.
> No more for us the fluttering of wings
> That whirred the air above us.
>
> Lo the fair dead! . . .
>
> No more the torrent
> No more for us the meeting-place
> (Lo the fair dead!)
> Tintagoel.[9]

The closing poem of the group, "Comraderie," follows as a nostalgic afterbeat; though the lovers are apart, their thoughts sometimes meet, and desire lingers at moments when "My pulses run, knowing thy thought hath passed / That beareth thee as doth the wind a rose."

The quasi-mystical settings of the following two pieces, "Ballad Rosalind" and the prose poem "Malrin," provide an interlude at precisely the center of the book, a device we have noted before and will see again in Pound's work. They fit into the framework, along with "Grace Before Song" and "Make-strong old dreams," rather than into the third or fourth group on either side of them, and they help to modulate between the two halves of the book-as-a-whole. In "Ballad Rosalind," the staunch "old Lord," "Silent and grey in his black oak throne," is replaced by Lady Rosalind, "fair as dawn and fleet as wind," echoing the promise in "Grace Before Song" to bring "bright white drops" of song to "this grey folk." Analogously, the strident and despairing tones that dominate the book's first two sections give way to a more buoyantly rapturous group centered on predominantly female figures at the end. "Malrin" reintroduces the artist's pride and defiance from the first group and, in sharing the dream of his creator and spurning all lesser forces, he reiterates the framework's promise of communion between the permanent world of divinity and the transient but spiritually receptive world of mortals. This anticipates the dominant thrust of the fifth group, with a paean to Swinburne at its center—a figure who shares many of Malrin's qualities.

But immediately following "Malrin," the fourth section—"Masks" through "Prometheus"—modulates to a consideration of the shifting uncertainty of the

artist's character, pondered with considerable fascination. "Masks" considers
the identity of the poet and myth-maker as "some soul from all the rest who'd
not forgot / The star-span acres of a former lot"—whose cosmic conciousness,
like Malrin's, retains contact with the world of the permanent, the realm of true
forms. "On His Own Face in a Glass," ironically echoing Whitman, playfully
explores the dramatic interaction of an array of varied selves of which the poet's
soul is constituted, as they "jest, challenge, counterlie." This complex identity
comprised of multiple, interchanging personalities allows for a fluid succession
of states of consciousness and metamorphoses among forms.[10] Hence the incan-
tation of the following poem, "The Tree," invokes a process of transformation
and exults in the knowledge it brings: "I stood still and was a tree amid the wood
/ Knowing the truth of things unseen before." It is through the wonder of this
imaginative and spiritual insight that man's soul "is a hole full of God," as
"Make-strong old dreams" affirms.

In the next poem, "Invern," this encompassing spirit links the renewing
force of spring with the revivifying power of verse, and "Plotinus" reinforces a
sense of artistic triumph with an image of comforting self-incarnation: "And
then for utter loneliness, made I / New thoughts as crescent images of *me*."
Finally, the creative spirit is made eternal through the immolation of wearily
sighing selves in "Prometheus." Though the cosmic setting of this group of
poems tends to draw them toward the sort of abstraction that Pound was later to
eschew, their unifying image of a free-floating, polymorphous consciousness
provides an early glimpse of the sensibility that emerges in later works, where,
as Kenner notes, "Personality, stripped of contingencies, has become at length
a point of light moving through possible worlds, a mode of consciousness
capable of being put to an indefinite number of uses" (*Poetry* 125).

"Aegupton," the first poem of the next grouping (through "The Decadence"), provides a transition by integrating the triumphant, cosmic expansiveness of the artist's spirit with more concrete language and imagery, evocative,
in places, of the *Song of Songs*.[11] This introduces the elegiac and celebratory
strains of the following five poems, mixed with a resurgence of pride and
defiance. These strains are brought together in the central poem, "Salve O
Pontifex!," a tribute to Swinburne and a prayer for his afflatus. He becomes a
sort of fertility figure, a harbinger of new force for the creative act:

> Look! Breathe upon us
> The wonder of the thrice encinctured mystery
> Whereby thou being full of years art young,
> Loving even this lithe Prosephone
> That is free for the seasons of plenty.

The closing poem of the group, "The Decadence," recapitulates the sacrificial self-destruction of "Prometheus" in a more concretely aesthetic context: "We see Art vivant, and exult to die."

The gloom of "The Decadence," Pound wrote Williams, "is answered and contradicted on the opposite page" by "Redivivus," which introduces the much more lighthearted spirit of renewal that dominates the book's final section (*Ltrs* 6). This is brought to its climax in an adaptation of a Provençal folk song, "La Regina Avrillouse," which, Pound speculates, "may have been used in connection with such fragments of the worship of Flora and Venus as survived in the spring merrymakings: the dance itself is clearly discernable in its verbal rhythm" (*SR* 39). The rapturous celebration of the force of earthly love and revelry, along with the recaptured dance rhythms in Pound's version, offset the suffering and sacrifice of wandering spirits in sections 1, 2, and 4. By echoing some of the imagery of the opening poem, "La Fraisne," the spring queen seems to offer a reconstitution of its broken spirit:

> Lady of rich allure,
> Queen of the spring's embrace,
> Your arms are long like boughs of ash,
> Mid laugh broken streams, spirit of rain unsure,
> Breath of the poppy flower,
> All the wood thy bower
>   And the hills thy dwelling place.

Thus, as in "Hilda's Book" and many of Pound's other sequences and volumes, the closing poems answer those of the opening group.

The final poem, "Oltre la Torre: Rolando," suppresses the spirit of gloom with finality, specifically in response to "Ballad for Gloom" and "For E. McC.," and offers in its stead the "drops that dream and gleam and falling catch the sun / Evan'scent mirrors every opal one" promised in "Grace Before Song":

> Yea I have broke my Lord Gloom's yoke
> New yoke will I have none,
> Save the yoke that shines in the golden bow
> Betwixt the rain and the sun.

In fact, this section is characterized by a sort of aesthetic ecstasy, as Pound wrote of a poem included among them in a letter to Viola Jordan, calling it "one of a series more nearly connected with what I had to say on ecstasy at the beginning" of the letter.[12]

In its movement as a whole, then, the book presents an intricate arrangement of successive blocks of tonal pattern-units that echo, answer, reinforce, and modify one another. Briefly, they course from nostalgia and regret, counterpointed against the bold, virile pride of the artist's spirit, in the first section, through the diminuendo of isolation and sacrifice in the second group; desire, displacement and loss in the third; the shifting uncertainty of complex, transforming, and unincarnate identities in the fourth; elegiac strains counterpointed against a celebratory and defiant affirmation of life-force and of the spirit of art in group 5; and finally to the buoyant sense of renewal that closes the volume. This overall movement from the dark opening strains to the ecstatic closing is encapsulated in the central pairing "Ballad Rosalind" and "Malrin," a strategy exploited further in later sequences and eventually in *The Cantos*.

Significantly, the book is dedicated as an elegy—*A Lume Spento* (*with tapers quenched*) is its full title—to the painter William Brooke Smith, of whom Pound later wrote, "I haven't replaced him and shan't and no longer hope to" (*Ltrs* 165). As a whole, it incorporates many of the conventions of traditional elegy: most important, it moves from the broken-spirited lament in its opening group to the forceful affirmation of life and faith in renewal at the close; it defies the power of death ("For E. McC."), the permanence of loss ("Comraderie"), and mutability ("In Tempore Senectutis"); and it establishes channels of contact between the dead and the living ("Salve O Pontifex!"). But the volume does not present the clear working-through of a single emotional issue, as "Hilda's Book" does in its progression from an optimistic assertion of love's continuity at its outset to the challenge at its close. *A Lume Spento* is developed through a far more complex patterning of moods, themes, and imagery that cannot provide the easy sense of balance or close on quite so facile a resolution as we find in "Hilda's Book." In this respect, its structure is closer to that of *The Cantos*, though it is hardly comparable to the range and depth of thought and feeling and the virtuoso manipulation of language and image in the later work. Its design may nonetheless have provided a useful model for Pound's reshaping of his long poem into its final form.

"San Trovaso Notebook" and *A Quinzaine for This Yule*

Pound's next volume, the "San Trovaso Notebook," is programmatic in design in a way similar to "Hilda's Book" and strikes a similar sort of balance—perhaps the reason it was disbanded within a few months of its assemblage, late in 1908, and unpublished until the 1976 *Collected Early Poems*.[13] But it is clear that Pound initially arranged the poems into a definite sequence, as his table of contents demonstrates:

Over the Ognisanti
Night Litany
Purveyors General

San Vio. June
Roundel for Arms

Aube of the West Dawn
Roundel. After Du Bellay
Sonnet of the August Calm
To Ysolt. For Pardon
For Ysolt. The Triad of Dawn
Piazza San Marco

Lotus-Bloom
For a Play (Maeterlinck)
The Rune
To La Contessa Bianzafior (Defense at Parting)
Narcotic Alcohol
Blazed
For the Triumph of the Arts

Alma Sol Veneziae
Fragment to W. C. W.'s Romance
Fragmenti
In That Country
Autumnus
Fratello Mio Zephyrus

For E. McC. *The Rejected Stanza*
Ballad of Wine Skins
I Wait
The Hour of Gold
Partenza di Venezia

Shallott
Essay
Azzuri e bianchi
Battle Dawn
Greek Epigram
Blue, grey and white
For Italico Brass (*CEP* 317–20)

Written for the most part in Venice during Pound's residence in the San Trovaso quarter of the city in 1908, many of the poems are superficially related to features of the area, and the overall movement is marked out and balanced by an entry to Venice from above, in "Over the Ognisanti," and a departure from Venice in "Partenza di Venezia" near the end. Much of the sequence is elegiac and lamentative, especially where concerned with the artist's removal from life and his struggle against hostile forces, though against this emotive pattern the book sets two sources of faith and renewal: love and the glory of creation as it is revealed in the splendors of dawn and Venice. In fact, dawn and Venice supply the dominant patterns of imagery, counterpointed by night scenes and passages of wandering and dislocation.

The opening five poems proleptically establish these major currents for the sequence as a whole. The first, "Over the Ognisanti," looks down over the Ognisanti area of Venice with the artist's privileged perspective ("alone with beauty most the while"), but also with a sense of removal from the stream of life, snatches of which will be garnered and echoed in the poems to follow. These will not be flashes from above of the divine world, as "Grace Before Song" promises at the outset of *A Lume Spento*, but exuberant moments captured from the mill of commonplace activity below:

> Also have I the swallows and the sunset
> And I see much life below me,
>   In the garden, on the waters,
> And hither float the shades of songs they sing
> To sound of wrinkled mandolin, and plash of waters,
> Which shades of song re-echoed
> Within that somewhile barren hall, my heart,
> Are found as I transcribe them following.

The next poem, "Night Litany," is a rapt, incantatory celebration, a prayer of thanks for the beauty of divine creation as embodied in the Venetian night and an invocation for a corresponding purity of heart:

> O Dieu, purifiez nos coeurs!
>   purifiez nos coeurs!
>
> Yea the lines hast thou laid unto me
>   in pleasant places,
> And the beauty of this thy Venice
>   hast thou shewn unto me
> Until is its loveliness become unto me
>   a thing of tears.

The third poem, "Purveyors General," imparts a sense of purpose to the artist's isolation in "Over the Ognisanti." He is engaged in the urgency of a search through chaos and distant "lands and realms / of the infinite" for "New tales, new mysteries, / New songs from out the breeze" to inform the "ease" and the "peace" of the "Home-stayers." What he brings are new imaginative forms; later in the sequence, "Ballad of Wine Skins" asserts that "The cry of the bard in the half-light / Is chaos bruised into form," and the process is described in a prose "Essay" near the end: "All art begins in the physical discontent (or torture) of loneliness and partiality. It is (was) to fill this lack that man first spun shapes out of the void." Thus through his anguished solitude the artist partakes of the glory of creation celebrated in "Night Litany" and in the two poems following "Purveyors General": "San Vio. June" and "Roundel for Arms." This rapid alternation between gloom and restorative brilliance is characteristic of Pound's sequences, including *The Cantos,* as is this intricate motivic patterning.[14]

In "San Vio. June" and "Roundel for Arms," the Venetian sun and waters afford solace and a spiritually and aesthetically invigorating sense of place. "San Vio. June" provides the wandering soul's *nostos:*

> Weary I came to thee, my romery
> A cloth of day-strands raveled and ill-spun,
> My soul a swimmer weary of the sea,
> The shore a desert place with flowers none.

"Roundel for Arms" finds substance, martial vigor, and—by implication, in "blood and body"—spiritual communion for song: "All blood and body for the sun's delight, / Such be the forms, that in my song bid spring. . . . "

The second group—"Aube of the West Dawn" through the short sequence "Piazza San Marco"—builds on this sense of renewal, primarily through mystic communion with the dawn, in "Aube of the West Dawn," and through love in the following five poems. The third group is characterized by defiance: of loss ("For a Play"), of detractors ("To La Contessa Bianzafior"), and of persecutors of art ("For the Triumph of the Arts"). Though not the most successful poem of the book, "Lotus-Bloom," which opens this section, is exceptional for its range, its allusiveness, and its associative leaps suggestive of the technique of later work. It defies Christian dogma, first of all, and—punning on the name of the magnificent Venetian theater it celebrates, la Fenicé (the phoenix)—reaches back behind "Matri Dei" to "Three Queens": Mary, Isis, and presumably Demeter. At the end, this process of "old imaginings" is compared to the rolling of the Giudecca canal and to the unraveling of an Old Testament scroll in a synagogue—certainly a use of subject rhyme similar to that in *The Cantos.*[15]

The fourth section finds sources of hope and renewal amid settings of despair, beginning, again, with the revivifying Venetian sun in "Alma Sol Veneziae," and ending with "Fratello Mio, Zephyrus," which pits the renewing force of love against autumn's decay. The fifth group, however, is strongly elegiac, framed by a lament for untimely death in "For E. McC. *The Rejected*

Stanza," at its beginning, and a tribute at parting, reluctantly, from Venice, at its close in "Partenza di Venezia":

> Ne'er felt I parting from a woman loved
> As feel I now my going forth from thee,
> Yea, all thy waters cry out "Stay with me!"
> And laugh reflected flames up luringly.

The remaining group draws together the various strains of the sequence and effects the book's symmetry by answering the poems of the opening. "Shallott," the next poem after departure from Venice, embraces the wandering of "Purveyors General," exulting in the discovery of "things long since forgot" and in the freedom of adventure "Oer land & sea." The closing poem, "For Italico Brass," returns to the artist's detachment from life that opens the volume in "Over the Ognisanti," but with a sense of triumph in the completeness and depth of the resulting vision:

> Some as I say
> See but the hues that gainst more hues laugh gay
> And weave bright lyric of such interplay
> As Monet claims is all the soul of art.
> *But I see more.*

The poem ponders the mystery of death and probes the aesthetic possibilities of reincarnation from "death's own isle," in answer to the elegiac strains of the preceding group, but closes with a restatement of the artist's painfully isolated perspective:

> When thou knowst all that these my hues strive say,
> Then shalt thou know some whit the pain
> That gnaws, then shalt thou
>   know some whit the strain
> That spite the palate
>   eats the heart away.

The balanced arrangement of the "San Trovaso Notebook," then, provides a sense of closure much like that of "Hilda's Book," though with a greater range and complexity. Its movement is marked out discursively by an entry to Venice at one end and a departure at the other, yet like the previous volumes its unity is essentially emotive, progressing by means of an alternation between elegiac strains on the one hand and more exuberant tonal patterns on the other: isolation is balanced by a sense of artistic purpose, and a contemplation of death is answered by locating sources of spiritual and emotional renewal in dawn, Venice, love, and the power of art.

Pound's next volume, *A Quinzaine for This Yule,* is comparable in scope but attains greater compression of overall design. Comparing it to *A Lume Spento* in a letter to his parents, Pound points out that the two books work together as complements and are designed to encompass between them man's "every mood and mental need." He cites two poems at opposite ends of the emotive spectrum of *A Quinzaine for This Yule,* stating his own preference for "Sandalphon" (which is closest to "the obvious rigor and virility of *A.L.S.*") and calling it "the biggest thing I have yet done":

> As for the "15": you need not be afraid of it; it lacks the obvious rigor and virility of *A.L.S.*, but the workmanship is finer and more finished and a great many people prefer it. While intended primarily for people who have already read the 1st book, it does no harm if it goes alone. The "Sandalphon" is quite sufficient and in many ways the biggest thing I have done. . . . Bill Williams takes "Nel Biancheggiar" as my best. . . . In a man's complete work there should be something for every mood and mental need. cf. Shakspeare. It is only the minor poet who fills one or two kinds of need. (YC)

The range of *A Quinzaine for This Yule* is attained partly by incorporating and building on the essential framework of the "San Trovaso Notebook"; its subtitle is *Being selected from a Venetian sketch-book, "San Trovaso."* Pound kept the opening contours of that sequence by placing its first three poems, intact and in the same order, at the head of the new volume: "Prelude. Over the Ognisanti," "Night Litany," and "Purveyors General." The next three are drawn from subsequent groupings of the "San Trovaso Notebook," so that the first six poems provide the major outline of the earlier book in a very brief space, using sometimes abrupt tonal juxtapositions unlike the careful modulations of *A Lume Spento.* Here is the order of the poems in *A Quinzaine for This Yule:*

Prelude. Over the Ognisanti
Night Litany
Purveyors General
Aube of the West Dawn. Venetian June
To la Contessa Bianzafior (cent. xiv.). (Defense at Parting)
  [I and II only]
Partenza di Venezia

Lucifer Caditurus
Sandalphon
Fortunatus
Beddoesque
Greek Epigram

Christophori Columbi Tumulus (From the Latin of Hipolytus
  Capilupus, Early cent. MDC)
To T. H. The Amphora
Histrion
Nel Biancheggiar

Thus the first section of the volume moves from an arrival in Venice and a sense
of the artist's privileged but anguished isolation to a nostalgic and reluctant
departure from Venice and from the reassurance and sense of place that Venice
provides. Between these, in rapid succession, are an invocational prayer for
purity of heart and inspiration, "Night Litany"; a projection of the urgency and
distress of the artist's search for form, "Purveyors General"; a sense of hope and
fulfillment through mystic communion, in "Aube of the West Dawn"; and a
defiant assertion of the value of poetic tribute, "To La Contessa Bianzafior."[16]
Spliced together in this way, these six poems provide an opening for the book,
and the emotive patterns they introduce are all recapitulated, varied, and developed in the following poems.

The defiant focus of the second section, the center of the volume, starts out
from the singer's insistent defense of his songs in "To La Contessa Bianzafior"
and brings the sequence closer to "the obvious rigor and virility of *A.L.S.*"; this
group spurns subjection and the limitations of both mortal vulnerability and
mortal boundaries of perception. Picking up the wandering motif of "Purveyors
General," the persona of "Lucifer Caditurus" (Lucifer overthrown) is a harbinger of divine illumination who refuses

> . . . to plod
> An huckster of the sapphire beams
> From star to star
> Giving to each his small embraced desire.

The prayer motif of "Night Litany" is reintroduced through the next poem,
"Sandalphon"; here, as Pound's note explains, the Talmudic angel of prayer
draws the new life of flowers and trees from the paeans of dying angels of wind
and fire, imparting poetic imagination to mortals out of his own creative ecstasy.

"Fortunatus" answers the sadness of departure in "Partenza di Venezia"
with a sense of inexorable impulsion, "resistless, unresisting," "towards my
triumph." The motif of wandering as part of the creative process is reiterated
briefly in the prose note that follows, and "Beddoesque" launches *in media res*
out of an undetermined past toward the empyrean, drawing timeless poetic
moments out of "new-old runes and magic of past time." In its sweep out of the
dark "sea deep" and its promise of "God's truth," it presents, in miniature, the
thrust of Canto I:

> —and going heavenward leaves
> An opal spray to wake, a track that gleams
> With new-old runes and magic of past time
> Caught from the sea deep of the whole man-soul,
> The "mantra" of our craft, that to the sun,
> New brought and broken by the fearless keel,
> That were but part of all the sun-smit sea,
> Have for a space their individual being,
> And do seem as things apart from all Time's hoard,
> The great whole liquid jewel of God's truth.

"Greek Epigram," drawn from the "San Trovaso Notebook," closes the second group on a further note of defiance, denying mortality and mortal limits of praise. It adopts the artist's distance from life of "Over the Ognisanti" and "Purveyors General," and its affirmation of unwavering praise opens out toward the dominant tone of the last section:

> So, when I weary of praising the dawn and the sunset,
> Let me be no more counted among the immortals;
> But number me amid the wearying ones,
> Let me be a man as the herd,
> And as the slave that is given in barter.

The closing four poems are aligned by their celebration of art's renewing power to illumine and sustain man's spirit. All that this volume offers to fulfill the promise of its occasional title, *For This Yule*, is contained in this section's assertion of a capacity to commemorate or revivify the past through moments of aesthetic contemplation or ecstasy. "Christophori Columbi Tumulus," first, laments the mortality of its adventuring hero but affirms his penetration to the otherworld beyond Oceanus's boundaries. The sonnet, "To T. H. The Amphora," resuscitates the past both in its form and in its lighthearted libation of Thomas Hood's poetry. "Histrion" modulates to a more contemplative mode and ponders the process by which the poet's spirit takes its form from reflections of past "Masters of the Soul." A shifting of the poet's identity is conceived of as taking place not through empathetic projection or the interplay of multiple selves, but through a kind of spiritual possession:

> 'Tis as in midmost us there glows a sphere
> Translucent, molten gold, that is the "I"
> And into this some form projects itself:
> Christus, or John, or eke the Florentine.

Finally, "Nel Biancheggiar" provides a sense of closure by relating the splendor of dawn to the sustaining power of music as a stay against the desola-

)

tion of "that somewhile barren hall, my heart" that echoes street-songs garnered from below in the opening poem, "Over the Ognisanti":

> As when the living music swoons
> But dies not quite, because for love of us
> —knowing our state
> How that 'tis troublous—
> It wills not die to leave us desolate.

A Quinzaine for This Yule, then, retains much the same contours as the "San Trovaso Notebook" and achieves a similar balance in fewer than half as many poems. This compression and the agility of its tonal shifts among sections and among individual poems point the way toward the technique of later volumes and sequences. The poems in this volume gain much of their continuity from a shared, limited array of themes, motifs, and perspectives, but these are not used to provide gradual, logically regulated transitions beneath its emotive leaps, as in *A Lume Spento.*

Personae and *Exultations*

It should be clear at this point that Pound's carrying over of some early poems but not others into subsequent volumes is not simply the result of a "process of excision," as Jackson claims (190), since omitted poems may reappear in later volumes. *Personae,* for instance, uses only some poems from *A Lume Spento* and the "San Trovaso Notebook," but the next volume, *Exultations,* includes a selection from *Personae* along with different poems from *A Lume Spento* and *A Quinzaine for This Yule.* Although Pound eventually dropped many of these works from the canon, he retained or omitted them in successive early volumes not solely on the basis of his qualitative judgments of them, but also according to the demands of the sequence worked out for each book-as-a-whole. This is aptly illustrated by a letter he wrote to his father while compiling the *Personae* (1926) collection; concerning the previously uncollected "To Whistler, American," he remarked that "I had some reason for rejecting [it] from *Lustra;* but don't quite remember what. It's just possible that it might fit the present collection" (YC).

Concomitantly, though Pound sometimes carried over groupings intact from one volume into another—the first three poems of the "San Trovaso Notebook" into *A Quinzaine for This Yule,* for instance—more often poems are separated from their original groupings and integrated into new ones. Thus, while *Personae* starts out with almost the same succession as *A Lume Spento,* it ends up as a different book-as-a-whole with a similarly symmetrical design. The first grouping omits only "In Epitaphium Eius," so that the book begins with the same cavalier spirit, the boisterous song and jaunty colloquialism, building up to the bold, virile pride of the artist and counterpointed against currents of nostalgia and loss, as in *A Lume Spento;* but the light, ironic pause supplied by "In Epitaphium Eius" is absent here. The next two groups of *A Lume Spento* are collapsed into one in *Personae* by excluding similarly ironic interjections ("Anima Sola" and "The Cry of the Eyes") and deleting all but the essential framework of the third group, drawn mostly from "Hilda's Book" and focused on a lover's tribute. Although several other poems from *A Lume Spento* are interspersed through the rest of *Personae* ("Masks," "Ballad for Gloom," "For E. McC." and "Motif"), they are taken up into new and distinct groupings:

Grace Before Song
La Fraisne
Cino
Na Audiart
Villonaud for This Yule
A Villonaud. Ballad of the Gibbet
Mesmerism
Fifine Answers

In Tempore Senectutis
Famam Librosque Cano
Scriptor Ignotus
Praise of Ysolt
Camaraderie

Masks
Tally-O
Ballad for Gloom
For E. McC.
At the Heart O' Me
Xenia [excerpted from "Lotus-Bloom"]
Occidit ["The Hour of Gold" in the "San Trovaso Notebook"]

Search ["Motif"]
An Idyl for Glaucus
In Durance
Guillaume de Lorris Belated. A Vision of Italy
In the Old Age of the Soul
Alba Belingalis

From Syria
From the Saddle
Marvoil
Revolt *Against the Crepuscular Spirit in Modern Poetry*
And Thus in Nineveh
The White Stag
Piccadilly

From its first section, *Personae* moves to a group that pits devotion and love against the force of time's erosion, carrying over the artist's struggle and the tonal focus on his sense of pride from group one. This section moves from "In Tempore Senectutis" to "Comaraderie," and at its center is "Praise of Ysolt," projecting love's compulsion and power of revivification.

The book is drawn together in the three subsequent poems, "Masks," "Tally-O" and "Ballad for Gloom," which embody its key tonal patterns and dominant themes. They present, respectively, a state of contemplation, a lighthearted spirit of renewal, and strident defiance of forces greater than man; and they are concerned with the nature of the artist and the creative act, love (in the heart's burgeoning with spring), and a battle for permanence. This key unit also draws together, from the book's framework, the promise of the opening "Grace Before Song" and the tenderness, verging on pathos, of the closing envoi, "Piccadilly." The volume's emotional unity is largely effected by the use of a focusing, pivotal group.

The next section consists of a series of tributes: to the dead ("For E. McC."), to a woman ("At the Heart O' Me," centered on love's vulnerability, and "Xenia"), and to the splendor of the setting sun and its evocation of pageantry and imaginative vigor ("Occidit"). From here the sequence shifts with "Search,"[17] whose title suggests the direction of the following poems, which attempt to locate means of overcoming mortal limitations and especially of breaking through barriers of circumstance, or of thought and feeling, that obstruct communion with others, divorce one from his own nature ("In the Old Age of the Soul"), or prevent the realization of an ideal of harmony and perfection ("Guillaume de Lorris Belated"). These poems strain against bounds of consciousness toward visionary states or toward transformation, with a desperate urgency climaxing in the almost hysterical pitch of "An Idyl for Glaucus":

> I wonder why the wind, even the wind doth seem
> To mock me now, all night, all night, and
> Have I strayed among the cliffs here.
> They say, some day I'll fall
> Down through the sea-bit fissures, and no more
> Know the warm cloak of sun, or bathe
> The dew across my tired eyes to comfort them.

> They try to keep me hid within four walls.
> I will not stay!
> Oimè!
> And the wind saith; Oimè!

Pound's explanation, in an unpublished letter to his parents, characterizes the state of consciousness dominating this group:

> First thought of doing the Glaucus myth on reading the lines from Dante quoted over it. The poem is supposedly a lament of the girl left behind when Glaucus was turned into a sea-god by eating a certain grass—or by allegory if one so choose to interpret it. Had an extention of consciousness which enabled him to experience the feelings of a sea-creature—a consciousness partly cosmic and the equation ought to hold good in any case where the man's further or subtler development of mind puts a barrier between him and a woman to whom he has become incomprehensible. (YC)

Thus the focus of the following poem, "In Durance," is a sense of entrapment among others who "reach me not" and longing for "kin of the spirit" who "have some breath for beauty and the arts," and whom the poem ultimately succeeds in conjuring:

> And yet my soul sings "Up!" and we are one.
> Yea thou, and Thou, and THOU, and all my kin
> To whom my breast and arms are ever warm,
> For that I love ye as the wind the trees. . . .

With this the section turns toward the reconciliation with life attained in "Guillaume de Lorris Belated," Pound's major excursion into the form of the medieval dream poem. But dreams come inexorably upon "the old age of the soul" in the next poem and bring not peace but "Some strange old lust for deeds" for which they finally provide a substitute.

"Alba Belingalis" picks up both the martial context and the wakening impulse from this poem and, presented as a translation "From a tenth century ms.," provides a transition into the final group. Like the opening section, this group consists of a series of "personae," mostly Provençal poets whose songs reach out past some immediate conflict, such as a crusade in "From Syria"; affirm a continuity of love, however compromised; and attest to the power of art to withstand defeat, exile, and obscurity. Thus Marvoil sings on despite separation from the object of his love, filling the emptiness within and around him with testaments of obsessional devotion; and the poet of "And Thus in Nineveh" sings from the tomb and gathers tribute for the works that will outlast him because of their strength and solidity of spirit:

"It is not, Raama, that my song rings highest
Or more sweet in tone than any, but that I
Am here a Poet, that doth drink of life
As lesser men drink wine."

This recapitulates the singer's pride from the first section and provides precisely what "Revolt," the focus of this last group, calls for, starting from a contemplative weighing of dreams against deeds and building up through its anaphoric repetition, "Great God," to its closing, indignant outcry:

Great God, if these thy sons are grown such thin ephemera,
I bid thee grapple chaos and beget
Some new titanic spawn to pile the hills and stir
This earth again.

The final two poems, "The White Stag" and "Piccadilly," are gentler afterbeats of this, hunting the poet's fame and commemorating what is beautiful but transient around him. Placed at the end of the book, "Piccadilly" closes on a poignant note in sharp contrast to the aggressive, declamatory spirit of much of the volume:

Beautiful, tragical faces,
Ye that were whole, and are so sunken;
And, O ye vile, ye that might have been loved,
That are so sodden and drunken,
Who hath forgotten you?

O wistful, fragile faces, few out of many!

Personae, then, like other volumes before it, especially *A Lume Spento,* and like the *Homage to Sextus Propertius* many years later, exhibits a roughly symmetrical structure: the opening and closing groups echo and answer each other's emotive patterns, themes and imagery, and the sequence is informed by a brief group near its center. There is also a more discursive symmetry in this volume: the first and last groups contain predominantly poems set in the past—Provençal personae, for the most part—while the poems between them are concerned with permanent (cosmic or mythic) contexts, or with recurrent states of consciousness. As early as 1909, this scheme begins to approximate the layering Pound pointed out much later, in *The Cantos,* of "the permanent, the recurrent, the casual" (*Ltrs* 239). There is little here of "the casual," which makes its first real entry in *Canzoni,* but a concern with the present is significantly in evidence in "Revolt," "The White Stag," and "Piccadilly." This helps to broaden the scope of the book and establishes a pattern that, though absent from *Exultations,* recurs in every volume from *Canzoni* through *The Cantos* and in many of the shorter sequences as well. The groundplan for *Personae* was apparently established at a very early stage of its assemblage. Commenting on "the formation and shaping of the book as a whole" as evidenced in extant drafts, C. G. Petter calls attention to "what appears to be an early plan for the book":

> The plan outlines three sections: the first containing three poems from *A Lume Spento;* the second, three poems from *A Quinzaine for this Yule,* and the third two new poems: "Marvoil" and "Piccadilly." . . . As the collection developed this original plan evidently was modified: the poems from *A Quinzaine for this Yule* were abandoned and the *A Lume Spento* and the new poems expanded. But the original concept of beginning with "Cino" or "La Fraisne" and ending with "Piccadilly" was maintained to the end. Nevertheless Pound was changing and adding poems within this framework right up to the last proof. (115–16)[18]

Clearly, while the details of the book's contents and organization could be changed at any stage, the general direction of its development was established and maintained from the beginning. This is very suggestive of the way successive cantos and volumes of cantos would unfold toward a determined end, although their exact route and their individual details could be altered as the process of composition demanded, beginning fifteen years later.

Exultations, published a few months after *Personae,* also clearly illustrates Pound's radical reworking of his sequences. Though nearly half its poems are drawn from previous books, only the faintest shade of an earlier grouping lingers. The central principle of organization of this sequence, however, is precisely the same as that of the volumes before and after it—that is, in terms of an emotional unity.

Here is the volume's table of contents:

Guido Invites You Thus
Night Litany
Sandalphon
Sestina: Altaforte
Piere Vidal Old
Ballad of the Goodly Fere

Hymn III
Sestina for Ysolt
Portrait From "La Mère Inconnue"
"Fair Helena" by Rackham
Laudantes Decem Pulchritudinis Johannae Templi

Aux Belles de Londres
Francesca

Greek Epigram
Christophori Columbi Tumulus
Plotinus
On His Own Face in a Glass
Histrion
The Eyes [The Cry of the Eyes]

Defiance
Song
Nel Biancheggiar
Nils Lykke
A Song of the Young Virgin Mother
Planh for the Young English King
Alba Innominata
Planh

In an unpublished letter to Viola Baxter Jordan, Pound describes the arrangement of this book-as-a-whole as a cycle designed to embody a "proportioned presentation of life"—to reflect, as he wrote of *A Quinzaine for This Yule,* man's "every mood and mental need." In the course of vindicating "Piere Vidal Old," under fire for its treatment of sexuality, Pound points out its place within the cycle and characterizes the successive "exultations" of the first grouping:

> Thus. Night Litany—Awe in the presence of beauty. Sandalphon—The joy of submission to an uncomprehended supreme power & wisdom.
> Altaforte—*Strife* & Love of strife for strife's sake. & if you will love of Blood.
> Vidal—sexual passion. The Goodly Fere—love of strength.
> What I mean by its position in the series—incomplete tho' the series still is—is that the collection as a whole should give a more or less proportioned presentation of life. Each poem is in some extent the analysis of some element of life, set apart from the rest, examined by itself. The only question to answer is "Do I present these things honestly? or do I try to persuade the reader to accept a false set of values." (YC; qtd. in McKeown 56)

The poem preceding these, "Guido Invites You Thus," serves as part of the volume's framework. As a riposte to Dante, it is faintly sardonic, but in keeping with what follows, it is an impetuous and adventurous invitation to vision and permanence through a knowledge of life and of the heart. It is, as Witemeyer notes, one of Pound's journey poems presenting the artist's quest, though it does not, as he suggests, exclude "the 'blind earth' of bourgeois society" (118); rather, it encompasses and moves beyond "Life, all of it, my sea, and all men's streams" in its trajectory toward a higher, more complete vision. This is the book's prefatory promise, and the first group of poems begins its fulfillment amid some of the earthiest of passions: blood-lust, sexual desire, and love of strength.

The central concerns of the next group—"Hymn III" through "Francesca"—are love, a sense of separation, and attempts to overcome it, through imagination in "Portrait" and "Fair Helena" and through visionary intensity and recollection in "Laudantes Decem." This movement is colored strongly by a physicality and immediacy of desire, focused particularly in the seventh section of "Laudantes Decem," as we saw in chapter 2. In contrast to the passions of the opening group, this section is informed by a strong current of tenderness, beginning with a sense of vulnerable fragility in "Hymn III."

The volume's vision-quest and the spirituality from which it is never very far removed dominate the third group of poems, all of which are drawn from earlier books. An immortal spirit's contemplation and praise of "the dawn and the sunset" in "Greek Epigram" begins this movement, which shifts to a pondering of the nature of the self and its fluid, uncertain identity in "On His Own Face in a Glass" and "Histrion" and closes with the self-ironic call back to life at the end of "The Cry of the Eyes."

The final grouping effects this return with exuberance and, correspondingly, is drawn together partly by its dominant imagery of dawn, just as the opening section is focused by the night setting of "Night Litany" and the "darker" strains of passion in "Sestina: Altaforte" and "Piere Vidal Old." This last group recapitulates the emotive patterns of love and tenderness at the book's center and directs its quest toward a means of sustaining and strengthening the purity of its gentler impulses—an extension of the prayer in "Night Litany" and a rounding off of the volume's cycle of passions.

"Defiance" and "Song" set dreams, as a force of continuity and a medium of spiritual communion, against the erosion of day and of "base love," and "Nel Biancheggiar," similarly, finds relief from desolation in the alliance of dawn, music, and love. "Nils Lykke" spurns the "black shadows" of memory that taint the experience of present love, and "A Song of the Virgin Mother" pleads with nature for protection of the Christ-child. The eulogy of "Planh for the Young English King" picks up earlier elegiac strains and extols the dead king, Henry Plantagenet, as a sustaining force of virtue for the living. The sequence's cycle is completed by a spirited celebration of love and of lovers' joyfully reciprocal play, persisting against the dawn that will separate them, in "Alba Innominata."[19]

The Yeatsian "Planh" closes the framework of the book and answers the opening "Guido Invites You Thus." It speaks from outside of experience, having passed through its gamut, lamenting sorrow and weariness and seeking respite especially from love. A relentless pursuit by the "white thoughts" in the forest leaves the sequence still amid its cycle of passions, however, and in search of escape instead of the encompassing, transcendent vision that "Guido Invites You Thus" sets out to attain. It ends, rather, with "thy heart and its desire":

> Aye! It's a long hunting
> And it's a deep hunger I have when I see them a-gliding
> And a-flickering there, where the trees stand apart.
>
> But oh, it is sorrow and sorrow
> When love dies-down in the heart.

Whether or not *Exultations* projects the completed cycle that a "proportioned presentation of life" implies is questionable, and Pound's letter expresses some reservation about this. For one thing, his medium was still limited by a persistence of archaisms in diction and syntax and by a use of abstraction to present the more mystic dimensions of experience; the technique of the poems had not yet reached the point where "the Image is itself the speech. The Image is the word beyond formulated language" (*GB* 88). The volume's presentation is also constrained by what now seem rather prudish boundaries of propriety; if "Piere Vidal Old" was subject to attack for its subdued treatment of sexuality, any more direct and explicit handling of this or other matters of passion would have been unthinkable. And the poems of this volume do not yet directly confront such taboos and the cultural marasmus of which they are symptomatic, as the poems of *Lustra* were to do; the immediate present was not yet as pressing a concern as the past or the timeless. Consequently, the volume's range is limited and it does not, in the end, lay claim to an encompassing vision, as a different arrangement might have done—say, by placing the ceaseless, unwearying praise of "Greek Epigram" or the "joy of submission to an uncomprehended supreme power & wisdom" of "Sandalphon" at the conclusion. Though Pound's next volumes present a more extended range, the completeness and depth that *Exultations* strives for is attained with certainty only in *The Cantos* and, perhaps, in *Hugh Selwyn Mauberley*.

Glancing back over the volumes discussed in this chapter, we find that virtually all of the major structuring devices of *The Cantos* were already operant, in rudimentary form, by 1909. First, the ideogrammic method, though not actually formulated till much later, is already at work both in the juxtaposition of tonal groups within each book and in the succession of poems within each group. For instance, the opening section of *A Lume Spento,* used again at the head of *Personae,* is characterized by strains of nostalgia, regret, and longing, counterpointed against the artist's pride, often boisterously expressed; but each of the poems projects a different combination and interaction of these tonalities. Metamorphosis is an important related principle, as in "La Fraisne," where it is a means of transforming regret into a form of contentment. "Cino" achieves an emotional transition to cavalier exuberance by similar means: through transformation of the lover into a careless, wayfaring singer and of the women into songs. The deceased troubadour of "In Epitaphium Eius" likewise converts his devotion through the permutation of one woman into many, and "Na Audiart," in turn, is playfully ironic in its concatenation of many women's features into one "dompna soiseubuda," and becomes regretful again in its vision of the future. All of these contribute slightly different dimensions and different nuances to the group as a whole, "presenting one facet and then another until at some point one gets off the dead and desensitized surface of the reader's mind, on to a part that will register" (*GK* 51). The ideogrammic method is also implicit in Pound's assertion that in *Exultations* "each poem is in some extent the analysis of some element of life, set apart from the rest, examined by itself," though further development will entail greater proximity among these elements.

The various personae contained within this group also present an intricate succession of subject rhymes: Miraut de Garzelas in "La Fraisne" struggling to suppress his memories of a lover rhymes with Cino turning remembered women and love into song, and these, in turn, rhyme with the troubadour and lover of "In Epitaphium Eius," Bertrans de Born in "Na Audiart," Villon, and Browning. One might not go so far as to agree that "subject rhyme is the basis for all of the structuring in *The Cantos*," but its importance there is obvious (Davis, *Fugue* 40). Relatedly, the figures in this group may also be said to trace "repeats in history," presenting exempla of the creative sensibility's exile that extend from mythic pre-history through Provence and medieval France to the immediate past.

Also, as Carne-Ross notes, "it is a basic principle of *The Cantos* that all related characters can merge, or melt, into one another" (139), and this, too, takes place among the figures within this early group of personae—not with the rapidity of "Then Actaeon: Vidal" in Canto IV, but rather in the way Odysseus, for instance, takes on a series of identities, including Elpenor's, in the course of *The Cantos*. *A Lume Spento* considers the processes of merging and metamorphosis explicitly in the group comprised of "Masks," "On His Own Face in a Glass," and "The Tree," and presents a similarly composite figure in "Plotinus."

In its overall movement from beginning to end, *A Lume Spento* follows the same general progression as *The Cantos* from darkness to light—in this case, from lamentation to ecstasy—though in both sequences it is not an orderly Dantescan rising but an advancement by means of alternation between the two. The movement through Venice, from "Over the Ognisanti" to "Partenza di Venezia," a somewhat programmatic dimension of the "San Trovaso Notebook" and *A Quinzaine for This Yule*, is roughly analogous to the periplum of *The Cantos*, which presents history, geography, economics, and so on "not as land looks on a map / but as sea bord seen by men sailing" (Canto LIX). Finally, and most important, in these early volumes as well as in *The Cantos* the primary organizational principle is the interaction and progression of tonal patterns that impart an emotional unity to each volume.

Obviously, however, we do not have *The Cantos* at this early date, even though its primary structural techniques are already emergent. This is partly because the devices used here are subsumed by the overall balance, almost a stasis, in the arrangement of each book-as-a-whole, and they are clearly not allowed to carry the movement of the sequence as they are in the more open, improvisatory unfolding of *The Cantos*. They are also held in check by the poems' abstractness, their often obstructive diction and syntax, their use of conventional forms, and their continual reference to regular iambic meter despite their frequent departures from it. Other developments, then, were needed before these devices could be employed efficiently, and chapter 5 will examine some of the advances made in Pound's next volumes.

5

"The Book-As-a-Whole," 1911–1919

Canzoni

Up through 1910, the missing element in Pound's work most needed for writing a "tale of the tribe" was a way of incorporating the present: a vantage point from which to assess contemporary moeurs, their relation to man's cultural and spiritual history, and their impact upon the individual sensibility acutely aware of that relation and of the heritage of the past.

It is not coincidental that a reorientation to the present was nearly contemporaneous with the formulation of absolute rhythm, with Imagism, and with an accelerated drive toward prose simplicity of diction and directness of syntax; this revamping of technique and its key emphasis on the "intellectual and emotional complex" made possible an expanded range of subjects and ideas without necessitating a compromise of the poems' emotive coherence. "Pound's demand for an absolute rhythm . . . is closely related to his belief that in poetry it is really the subjective, emotional, subconscious strata that validate whatever ideas are advanced" (Hesse 21). As Pound put it, "The artistic statement of a man is not his statement of the detached and theoretic part of himself, but of his will and of his emotions" (*SP* 130). Facts, ideas, judgments, observations, historical analysis, and a range of other materials become accessible as statements of will and emotions, and Pound's poetics is well on the way toward the realization of "a form that wouldn't exclude something merely because it didn't fit." This begins to take place recognizably in *Canzoni* (1911) and evolves steadily through *Ripostes, Lustra,* and *Quia Pauper Amavi.*

Pound's next volume after *Exultations* was actually *Provença* (1910), the first selection of early poems and the first volume printed in America. As a selection, it will not detain us as long as other volumes, but it is important to note that its last section, "Canzoniere" (perhaps named after Petrarch's collection), is the seed of *Canzoni* and contains most of that book's first two groupings.[1] "Canzoniere" begins with "Octave," an introductory piece that announces the following poems as songs of tribute, while *Canzoni* drops this introduction and begins with "Canzon: The Yearly Slain." This provides an initial matrix capable of broader development and directly introduces the central concerns of the book-as-a-whole: love, its transience, sorrow and power of renewal, devotion, vision and song, and the effort to locate sources of permanent value amid the flux of life and feeling. Starting with a poem that both launches the book's forward movement and announces the direction of what follows, instead of with a prefatory framework, is an important strategy in *Canzoni*, repeated in subsequent volumes and in *The Cantos*.

The six sections of the book are arranged partly in answer to the sense of loss introduced in the first poem:

Canzon: The Yearly Slain
Canzon: The Spear
Canzon: To Be Sung beneath a Window
Canzon: Of Incense
Canzone: Of Angels

To Our Lady of Vicarious Atonement
To Guido Cavalcanti
Sonnet in Tenzone
Sonnet: Chi è questa?
Ballata, Fragment
Canzon: The Vision
Octave
Sonnet
Ballatetta
Madrigale
Era Mea

Threnos
The Tree
Paracelsus in Excelsis
De Aegypto

Li Bel Chasteus
Prayer for His Lady's Life
Speech for Psyche
Blandula, Tenulla, Vagula
Erat Hora
Epigrams

La Nuvoletta
Rosa Sempiterna
The Golden Sestina
Rome
Her Monument, the Image Cut Thereon
Victorian Eclogues

A Prologue
Maestro di tocar
Aria
Leviora [withdrawn except for L'Art]
To Hulme (T. E.) and Fitzgerald [withdrawn]
Song in the Manner of Housman
Redondillas or Something of that Sort [withdrawn]
Translations from Heine
Und Drang.[2]

The first group consists of five canzoni ("Canzon: The Yearly Slain" through "Canzone: Of Angels"), a form that Pound called, in a cancelled note, "rather a ritual, the high mass, if you will, of poetry, than its prayer in secret" (*CEP* 305). Accordingly, the dominant mode of this group is the ritualistic declamation of a high mass, beginning with the first word of "Canzon: The Yearly Slain":

> Ah! red-leafed time hath driven out the rose
> And crimson dew is fallen on the leaf
> Ere ever yet the cold white wheat be sown
> That hideth all earth's green and sere and red.

This initial, lamentative outburst introduces motifs of "the fair dead," memory of her, and devotion to her, which are woven into a unifying network in the course of the volume. Korè's demise is quickly generalized and internalized here in a consideration of love's transience and its resistless compulsion:

> Love that is born of Time and comes and goes!
> Love that doth hold all noble hearts in fief!
> As red leaves follow where the wind hath flown,
> So all men follow Love when Love is dead.

The following canzoni trace a movement from Korè's sojourn in the underworld and a corresponding sorrow and barrenness of heart to love's aetherial guides in "Canzone: Of Angels," ascending by means of the lover's vision and constancy of devotion. Consequently, the focus of the group is the lover's experience projected through the oratorical strains of the "high mass," and Korè, or the beloved, is held in memory only and addressed, for the most part, in third person. In the second poem, "Canzon: The Spear," her image is internalized and becomes a beacon "That steadfast gloweth o'er deep waters," dispelling fear, lending spiritual guidance, and providing a basis for love's renewal. The spring imagery that embodies her in this poem directly answers the loss of "Canzon: The Yearly Slain."

"Canzon: To Be Sung beneath a Window" focuses on the songs' act of tribute and voices the reverence, awe, and humility of the high mass. In "Canzon: Of Incense," the woman's exotic charms rise like ritual burning incense, and memory is enjoined to body forth the spirit of love's renewal: "Fragrant be thou as a new field one moweth." "Canzone: Of Angels" concludes the group with a divinely empowered vision of spirits of love, and the force of renewal in the woman's mystic radiance is traced through a conceit of metaphysical complexity comparing her emergence to the rising of "The diver at Sorrento from beneath /The vitreous indigo." Thus this group moves from Korè's descent to the under-world and the decay of life force to her resurgence through divine power in-voked by the mystic vision and ritual of the canzone. The sequence opens on a negative note, as McDougal notes, "with the death of everything spring repre-sents" (82), and begins to locate sources of renewal and permanence through memory, vision, and spiritual receptiveness. The rest of the book is developed largely in terms of these patterns explored through a series of contexts.

The second group picks up the religious implications of the first, beginning with a tribute to "Our Lady of Vicarious Atonement," a source of healing and redemption, and closing with the litany of "Era Mea." The first group ends by announcing that "Voices at last to voice my heart's long mood— / Are come to greet her in their amplitude," and the poems that follow are accordingly more dramatic and direct. "To Our Lady of Vicarious Atonement" addresses the lady directly and turns from questioning to meditation upon the spirit's burden of sin; like the first group, the second begins in this poem on a darker note: "Where lips awake our joy / The sad heart sleeps / Within."

The next poem addresses Guido Cavalcanti, beseeching initiation to a re-newing vision of love and constancy, and the succeeding poems refer increas-ingly to the sustaining power of art through homage, allusion, and translation. In the conflict of "Sonnet in Tenzone," for instance, the heart responds to the mind's challenge by alluding to Ronsard: "'If naught I give, naught do I take return. / 'Ronsard me celebroit!.'" For art embodies and sustains beauty, its emotional power and its spiritual dimensions. This celebratory movement is qualified by "joy's bitter cost" in "Ballata, Fragment," and the group turns through the accusational closing of "Octave"—"Defaulter do I call the knave who hath got / Her silver in his heart, and doth her wrong"—toward its strident climax in "Sonnet":

If on the tally-board of wasted days
They daily write me for proud idleness,
Let high Hell summons me, and I confess,
No overt act the preferred charge allays.

The final three poems of this group are a gentle decrescendo celebrating the woman's grace and delicacy. "Ballatetta" and "Madrigale" focus on her movement and associate her with imagery of nature, drawing together the sequence's images of her as a harbinger of fertility (Korè) and as an object of vision and mystic devotion. This resurgence is momentarily reversed, then reinforced, in group three, which steps back from the focus in previous sections on love and the beloved and traces a descent into Korè's "dark lord's demesne": the realm of the dead and disembodied spirits, but also of metamorphosis, spiritual purification and expansion, and hence renewal. The group moves from a lament over separation and "the fair dead" in "Threnos," through an exultant consideration of the encompassing unity and composure of a spirit outside of life in "Paracelsus in Excelsis," to an affirmation of the artist's creative power and transcendent perspective in "De Aegypto."

The fourth group—"Li Bel Chasteus" through "Epigrams"—returns to earth and to love with a strengthened sense of physicality, and explores the relations between human and otherworldly forces. The gods are viewed in conflict with love (in "Prayer for His Lady's Life") or in union with it (in "Speech for Psyche"), or as distant and envious observers (in "Erat Hora"). This group commemorates the ecstatic moment of earthly love and through it locates the wholeness and tranquility of a "paradiso terrestre," especially in "Li Bel Chasteus" and in "Blandula, Tenulla, Vagula," where the earthly splendor of Sirmio is set against the promises of heaven. In "Erat Hora," a permanent spiritual consummation is attained through the heightened though transient experience of love and its reverberations in memory:

"Thank you, whatever comes." And then she turned
And, as the ray of sun on hanging flowers
Fades when the wind hath lifted them aside,
Went swiftly from me. Nay, whatever comes
One hour was sunlit and the most high gods
May not make boast of any better thing
Than to have watched that hour as it passed.

This is the sequence's emotional zenith, answering the loss and anguish of "Love that is born of time and comes and goes!" in "Canzon: The Yearly Slain."

"Epigrams," closing this group, reintroduces the visionary inwardness of the opening canzoni and serves to modulate toward group five, "La Nuvoletta" through "Victorian Eclogues." This group begins with elegiac tributes to the emotional and visionary force of a distant woman, in "La Nuvoletta," "Rosa Sempiterna," and "The Golden Sestina," all translations or imitations of Dante and Mirandola. But the following three poems—"Rome," "Her Monument," and "Victorian Eclogues"—focus again on mutability and loss, and their dominant tone is lamentative and wistful, brooding over what is past and irrecoverable or on the fragments that remain, charged with nostalgic resonance; all three build upon a disparity between the barrenness of the present and the richness and vitality of a recollected past. "Rome," a translation from Ronsard, begins with an epitaph for the ancient city—"O thou new comer who seek'st Rome in Rome"—and turns to lament time's destructive power:

> O world, thou unconstant mime!
> That which stands firm in thee Time batters down,
> And that which fleeteth doth outrun swift time.

"Her Monument," translated from Leopardi, meditates first on the discrepancy between a woman's death and decay and the completeness of her former beauty, then on the irony of man's nobility joined to his mortal frailty. And "Victorian Eclogues" moves in its three sections from the rejection of one love for another, to yearning for a past love, and finally to Abelard's prayer for Héloise's protection, since they are vowed to separation. The span of this group, then, begins in "La Nuvoletta" with the inner vision of the canzone's ethic of *fin' amor* and turns to a more external focus on life's unconstancy and human limitations.

This broadening of scope helps to prepare for the final group, but the shift to contemporania here is startlingly abrupt despite this preparation and despite the discursive foundation on which, as we shall see, this shift is mounted. "A Prologue" is transitional, announcing the onset of a new dispensation heralded by Christ's Nativity and by the demise of Diana in Ephesus—one among the old order of gods whose presence in group 4 marks the volume's high point. This form of Diana is a harbinger of natural growth and human fertility, and beneath the triumphant, celebratory voices of heaven and earth, her debacle is portentous.

The rest of this group develops the focus on song and the sense of a new order introduced here. In the tribute of "Maestro di tocar," song is a source of permanence and a medium for spiritual uplift beyond the flux of mortality, but this gives way to the irony and urbanity with which art, especially poetry, and love, are next considered, beginning with "Leviora." The focus turns toward the state of the present age, moving from the jaunty burlesque of "Leviora" and the playful reworking of Robert Burns in "To Hulme (T. E.) and Fitzgerald" to the sardonic parody of "Song in the Manner of Housman" and the discursive, self-ironic expostulation of "Redondillas, or Something of That Sort." "Translations from Heine" reintroduces the personal experience of love, combining tenderness and strength of passion with a cynically distanced wit and sophistication, and the group ends in "Und Drang" by deriding the age, its moeurs and its sterility in art and love, and searching for sources of permanent value and spiritual richness.

"Und Drang" begins with a lament over the mutability and limitation of life and feeling, over "Love that is born of time and comes and goes!" and attains a tentative reconciliation beginning in section IV:

> All things in season and no thing o'er long!
> Love and desire and gain and good forgetting,
> Thou canst not stay the wheel, hold none too long!

As we saw in chapter 2, a "passing through" beyond mutability and loss is effected through the transforming ecstasy of love and its memory, braving time, in section IX ("Horae Beatae Inscriptio"), a recapitulation of the volume's momentary acme in "Erat Hora": "How will this beauty, when I am far hence, / "Sweep back upon me and engulf my mind!"

The last sections deride the current age and affirm "a few dozen verities / That no shift of mood can shake from us" ("Au Salon"), and "Und Drang" closes with a riposte to Yeats's "The Cap and Bells" in "Au Jardin" (XII), just as the volume began with a riposte to Manning in "Canzon: The Yearly Slain." Both ripostes confront and reject accepted manners of the time: "Canzon: The Yearly Slain" does so through its technical mastery, and "Au Jardin" does so by dismissing both the sentimental image of the lover whose unqualified devotion is never consummated, except perhaps "symbolically," and a purely physical mode of love that is denuded of its spiritual dimension, a love that will "all come right / O' Sundays."[3] Instead, the sequence embraces a broader perspective and comes to rest on its unifying image of "a pink moth in the shrubbery": Korè reborn, vivacious but fragile, transient and ungraspable except in the image itself:

> And I loved a love once,
> Over beyond the moon there,
> I loved a love once,
> And, may be, more times,
>
> But she danced like a pink moth in the shrubbery.

In this closing poem, then, the volume rejects both the visionary inwardness of the courtly lover's devotion in its opening and the vapidity of the contemporary age. It accepts to some degree the transience and mutability lamented at the outset in "Canzon: The Yearly Slain" and confronted at several points along the way; and it establishes touchstones of permanent value in the intense perception of beauty, the heightened and spiritually informed experience of love, and the sustaining forces of memory and art. Pound's cancelled note to the volume points to this focus on "the permanent part of oneself":

> I ask you to consider whether it be not more difficult to serve that love of Beauty (or, even of some particular sort of Beauty) which belongs to the permanent part of oneself, than to express some sudden emotion or perception which being unusual, being keener than normal, is by its very way being, clearly defined or at least set apart from those things of the mind among which it appears. (*CEP* 305)

This accounts for the inward focus of much of the volume, broadened as it unfolds.

There is also a discursive schema in *Canzoni*. McKeown was first to note that its structure "is roughly chronological, moving from 11th century Provence to 20th century England" (74). Since then, a letter to Dorothy Shakespear has surfaced which details the groundplan of the volume and confirms this observation:

> The masterpiece was to have been the table of contents but some of the poems got on my nerves & I cut out 15 pages of 'em at the last minute. I tried to get an arrangement that would do a little of what Hugo botched in his Legend des Siecles. Artistically speaking its supposed to be a chronological table of emotions: Provence; Tuscany, the Renaissance, the XVIII, the XIX, centuries, external modernity (cut out) subjective modernity. finis. . . . I dont suppose any body'll see it—the table of contents—in this light but when my biographers unearth this missive it will be recorded as an astounding proof of my genius. The plan is filled in, as you see, with translations & old stuff more or less revised.

Pound goes on to offer two more remarks about the volume's design. First, he suggests that "the Canzoni is a sort of Purgatorio with the connecting links left out. I feel now . . . as if I were 'sul monte' & out where I could breathe." And commenting on "Victorian Eclogues," he notes, "The 'Eclogues' are I think over-strained & morbid but part of my criticism of emotion, the whole book is in sort that—to the working out from emotion into the open" (*EP/DS* 37–38).

More recently, James Longenbach has analyzed *Canzoni* in terms of the historical categories listed in this letter, suggesting groupings of poems largely different from those outlined here and concluding that

> throughout *Canzoni* Pound's sense that in some way "all ages are contemporaneous" conflicts directly with his designs for a "chronological table of emotions." . . . *Canzoni* is a record of what endures, and consequently it is not so much an expression of what Pound calls his "sense of history" as it is of his "historical sense." The poems are positioned in the schema not simply to evoke one particular moment in the past; more often, they are placed in order to express the continuities between several moments in time—what endures throughout the centuries of historical change. ("Toward" 396–97)

    While there is certainly a general, chronological movement from Provence in the first group of poems to the twentieth century in the last group, it is very difficult to categorize the poems between these in terms of any precise historical sequence. For instance, there is no clear reason, according to this scheme, why an adaptation of Propertius ("Prayer for His Lady's Life") and an improvisation on Apuleius, based on a translation by Pater ("Speech for Psyche"), are set together where the eighteenth century shifts into the nineteenth, or why "Rome," an adaptation of a poem by Ronsard referring to antiquity, is placed in the middle of the nineteenth.[4] Viewed in strictly chronological terms, the placement of the Nativity in the twentieth century, in "A Prologue," is incongruous at the least. At some level, then, this discursive framework is present in *Canzoni* but is clearly not adhered to very rigorously and does not in itself provide an accurate sense of the book's arrangement.

    More cogent, perhaps, is Pound's description of its movement as "a working out from emotion into the open." Its progression from the visionary inwardness and the constraint of the canzone form in the first group to the urbanity, the contemporary focus and the more open forms of the last is immediately apparent, and there is a fairly steady broadening and externalizing of perspective from the outset of the book to its close. It traces a form of ascension, "a sort of Purgatorio with the connecting links left out," and ends "sul monte"—not exactly amid a paradisal vision but with an overview of past and present and their relations, and of the course of the emotions that have been worked through. Thus the progression from Provence to the present is partly a movement away from the idealization and ethic of delay in the Provençal conventions of *fin' amor* toward a more modern insistence on immediacy and a corresponding quality that Pound called "hardness"—a reorientation capable of retaining the integrity of Provençal aesthetic and spiritual values in the twentieth century and using them as a standard against which contemporania may be assessed. This final vantage point, then, gives rise to the ironic and satiric strains of the closing group. "Und Drang" draws together the book's central concerns and glances with a qualifying distance at both the Provençal setting of the opening and the modern setting of the close.

    In "Cavalcanti," an essay Pound began almost contemporaneously with *Canzoni,* he uses what he there calls a "historic method" to distinguish the aesthetic orientations of a number of eras, much as his description of *Canzoni* suggests that its "chronological table of emotions" is designed to do. An application of these distinctions does not provide a rigidly schematic framework for *Canzoni,* but it helps to account for the placement of some poems in relation to others and to suggest the range of the volume. Provence, where *Canzoni* begins, is characterized by its concern with "the fine thing held in the mind" and is distinguished from the asceticism advanced by the church fathers; from the Greek aesthetic of "plastic moving toward coitus" or "the inferior thing ready for instant consumption," also characteristic of Roman poets including Propertius; and from the modern frame of mind where "we appear to have lost the radiant world where one thought cuts through another with clean edge, a world of moving energies . . . magnetisms that take form, that are seen, or that border the visible. . . ." (LE 150–54). This suggests the oppositions that mark out the movement of Canzoni, from "the fine thing held in the mind" to a modern loss of acute perception and vision heralded by the Nativity in "A Prologue"—back to the Greek "plastic plus immediate satisfaction"—and to a search for means of recapturing and preserving "the fine thing held in the mind" in a contemporary context.[5]

Thus the "chronological table of emotions" in Canzoni seems only tangentially related to history or a historic sense, following not a strict progression through successive eras, but a movement from one polarity of sensibility to another, from Provence to the modern world, by presenting luminous poetic details characteristic of these extremes and a series of gradations between them. In "Und Drang" the two extremes are superposed and allowed to reflect upon one another, as are the other counterpointed patterns of the book-as-a-whole: passion and disillusionment, loss or death and renewal, transience and continuity, spiritual and emotional fecundity and sterility, physical immediacy and memory or vision. At its close, the volume's resolution in its unifying image of the "pink moth in the shrubbery" recovers the aesthetic of "the fine thing held in the mind" for the present age. This highly charged confluence of disparate streams distinguishes the method of Canzoni from that of Exultations, where each poem presents "some element of life, set apart from the rest, examined by itself," so that components are ideogrammically joined within the volume but not set in resonant proximity, as here. The technique of Canzoni's closing group points the way to the Poetry sequences of the next few years and ultimately to The Cantos.

Canzoni's idiosyncratic incorporation of a historical scheme also looks forward to The Cantos, a "poem including history," and its rather broad reference to Hugo's La Légende des siècles suggests the ways in which the Odyssey and La Divina Commedia enter the structure of The Cantos but do not in any clear sense determine it.

Finally, the search for a "permanent basis in humanity" (SR 91) to set against the flux of mortality and against chaotic modern fragmentation establishes what is essentially a mythic order that helps to impart unity to the volume. Canzoni seeks to locate sources of continuity amid contemporania, the casual and its effects, rather than by exclusion or abstraction, as the earlier poems and sequences did. The final movement of the book thus "passes through" from "the merely haphazard or casual" to the recurrent and permanent, and emerges "sul monte."

Ripostes

Ripostes, Pound's next volume, begins in some ways where *Canzoni* leaves off. From its outset, it shares the contemporary orientation of the end of *Canzoni* and the overview of past, present, and their relations which that volume attains; *Ripostes* begins "sul monte." It builds on the external focus and the emotional openness that *Canzoni* works toward, reflected in the dominant mode of most of the poems: a direct address to the person, thing, or vision at the focus—to the vision of "Apparuit," for instance, to the corpse of "The Tomb at Akr Caar," and to the fragmented woman of "Portrait d'une Femme." As the title and epigraph— *"Gird on thy star, We'll have this out with fate"*—suggest, *Ripostes* is confrontative and built upon a few central contrasts. The most important is an opposition between the vitality and purity of the artist's vision and his spirit of adventure and emotional receptiveness, on the one hand, and, on the other, sterility and stagnation, especially as evidenced in contemporary characters bound by quotidian, by failures of perception and by clinging to the past.

But this sense of "riposte" is less a matter of satirical attack—for the satires occupy a relatively small proportion of the volume—than an insistence upon accurate perception and characterization and a refusal to idealize or qualify what is perceived. There is a corresponding insistence on distinctions of feeling, a disavowal of emotions that have lost their force, and a condemnation of this and other inadequacies of heart in the more satiric pieces. While *Canzoni* reaches a point of reconciliation with transience, *Ripostes* comes to insist upon it as the natural course of human affairs and to set against it the permanence of epiphanic moments and the enduring vision of the artist.

We have already seen, in chapter 1, how these key dimensions of the book are introduced through its first poem, "Silet," a sonnet that uses convention as a means of rejecting conventional pretensions: "When it is autumn do we get spring weather. . . ?" The balance of the first group (through "Portrait d'une Femme") and of subsequent groups develops the central concerns and tonal pattern-units introduced in this poem from a few different vantage points. The book falls roughly into two parts, the first consisting of two sections with a concentration of satirical pungency, and the second of three sections unified by a more positive orientation, consisting predominantly of praise, visionary moments, and affirmations of devotion:

Silet
In Exitum Cuiusdam
Apparuit
The Tomb at Akr Caar
Portrait d'une Femme

N.Y.
A Girl
Phasellus Ille
An Object
Quies

The Seafarer
Echoes [I and II]
An Immorality
Dieu! Qu'il la Fait
Salve! O Pontifex

Δώρια
The Needle
Sub Mare
Plunge
A Virginal

Pan is Dead
The Picture
Of Jacopo del Sellaio
The Return
Effects of Music Upon a Company of People

"Silet" ends with an indignant refusal to cling to and commemorate the past—"And who are we, who know that last intent / To plague to-morrow with a testament!"—and "In Exitum Cuiusdam," a riposte to Yeats's "A Lover Pleads with His Friends for Old Friends," carries this indignation from a personal into a social context. The poem dismisses the outworn or outlived affection of past friendships with a mordant, worldly sophistication in its rejection of loyalties preserved for convention's sake.[6]

This opening orientation is interrupted by the transient visionary richness of "Apparuit," as if the intensity and vividness with which the past here takes form answers the more superficial adherence to it spurned in the preceding poems. But dramatically realized as it is, the vision is qualified by an undertone of doubt and astonishment at the vitality of this resurrection and its concomitant rapture:

> Clothed in goldish weft, delicately perfect,
> gone as wind! The cloth of the magical hands!
> Thou a slight thing, thou in access of cunning
> dar'dst to assume this?

In the next poem, "The Tomb at Akr Caar," the moribundity of past earthly experience that cannot be revived is set alongside the vibrant awareness of the soul. The poem builds on the tremendous irony of this juxtaposition, at times somewhat whimsically:

> I have been kind. See, I have left the jars sealed,
> Lest thou shouldst wake and whimper for thy wine.
> And all thy robes I have kept smooth on thee.

Through the soul's almost perverse misdirection, it is entrapped and languishing—"there is no new thing in all this place"—as is the woman at the focus of the next poem, "Portrait d'une Femme." She too, in her way, is a corpse, addressed with much the same tone of compassion as in the soul's monologue to the empty body in "Tomb at Akr Caar":

> Your mind and you are our Sargasso Sea,
> London has swept about you this score years
> And bright ships left you this or that in fee.

This poem marks the end of the first group with its key contrast to "Apparuit"; the mystically envisioned woman there taking form is in dynamic opposition to the earthbound dullness of this figure, of whom no idealization or vision is possible, but only recognition and compassion beneath its light derision.

"N.Y." heads off the more pointedly satiric third group (through "Quies"). This poem is playfully mocking and self-mocking in its personification of the city as a girl and its tongue-in-cheek proposal to inspire her; its mid-course interjection of wonder at the absurdity of the proposition; and then its plunge forward into the impossible, a qualified but dauntless effort. This playfulness extends into "A Girl," imaginatively entering the experience and spiritual richness of its subject with a completeness of empathetic penetration much like that of "The Tree," though not as convincingly. The end of "A Girl" turns to satirize the obtuseness of a world incapable of apprehending the spirit's simple but genuine sense of participation in natural forces, particularly of growth:

> Tree you are,
> Moss you are,
> You are violets with wind above them.
> A child—*so* high—you are,
> And all this is folly to the world.

The sardonic point of the last line is sharpened in the rest of this group, in the caricature of "Phasellus Ille" and in the following two epigrams. "Phasellus Ille" mocks the "modern" editor's unthinking adherence to outworn convention, his recalcitrance to change, and his asexual automatism; nothing can "Shake up the stagnant pool of its convictions." "An Object," like "In Exitum Cuiusdam," rejects social conventions that would substitute perfunctory loyalty for genuine affection, and "Quies," closing the group, spurns the traditional sentimentality of elegy, from which it pivots wittily on the repetition of its key phrase to an unexpectedly lighthanded dismissal:

> This is another of our ancient loves.
> Pass and be silent, Rullus, for the day
> Hath lacked a something since this lady passed;
> Hath lacked a something. 'Twas but marginal.

"The Seafarer" initiates the third group (through "Salve! O Pontifex") and announces the shift in focus of the second part of the book, away from the disparagement of conventionality in the previous section. The difference between the two major parts of *Ripostes* is encapsulized by the contrast between the poems that introduce them: the urbane self-irony of "Silet"—"Why should we stop at all for what I think? / There is enough in what I chance to say"—and the boldness and vigor of sincerity announced in "The Seafarer": "May I for my own self song's truth reckon." The poem embraces the adventurousness and spiritual promise of the mind's and heart's quest:

> . . . Nathless there knocketh now
> The heart's thought that I on high streams
> The salt-wavy tumult traverse alone.
> Moaneth alway my mind's lust
> That I fare forth, that I afar hence
> Seek out a foreign fastness.

Though the archaic Anglo-Saxon rhythms and diction may seem incongruous in a poem that sets out in search of the new, they reflect the emotional and intellectual daring of the quest and their rocking motion helps to realize the poem's sustained metaphor of a sea-journey. This and the following poems of group three all refer to, translate, or adapt the work of earlier poets. Like "Apparuit" and, later in the book, "The Return," they discover vital moments of the past and recapture them for the present.

The next poems build on the "song's truth" invoked in "The Seafarer." "Echoes" juxtaposes two adaptations; the first, "Guido Orlando, Singing," reiterates song's truth in its courtly praise and devotion: "Worthy to reap men's praises / Is he who'd gaze upon / Truth's mazes." The second ("Asclepiades, Johanius Aegyptus") is a pointed *carpe diem:* "Think'st thou that Death will kiss thee?" "Echoes," then, momentarily superposes the two polarities of *Canzoni,* "the fine thing held in the mind" and "the inferior thing ready for instant consumption." "An Immorality," next, sets the value of "love and idleness" against martial prowess, and "Dieu! Qu'il la Fait" makes new a song of admiration and praise from Charles d'Orleans, finding in a woman's form the wonder of her creation. "Salve! O Pontifex" closes this group with a paean to Swinburne and an invocation to his spirit for afflatus.

Thus the third group voyages through the past and recovers illumined, enduring poetic moments and their spiritual richness. This appeal to the past and to the dead prepares the way for the fourth group, "Δώρια" through "A Virginal," which continues this exploration in a descent to the underworld and to marine depths of consciousness, discovering there the bases for emotive richness and renewal and sources of continuity amid flux, much in anticipation of Cantos I and XLVII. "Δώρια" appeals to chthonic powers as a source of continuity—"Let the gods speak softly of us / In days hereafter"—and "The Needle" seeks to preserve "the good hour" between lovers amid change that they are helpless to control.

The next three poems, "Sub Mare," "Plunge," and "A Virginal," form a triad linked by their focus of tribute and constancy of devotion, perhaps designed to set off the satiric triad that closes the second group. "Sub Mare" reaches down through consciousness to a marine landscape of eternity, partly through the experience of love: "Since you have come this place hovers round me." "Plunge" transfers the fertility of this setting to more solid ground, and with heightened urgency spurns the city in pursuit of pastoral nourishment. And "A Virginal" shifts to a mystic, hymn-like rapture of devotion; love and the reciprocal understanding between lovers are a basis of growth and of a sense of steadfast purity:

> No, no! Go from me. I have still the flavour,
> Soft as spring wind that's come from birchen bowers.
> Green come the shoots, aye April in the branches,
> As winter's wound with her sleight hand she staunches,
> Hath of the trees a likeness of the savour:
> As white their bark, so white this lady's hours.

The final group begins with a momentary reversal of this flourishing life-force by winter's onset in "Pan Is Dead."[7] But the balance of this group is centered on the power of the artist's vision to recapture, renew, and sustain the vitality of the past and to transcend the limitations of the mundane. "The Picture" and "Of Jacopo del Sellaio" work together as a meditation on the love and desire embodied and kept vital by an artist's vision in his painting. "The Picture" projects the immediacy of the observer's experience, with awe at the way "The eyes of this dead lady speak to me." "Of Jacopo del Sellaio" attributes the strength of this experience to the painter's vision, turns on a recognition of how the subject of the painting, though long dead, comes to life again in the present moment, and closes with a reiterated exclamation of wonder and an affirmation of the power of art to convey emotion:

> This man knew out the secret ways of love,
> No man could paint such things who did not know.
>
> And now she's gone, who was his Cyprian,
> And you are here, who are "The Isles" to me.
>
> And here's the thing that lasts the whole thing out:
> The eyes of this dead lady speak to me.

From here, the shift to the immediacy of a pure vision of spirits of the past momentarily taking form and life amid the flux of consciousness, in "The Return," is a highly congruent one. The movement of this poem follows the unfolding of its vision, "one and by one," beginning at its highest pitch of dramatic intensity in the excited repetition of "See, they return." It reaches toward its moment of fullest realization and its climax of nostalgic awareness— "These were the 'Wing'd-with-Awe,' / Inviolable"—and then falls off with the receding of the vision and a recognition of its transience. Unlike the vision of the woman limned and kept alive by the painter's insight in the two preceding poems, that of "The Return" emerges fleetingly but with full-bodied force that resonates beyond its close:

> Haie! Haie!
>   These were the swift to harry;
>   These the keen-scented;
>   These were the souls of blood.
>
>   Slow on the leash,
>   pallid the leash-men!

This visionary movement is sustained, with qualification, into the final poem, the short sequence "Effects of Music Upon a Company of People." Art again provides the basis of vision, which traces the fluid movement of souls ecstatically released by music and surging upward, away from physical boundaries. But they are ultimately returned to the level of the mundane:

> Then came a mer-host,
> And after them legion of Romans,
> The usual, dull, theatrical!

This supplies a diminished cadence for the volume and closes it on a note of confrontation in its distinction between vision and banality, lightly echoing the satiric focus of the second group.

This helps to reinforce the approximate symmetry of the book's arrangement. Its purest, most dramatically immediate moments of vision, "Apparuit" and "The Return," were originally published together but are here separated and used to focus the opening and closing groups.[8] "Apparuit," amid the surrounding poems, offers an alternative to forms of sterility, dullness, self-delusion, and confinement, and "The Return" serves as the climactic fulfillment of a capacity for vision affirmed in the closing group. Other, less exact pairings are also set up between the first and last groups: in both "The Tomb at Akr Caar" and "Effects of Music Upon a Company of People," for instance, vibrant spirits are released from decaying bodies but ultimately reentrapped. "Portrait d'une Femme" at one end and the paired "The Picture" and "Of Jacopo del Sellaio" at the other present a theme and its inversion that are also echoed less explicitly throughout the volume: "Portrait d'une Femme" depicts a woman physically alive but spiritually and emotionally stagnant, and projects along with her portrait the observer's experience of her, while the answering pair present a woman long dead yet vividly present. The artist's vision of her reflects the strength of her love and desire as they come to life again: "The eyes of this dead lady speak to me."

In fact, although the first part of the book is most satirical and the second generally more positive, there are positive notes at the beginning, in "Apparuit" and "A Girl," and a final parry and thrust at the end, in "Effects of Music Upon a Company of People." The volume is not arranged in terms of simply contrasted blocks, but contrapuntally: its two most prominent tonal motifs, a confrontation with dullness and a vital projection of vision, are introduced through an exchange, then developed in the book's two main movements and brought together for a final interchange and resolution in the coda. We have already noted a use of musical principles in the arrangement of Pound's volumes as early as *A Lume Spento,* and the construction of *Ripostes* is a further step toward the elaborate, fugue-like development of *The Cantos.* The bipartite organization of this volume also links it to *A Lume Spento* and points the way toward *Hugh Selwyn Mauberley;* its implications for *The Cantos* will be considered in chapter 6.

William Carlos Williams, to whom *Ripostes* is dedicated, was apparently quick to recognize its integrity; in an unpublished reply, Pound seems rather pleased by his observation:

Your perception of the "unit" is the most gratifying. That of course is the artistic triumph—to produce the whole which ceases to exist if *one* of its component parts be removed or permuted = or rather the "whole" that has no "parts." (YC)

Lustra and *Quia Pauper Amavi*

The technique of *Lustra*, Pound's next volume, though a logical development of the strategies used in previous volumes, is in some respects a departure from them. The dominant principle of movement among poems and groups remains juxtaposition, but the transitions are less often abrupt or distant leaps than gradual shifts. In this respect, *Lustra* recalls the mode of proceeding in *A Lume Spento*, but while the earlier volume builds on logical continuities of theme, context, and imagery, the coherence of *Lustra* is attained through the use of subtle emotive gradations, so that central tonal currents are sustained but varied in focus, emphasis, and proportion among poems, much as in the *Homage to Sextus Propertius*. The primary oppositional patterns of *Ripostes,* for instance, the confrontative and the visionary, are developed in *Lustra* through more gradual variations and are more fully interwoven. They operate not like focusing lenses for different blocks or movements, but more on the analogy of prisms whose mingled spectra generate a range of tonal colors and subtly varied hues. The importance of this shift in design for Pound's eventual long poem strategy can hardly be overstated; as Kenner notes, "The *Cantos* will before long be working in this way, setting like beside almost like, to delineate losses and gains, new delicacies, lost intensities" (*Era* 64).

The continuous recapitulations and variations implicit in this method are ideally suited to an extended structure such as that of *The Cantos* or that of *Lustra* which, with eighty-six poems and sequences in its final form, is by far Pound's most expansive effort prior to *The Cantos*. Crucial gradations, distinctions, and contrasts can be established and sustained by this means throughout "a poem of some length" much more readily than through movement in blocks alone.

Lustra evolved through four versions between 1916 and 1917: two English editions, consisting of "300 copies printed almost unabridged at Mathews expense and . . . the rest *castrato*" to placate readers' moral squeamishness (*P/L* 39); and two American editions, where the volume was published together with a selection from earlier works and with Ur-Cantos I–III. The additions to *Lustra* proper in the 1917 American printings suggest that this is its final form, and the following discussion will be concerned with the second impression. This is identical to the first in all respects except for the deletion of "The Temperaments" at the end, so that the volume closes with "Impressions of Voltaire."[9]

Pound's meticulous care in the arrangement of *Lustra* is apparent, first of all, in the way some of the periodical sequences published between 1913 and 1916 were rearranged or disbanded in order to fit them into the book-as-a-whole, while others were retained as the foundation for some of the volume's final groupings. Second, when Pound added poems in the American edition, he did not simply append them but positioned them within the sequence so that they fit into, and contribute to, its integral curve of movement. The considerable thought that went into the selection and arrangement of poems is also apparent in a preliminary table of contents that suggests the process of shaping a group through the deletion of some poems and the repositioning of others.[10] And finally, Pound's battle to get the volume printed intact and in the order he wanted is documented in his letters to Elkin Mathews, publisher of the English editions, printed in an appendix to *Pound/Joyce*. In defense of the book against possible action by censors, he pleads that "there is no immoral tone in Lustra. There is open speech, that is all, that is the whole of any possible complaint"; and he goes on to explain the need for

> such poems as "Further Instructions" or the "Cabaret" poem, . . . [and] the prefatory poems, though I do not consider them as good poetry as some containing more concrete expression. Still they act as a preface and are necessary to the form of the book. Beauty unrelieved goes soft and sticky. (283)

In the course of his defense he characterizes the volume in much the same terms he used to describe *Exultations:* "This book is, I hope, not a dull book. I believe it shows life fairly, and without slush and sentimentality. . . . If the book is not dull, neither is it trivial, nor undertaken in a trivial spirit. It expresses, I believe, a 'philosophy of life', or what I would rather call a 'sense of life'" (284–85). And his final, most important plea is for its integrity:

> Do try to think of the book as a whole, not of individual words in it. Even certain smaller poems, unimportant in themselves have a function in the book-as-a-whole. This shaping up a book is very important. It is almost as important as the construction of a play or a novel. . . . I am thinking of a few short satirical lines, when I ask you to consider this question of the "Book-as-a-whole." (285)

Clearly, the main concern is for a balance and a particular progression among tonalities, and though a compromise was struck providing for the two editions, Pound still complained that "My *Lustra* is all set up, and I find I have been beguiled into leaving out the more violent poems to the general loss of the book, the dam'd bloody insidious way one is edged into these tacit hypocrisies *is* disgusting" (*Ltrs* 81).

Pound's care in arranging the volume has won only marginal recognition from his readers to date, however. Kenner first noted a central group of five poems (from "Papyrus" through "To Formianus' Young Lady Friend") and observed how their progression typifies that of the volume as a whole (*Era* 62–64). More recently, Alexander has located groupings of poems according to their continuities in form:

> I believe that the sequence of poems is arranged in a pattern, which one might recapitulate thus: preliminaries and announcements; 'The Spring'; further announcements; love-visions; egotistical variations; epigrams; 'imagisms'; social sketches; love-visions; sketches and epilogue. *Lustra* is organized around the blocks of love-visions and epigrams, with a calculated variation of intensity, subject, type, tone and length, though all in the key of Eros. (88)

These groupings are applicable and useful, though it seems unlikely, in view of Pound's emphasis on an emotional unity and in light of his comments on the volume, that the poems would be arranged quite so categorically, in terms of subject and outer form alone.

In fact, the tonal continuities and shifts in *Lustra* develop the dominant tonalities that inform the organization of *Ripostes*. While *Ripostes* approaches contemporania through confrontation and insistence on vital distinctions, *Lustra* is both more aggressively confrontative and more bitingly satiric. Yet it is also more delicate and understated in its moments of vision and deeply-felt realization, and hence its key contrasts are more sharply defined, though more gradually developed.

The book's nine groups build on these contrasts through variations in proportion and emphasis and through a contrapuntal development of related themes. The first group is primarily satiric, though this is punctuated by notes of ecstatic appreciation and contrasting notes of loss. The more personal focus of the second group permeates even its satiric elements and helps to modulate toward the aesthetic orientation of group 3. Group 4 is the book's elegiac center, and this tonal element builds in emphasis through the rest of the volume, becoming dominant once again in the final group. Group 5 presents an exuberant resurgence of life-force, but the energies of group 6 find expression in a mixture of satire and notes of longing. The social commentary that courses throughout the volume becomes dominant in group 7, and group 8 views contemporania from an aesthetic perspective. This recapitulates the focus of group 3 and provides a transition into the final group 9, which, though primarily elegiac, draws together all of the volume's tonalities and themes. The contents of these groups are as follows:

Tenzone
The Condolence
The Garret
The Garden
Ortus
Salutation
Salutation the Second
The Spring
Albâtre

Causa
Commission
A Pact

Surgit Fama
Preference

Dance Figure
April
Gentildonna
The Rest
Les Millwin
Further Instructions
A Song of the Degrees
Ité
Dum Capitolium Scandet

Tò Καλόν"
The Study in Aesthetics
The Bellaires
The New Cake of Soap
Salvationists
Epitaph
Arides
The Bath Tub
Amitiés
Meditatio
To Dives
Ladies
Phyllidula
The Patterns
Coda
The Seeing Eye
Ancora

Dompna Pois de Me No'us Cal
The Coming of War: Actaeon
After Ch'u Yuan
Liu Ch'e
Fan Piece, for Her Imperial Lord
Ts'ai Chih
In a Station of the Metro

Alba
Heather
The Faun
Coitus
The Encounter
Tempora

Black Slippers: Bellotti
Society
Image from D'Orleans

Papyrus
Ione, Dead the Long Year
'Ιμέρρω
Shop Girl
To Formianus' Young Lady Friend
Tame Cat

L'Art, 1910
Simulacra
Women Before a Shop
Epilogue
The Social Order
The Tea Shop

Ancient Music
The Lake Isle
Epitaphs
Our Contemporaries
Ancient Wisdom, Rather Cosmic
The Three Poets

The Gypsy
The Game of Chess
Provincia Deserta
Cathay
Near Perigord
Villanelle: The Psychological Hour
Dans un Omnibus de Londres
Pagani's, November 8
To a Friend Writing on Cabaret Dancers
Homage to Quintus Septimius Florens Christianus

Fish and the Shadow
Impressions of François Marie Arouet (de Voltaire)

The volume's confrontative mode begins in its title and explanation: it is to be "an offering for the sins of the whole people"—the sins, as the poems that follow make clear, of dullness, imperception, and repressive conventionality.[11] The first group, "Tenzone" through "A Pact," picks up this note and launches a full-bodied attack in the direct challenge of the first poem, using Whitmanesque diction and constructions to set moral freedom and freedom of expression against the prudery of contemporary moeurs. "Tenzone" introduces a link among vital sexuality, a corresponding richness of feeling, and art, and a distinction between these and the sterility of social pretense. These crucial concerns are developed in the rest of the volume, and their importance persists throughout Pound's work. Clark Emery finds, for instance, that one of the key tensions in *The Cantos*

> is the effort to bring together the Eleusinian (or Dionysian) concept of natural fecundity and the Confucian concept of human ordering. Prudery, of course, is an enemy of the former drive, distorting and making it shameful. . . . On the one hand it completely falsifies and commercializes the concept of love . . . ; on the other, it betrays the idea of individual liberty as the right to do anything that does not injure others. . . .(5)

The transition between this poem and the next, "The Condolence," is typical of the method of *Lustra*, "setting like beside almost like." While the first poem attacks the reading public for their prudishness, the second attacks the procured audience for misreading the poems' "virility." Though the poems themselves insist on the importance of this element, "The Condolence" raises an indignant outcry at their categorization, the resulting compromise of the individuality they insist on, and the mistaking of delicacy and fertility of feeling for boorish hedonism.

The remainder of this group follows the central contour of the "Contemporania" sequence on which it is built, with a few important rearrangements that result in a more balanced alternation between "orations" and "pictures" than in "Contemporania," and correspondingly between satiric attacks and moments of vision.[12] "The Garret" begins with the same mode of address as the first two poems, setting up the expectation of another attack—"Come, let us pity those who are better off than we are"—but shifts to an image of delicately rapturous fulfillment in the communion between lovers at dawn's illumined moment. This poem is poised on the graceful motion of its central simile, "Dawn enters with little feet / like a gilded Pavlova," and on this it pivots into "The Garden." By contrast with the dawn's and the dancer's natural grace, the woman's gait in "The Garden" is helplessly self-conscious, and her inhibited, anemic constitution is set off by the emotional richness of "The Garret," where "I am near my desire." Clearly, these poems gain enormously in depth from their juxtaposition. The third "picture," "Ortus," addresses a woman much like that of "The Garden" in a mockingly affectionate attempt to impart form and spirit to her shapeless, diffusive flux. As if out of frustration, the next poem, "Salutation," derides the "generation of the thoroughly smug / and thoroughly uncomfortable" and confronts artificial class distinctions, disparaging the upper class, admiring the natural ease of fishermen and their families, and setting the nude fish, in harmony with their surroundings, above both. This image of fish as an ideal of composure and harmony becomes a significant motif, and its use here is echoed in the last group by "Fish and the Shadow." "Salutation the Second" strips away the clothing of upper-class, sentimental conventions ("the Picturesque" and "vertigo of emotion") and offers up the songs as naked, impudent celebrations of life force, dancing the cordax and disrupting prudish complacency with their insistence on "the indecorous conduct of the gods"—on the sensual elements of permanent human "states of mind."

But the emotional openness these poems embrace also has its perils. "The Spring" begins with a celebration of the season's growth but turns with an apprehension of irrecoverable loss, unanswerable desire, and their resulting anguish "like black lightning," a destructive element of the season's fertility:

> And wild desire
> Falls like black lightning.
> O bewildered heart,
> Though every branch have back what last year lost,
> She, who moved here amid the cyclamen,
> Moves only now a clinging tenuous ghost.

This introduces the volume's first elegiac note, to be developed more fully in group 4. "Albâtre" offers a contrast to the "black lightning" in its calmly distanced observation of whiteness in a woman who "Is, for the time being, the mistress of my friend," a purity distinct from the repression of moral prudery. The intimacy of this setting is carried over to the lightly mocking, lightly regretful sense of the exile's exclusiveness in "Causa."

"Commission" draws together the orations of the first group in speaking out "against all forms of oppression" and in particular against the sterility and enslavement of social institutions that provide a partial death; a family with three generations under one roof is "like an old tree with shoots, / And with some branches rotted and falling." The group turns from the Whitmanesque construction of this poem to end on a conciliatory but backhanded tribute to Whitman, "a pig-headed father." While in "Commission" adherence to the past out of convention is like a half-rotted tree, in "A Pact" the past is a fertile heritage that nurtures new growth—"We have one sap and one root"—and new means of creativity: "It was you that broke the new wood, / Now is a time for carving." The second group plays off the first by rehandling the same elements, in a different succession and with different emphases. Its movement is also marked out by an alternation of "orations" and "pictures," though the latter are clearly dominant; the attacks are more indirect and the visions more vibrant and fully developed. Like the first group, the second ends with a homage to Whitman, "Dum Capitolium Scandet," echoing "Crossing Brooklyn Ferry" and welcoming the poems' poetic progeny. It begins, however, on a different but related note in "Surgit Fama," which picks up "a pact with you, Walt Whitman" from the previous poem and works it into "a truce among the gods," playfully celebrating the fertility and free interplay of reemerging "eternal states of mind."[13] Like "Tenzone," this is an exhortation to the poems that follow—"Do thou speak true, even to the letter"—and sincerity is related to the earth's fertility and richness of life-impulse:

> The corn has again its mother and she, Leuconoë,
> That failed never women,
> Fails not the earth now.

Images of fertility and growth and contrasting images of destruction and sterility, with their related colorations, are a central part of the contrapuntal movement of this group and of the book.

In "Preference," fascination and mystified wonder at a woman's persistence in mind draw in toward the more personally involved perspective of the rest of this group, especially in the self-ironic turn at its close: "And I, who follow every seed-leaf upon the wind? / You will say that I deserve this."[14]

"Dance Figure," "April," and "Gentildonna" form a triad that moves from a celebration of fertile life-impulse to a sense of horrified loss in its passing, and finally to an apprehension of its power of recurrence—a much more effective rehandling of the Korè motif that courses through *Canzoni*. "Dance Figure" is an energetic song of admiration and desire focused by its image of graceful motion and built up through its accomplished handling of absolute rhythm and its modeling on the *Song of Songs*.[15] Loss and yearning are then externalized in the carnage of stripped olive boughs in "April" and reversed through the resurrection of a dead lover out of memory in the once more flourishing olive of "Gentildonna."

The next three poems, "The Rest," "Les Millwin," and "Further Instructions," form a contrasting triad that homes in on the position of art and artists in their contemporary social context and focuses on the obstacles that impede them. "The Rest" laments the condition of the arts in America but ends on a more hopeful note: "Take thought: / I have weathered the storm, / I have beaten

out my exile." At the center, "Les Millwin" presentatively but mockingly depicts a ballet audience whose souls are dislocated and art students similarly
self-dismantled, "With arms exalted, with fore-arms / Crossed in great futuristic
X's." And "Further Instructions" closes the triad, inveighing against social
moeurs and conventional expectations of poetry through an ironically affectionate address to the poems: "You do not even express our inner nobilities, / You
will come to a very bad end."

This triad, originally gathered under the heading "Lustra," focuses the
satiric dimension of the volume and attains what Pound specified as the object
of satire: "Satire reminds one that certain things are not worth while. It draws
one to consider time wasted" (*LE* 45). It also embodies much of what Pound
called the "cult of ugliness." In *Lustra,* as Witemeyer notes, this is in direct
opposition to a celebration of life force, as in the preceding triad of poems:
"Instead of celebrating the life force through fertility themes, the cult of ugliness
reveals death in contemporary life and letters. This death is both psychic (a
spiritual or cultural desiccation) and physical (an emotional and sexual impo-
tence). The characters satirized are incomplete, lacking the vital unity or *virtù*
of the Poundian goddess" (130). The setting up of this opposition in contrasting
triads is indeed a conventional figure made new, and this structural motif is
picked up and worked through fully in "Cathay," as we have seen, and comes to
play a still more significant role in later works.

The closing of "Further Instructions" defiantly introduces the motif of
"Chinese colours," which "Song of the Degrees," typically, carries over. Here
critics' expected "vertigo of emotion" is supplanted by a response to pure form,
color and light: "O glass subtly evil, O confusion of colours!" (cf. Zimmermann). The motif is again rehandled in the "hard Sophoclean light" of "Ité," as
the light of perfection but also of an undeluded recognition of emotion and
understanding of human experience.

The third group is more epigrammatic and is distinguished by its play of
wit, its range of subtle ironies, and its aesthetic preoccupations. The deceptive
simplicity of "Tò Καλόν," at the start, gives way to a more complex inner layer
of self-irony. The idea that "beauty is difficult" and the frustration of a desire to
attain it, the most readily apparent dimension of the poem, becomes a dominant
concern in the fourth group and in "Cathay," and a keynote in virtually all of
Pound's work from this volume onward, taken up as a leitmotif in the *Pisan
Cantos.* But here Beauty is addressed not through its embodiment in a particular
woman or goddess, in a set of emotions or in aesthetic achievement, but through
a slightly absurd personification as a coy mistress whom the poet has failed to
seduce and even to dream of seducing; he is the butt of her whimsy and accepts
instead of her the compromise of the "handmaids" she sends him:

> Even in my dreams you have denied yourself to me
> And sent me only your handmaids.

The immediacy of presence with which Beauty appears elsewhere is lacking, and her suitor is curiously helpless, dreaming rather than actively seeking her. Also absent are the vulnerability and the sense of personal peril that usually accompany this pursuit, in "The Spring," for instance, and most notably in the Actaeon motif of "The Coming of War" and the later Canto IV.

Self-irony is built up further and more explicitly in "The Study in Aesthetics," where a small child's "unusual wisdom" appears in his simple, ingenuous, excited apprehension of beauty, which seems a negative comment on the poet's sophistication: "And at this I was mildly abashed." This affect is echoed with a wry, gnomic twist near the end of this group in "The Seeing Eye": "It is only in small dogs and the young / That we find minute observation."

The following poems, as if in response to this self-irony, are directed outward in the delineation of contemporary sterilities. First, "setting like beside almost like," the enviable simplicity of the child in "The Study in Aesthetics" is followed by a more crippling simplicity in "The Bellaires," a sardonic caricature of the outworn ideal of a leisure class, an aristocracy caught chaotically between a past order no longer valid and a present world it is unprepared to cope with. Yet beneath the cutting edge of this poem is a note of genuine compassion; "the good squire Bellaire," though in no sense an artist, is victimized and exiled in a similar way by mercenary values, and his wanderings are reminiscent of those traced in "Provincia Deserta":

> To Carcassonne, Pui, and Alais
> He fareth from day to day,
> Or takes the sea air
> Between Marseilles
> And Beziers.

This combination of satire and compassion is developed through a counterpoint in the following epigrams. Swift, wittily mocking jabs at sterility, obtuseness, and other inadequacies of the age and its pretensions—especially in "The New Cake of Soap," "Epitaph," "Arides," and "The Patterns"—are played off more subtle ironies and undertones of loss and exile, as in "Salvationists," "The Bath Tub," "Amitiés," "To Dives," "Ladies," and "Phyllidula." These two dominant strains are brought together briefly near the end of the group, in "Coda," where the poems' often caustic confrontativeness seems to arise from a sense of loss:

> O my songs,
> Why do you look so eagerly and so curiously
>   into people's faces,
> Will you find your lost dead among them?

This motif of the "lost dead," introduced in "The Spring" and "Gentildonna," comes almost to dominate the volume from this point on, and the question raised in this poem—"Will you find your lost dead among them?"—is answered in the affirmative near the end of the book, in "Dans un Omnibus de Londres." In the particular context of this third group, the "lost dead" becomes tremendously evocative, referring not only to the literal dead, but to experience past and irrecoverable and to a poetic heritage that is no longer a lively part of contemporary awareness. The final poem of this group, "Ancora," announces a living connection with the past, "When we splashed and were splashed with / The lucid Castalian spray." The next group sets out to recover the past and to explore the degrees and range of its loss and the forms of beauty and life force, and the perception of them, that remain.

The volume's first group introduces its major set of tonalities; the last intensifies and draws them together; and the concentratedly elegiac fourth group, near the center, focuses and informs the full emotive expanse of the book. "Dompna Pois de Me No'us Cal," at its start, obliquely praises the woman at its focus, Maent, through its teasing assemblage of an ideal woman to substitute for her. The aesthetic of the search for fit components and their synthesis into a living whole is energized by a sense of loss and rejection, and by a recognition, again, that "beauty is difficult" and ultimately attainable only in part (or parts) and in fragmentary glimpses, as in the surrounding poems, of whose *modus operandi* this aesthetic is emblematic.

"The Coming of War: Actaeon" presents a recapturing of the mythic past and proceeds through the unfolding of a vision, momentarily halted and focused by a recognition of Actaeon:

An image of Lethe,
     and the fields
Full of faint light
     but golden,
Gray cliffs,
     and beneath them
A sea
Harsher than granite,
     unstill, never ceasing;
High forms
     with the movement of gods,
Perilous aspect;
     And one said:
"This is Actaeon."
          Actaeon of golden greaves!
Over fair meadows,
Over the cool face of that field,

> Unstill, ever moving
> Hosts of an ancient people,
> The silent cortège.

Actaeon, whose hapless encounter with beauty in the form of Diana bathing provoked his destruction, embodies the precariousness and vulnerability implicit in the heightened urgency of the artist's pursuit and in an awareness so acutely activated that it moves in constant peril of a self-destructive reversal of its own energies. Actaeon represents not the lethargic dreamer of "Τò Καλόν" but the fully mobilized hunter: two poles of sensibility that answer one another in Pound's work from the beginning through the end, as in the two parts of *Hugh Selwyn Mauberley*. In "The Coming of War: Actaeon," this urgency suggests a basis for the restless agitation and the eternal displacement of "the silent cortège," in continual pursuit of what can only be glimpsed in part and relinquished.[16]

This establishes the focus for the following five poems, built on Chinese models and exploiting the technique of superposition. They project glimpses of beauty captured through keenly engaged perception of nuances of appearance and circumstance, and celebrate it while lamenting its transience, elusiveness, and loss through neglect or decay. While the form of the classical epigram in the preceding group is an apt means of conveying the force and suddenness of the satiric boxer's jab, the superpositional method is well suited to the brevity of the glance it records and the immediacy of recognition and insight it leads to: "the precise instant when a thing outward and objective transforms itself, or darts into a thing inward and subjective" (*GB* 89). Though the tragic austerity of "The Coming of War: Actaeon" is briefly reversed in the exuberant "After Ch'u Yuan"—"I will walk in the glade, / I will come out from the new thicket / and accost the procession of maidens"—the following four poems build in poignancy of loss toward "In a Station of the Metro."

The fifth group, "Alba" through "Image from D'Orleans," develops the dominant tonality of "After Ch'u Yuan": a Dionysian celebration of recaptured spirits and resurgent life-force. "Alba" uses the superpositional technique of the preceding group to present an image of love's fulfillment apprehended and nurtured in memory:

> As cool as the pale wet leaves
> of lily-of-the-valley
> She lay beside me in the dawn.

This gives way to the visionary state of consciousness of "Heather," to the celebratory hymn in "Coitus" for the fertile Dione—the positive aspect of Diana's force—and to the energy of "the bright new season" in "Image from

D'Orleans." But this dimension is set in humorous juxtaposition with contemporary counterparts offered in other poems of this group. In "The Faun," the lascivious creature emerges incongruously into the present—"And what, pray, do you know about horticulture, you capriped?"—and a modern dryad in "Tempora" offers a querulous substitute for ancient fertility rites: "Oh, no, she is not crying: 'Tamuz.' / She says, 'May my poems be printed this week? . . . '" "The Encounter," "Black Slippers: Bellotti," and "Society" similarly present females whose fecundity is repressed or perverted by social conventions, and the key tone here is whimsically amused rather than caustic.

Moving into the sixth group ("Papyrus" through "Tame Cat"), the juxtaposition of "Image from D'Orleans" and "Papyrus" recapitulates the shift, in "The Spring," from a celebration of "the bright new season" to a bitter intensity of unfulfilled desire. As Kenner suggests, the two poems that follow, "'Ione, Dead the Long Year'" and "'Ἱμέρρω,'" present a locus of purity of desire in their restrained understatement, while the next two, "Shop Girl" and "To Formianus' Young Lady Friend," trace a progressive decline of sensibility in the present: "O most unfortunate age!" (*Era* 62–64). "Tame Cat," closing the group, comments ironically on the matter; the last stronghold of taste is in a sort of animal ingenuousness: "It rests me to be among beautiful women. / Why should one always lie about such matters?"

The brief seventh group, "L'Art, 1910" through "The Tea Shop," looks askance more explicitly at the age, its sterility, and its inadequacy of taste. In answer to its failures is the affirmation in "Epilogue" that "Only emotion remains," and this carries through the curious mixture of light irony and lamentation in the next two poems' apprehension of transience: in the barren legacy of a woman in "The Social Order" who "has left on this earth / No sound / Save a squabble of female connections" and in the common but genuine beauty of a waitress in "The Tea Shop" who, like those she charms for the moment, "also will turn middle-aged."

The eighth group, "Ancient Music" through "The Three Poets," shifts to an aesthetic context, juxtaposing moments evoked from poetic tradition with present orientations, as in "Ancient Music," "Epitaphs," and "Ancient Wisdom, Rather Cosmic," or else mocking the age less obliquely, as in the caricature of Rupert Brooke in "Our Contemporaries." Though this poem is essentially humorous, it levels a charge that informs Pound's critiques in this volume and underscores its central orientations: Brooke is condemned for a failure to fully engage with Beauty, to meet her advances and to make her his own. Rather than accepting the pursuit and its perils, he turns away and veils his resulting lack of substance in saccharine ornamentation: "he returned to this island / And wrote ninety Petrarchan sonnets." Similarly, the group closes in "The Three Poets" with a triad of jilted lovers, two of whom couch their loss in conventional artifice and abstraction, while the third, in keeping with the mode of *Lustra,* rebukes the woman directly.

The final group, "The Gypsy" through "Impressions of François-Marie Arouet (de Voltaire)," containing all of the volume's longer sequences, draws together and strengthens its key tonal currents. "The Gypsy" and "The Game of Chess" head off this group, introducing its central mode of the encounter, its focus on perception of form and motion, and its emphasis on crucial distinctions of sensibility. The dominant perspective is that of the wanderer who registers orientations of the past and their distances from the present, and who knows the cities and manners of many men. An encounter in "The Gypsy" opens out to a broader context in time and space, conferring dignity on the gypsy not only through its admiring description, but also by locating him in his cultural and historical setting. The gypsy's sense of loss and displacement, his struggle to reestablish his coordinates and a connection with others of like mind, and his persistence, like the speaker's, through social and natural adversities, course implicitly through the book-as-a-whole and are the life-blood of this final group, with "Cathay" at its heart. With the addition of an emphasis on acuteness of perception of form, color, and motion in "The Game of Chess," the matrix for the group is virtually completed.

"Provincia Deserta" carries over the wandering of "The Gypsy"—the geography is the same—and builds from a sense of loss of the Provençal heritage, through a personal encounter with the present state of its setting, toward its partial recovery:[17]

> That age is gone;
> Pieire de Maensac is gone.
> I have walked over these roads;
> I have thought of them living.

This poem's immediacy is dramatically heightened in "Cathay," which transposes its wanderings and its effort to overcome a sense of displacement into a Chinese past and a martial context, with its implicit bearing on the European present. The struggle to sustain a spiritual and emotional balance in the face of an intractable sense of exile, loss, and the wastage of civilization and of human potential, through memory, vision, and receptiveness to experience, resonates throughout the group and back through the entire volume. As noted earlier, "Near Perigord" explores and revivifies the Provençal past much as "Provincia Deserta" does, but through an imaginative and aesthetic penetration of its *documented* heritage.

"Villanelle: The Psychological Hour" continues in the literary context of "Near Perigord," transposed to a London milieu. The poem's movement recapitulates that of "Cathay," with a more private focus: the opening echoes its major streams of exile, displacement, isolation, and loss, and the end attains a tentative resolution in its blunt recognition of displacement as a social constant, at least among artists.

"Dans un Omnibus de Londres" continues the wandering, the mode of encounter, and the increasingly personal focus of this group. Here, wandering takes place in memory, evinced by a sudden apparition of the past and its evocation of anguished loss, "Les yeux d'une morte / M'ont salué," then sustained through successive recollections introduced by the anaphoric "Je vis. . . ." The unfolding reminiscences are commonplace enough, but their projection of nostalgia is unmistakable:

> Je vis le parc,
> Et tous les gazons divers
> Où nous avions loué des chaises
> Pour quatre sous.

This is the last of the volume's recapitulations of yearning for the "lost dead," drawing together its earlier occurrences in "The Spring," "Gentildonna," "Coda," "Liu Ch'e," "'Ione, Dead the Long Year,'" and "Cathay."[18] Here, as in moments of the *Pisan Cantos*, French is used to impart restraint to the poem's emotions and to block sentimentality; it helps to objectify an acutely personal stream of recollections.[19]

"To a Friend Writing on Cabaret Dancers" shifts to a lighter encounter, finding in the commonplace nothing extraordinary enough even to supply a basis for romantic illusion, hence recounting emptiness in its own way. "Homage to Quintus Septimius Florens Christianus" continues in a lighter ironic vein, but with a poignant focus in the *ubi sunt* lament of the fourth poem that is sharpened by the context of this group:

> Time's tooth is into the lot, and war's and fate's too.
> Envy has taken your all,
> Save your douth and your story.

Finally, the placement of "Impressions of Voltaire" at the conclusion, in the same group and aligned along the same vector with "Cathay," "Near Perigord," "Villanelle: The Psychological Hour," and "Homage to Quintus Septimius Florens Christianus," is the master stroke of the volume's arrangement. In its context, the movement of the three poems in "Impressions of Voltaire," examined in chapter 3, becomes more sharply delineated and far more resonant. In poem I, Phyllidula's defection from love in favor of riches cuts more deeply because it epitomizes the age's decay and pretentiousness that much of the volume pinpoints; she is a paradigm of the "cult of ugliness" and an antithesis of the female purity and fecund vitality of the book's more Dionysian movements. Similarly, poem II draws to a focus and climactic plangency the sense of loss and decay, the horror at time's wastage, and the urgent longing for what is irretrievable that course throughout the book and especially through "Cathay." But the sequence's final poem turns and closes the book with a courageously exuberant affirmation of hope and continuing vitality of feeling—"Only emotion remains"—in the face of all loss, however resistless:

> You'll wonder that an old man of eighty
> Can go on writing you verses. . . .
>
> Grass showing under the snow,
> Birds singing late in the year!

Thus the movement of the book-as-a-whole, and especially of its last group, fulfills the promise of its opening: "the hidden recesses / Have heard the echoes of my heels / in the cool light, / in the darkness." Its exploration of past and present, through "the hidden recesses" of feeling and an enormous range of its subtle gradations and nuances, exhibits a more complex emotional coherence than any of Pound's earlier books, and it surpasses the next two, *Quia Pauper Amavi* and *Poems, 1918–1921,* though not, of course, *The Cantos.* There is an incontrovertible emotional logic in the way each key tonality in the volume is developed through a spectrum of degrees, perspectives and contexts and is answered by related and contrasting tonal movements. This is reinforced through a continuity and development of themes and imagery; through intermittent gatherings of poems into logically or formally unified groups, such as the epigrams of group 3 and the superpositional poems of group 4; through an extensive use of structural motifs, especially of triadic units; and through the arrangement of similar tonal elements in successive groups in sometimes parallel or inverted order. Clearly, *Lustra* employs most of the techniques of *The Cantos,* and it is small wonder that Pound insisted on its arrangement as "almost as important as the construction of a play or a novel."

Published two years later, Pound's next volume, *Quia Pauper Amavi,* is a sequence of sequences: on a smaller order, precisely what *The Cantos* were to become. By juxtaposing "Langue d'Oc," "Moeurs Contemporaines," "Three Cantos," and the *Homage to Sextus Propertius,* the book returns to a structure built up in successive blocks that was the dominant mode of arrangement in the volumes before *Lustra.* Yet the sequences that constitute each block are also developed largely in terms of gradations and degrees of their major emotive pattern-units; by coordinating these two methods, Pound was able to "get a form" that could contain larger movements and their interaction without the loss of more subtle distinctions and definitions. This is very nearly a form "that wouldn't exclude something merely because it didn't fit." Though many structural influences and further experiments no doubt played their part in the reworking of the Ur-Cantos toward their final form, as Bush has comprehensively demonstrated (*Genesis*), this coordination of architectonic strategies in *Quia Pauper Amavi*, in 1919, was the most important step toward the expansiveness and flexibility of *The Cantos'* ultimate form. Further, intermediate developments are apparent in *Hugh Selwyn Mauberley* and *Poems, 1918–1921*, and chapter 6 will return to a more extensive consideration of this issue.

Another element in *Quia Pauper Amavi* that contributed significantly to the emergence of *The Cantos* is its use of what Pound called in *Canzoni* a "chronological table of emotions." This is implicit in the past tense of the title and its provenance in Ovid's *Ars Amatoria—Quia Pauper Amavi*, "when I loved I was poor"—which introduces the erotic focus of most of the volume as well. Of course, with "Langue d'Oc" at the head of the book and the *Homage to Sextus Propertius* at the end, it hardly presents a literal chronology of settings; like *Canzoni*, rather, it follows a movement between polarities of sensibility and functions through juxtapositional contrasts. Diction and syntax are modulated accordingly, so that the volume moves from the rapturous celebration of life-force and a relatively pure form of devotion in "Langue d'Oc," with a corresponding archaism, to a more colloquial and cutting overview of the present state of affairs in the caricatures of "Moeurs Contemporaines." "Three Cantos," positioned at the focus, shifts to a more explicitly aesthetic context, and by invoking Browning's *Sordello* first, it launches out from the recent past back to the nekuia, before Homer, through virtually all intervening ages and forward to the present and to the future of the poems it announces are still to be written.[20] This section captures the paideuma of each age it considers through a collocation of luminous details and a projection of distinctive responses to them. Thus, it coordinates a personal dimension with a more objective overview: two elements that complement one another in the most important and most successful achievements in the form of the poetic sequence.

Homage to Sextus Propertius, the last section of the volume, draws together its erotic and aesthetic dimensions, along with the social concerns of "Moeurs Contemporaines," and adds to these a substratum of political awareness, using a controlled, subtly ironic manipulation of language exploited still more fully in *Hugh Selwyn Mauberley*. It is toward that work and toward *The Cantos* that the final movement of the *Homage* opens out, with its proud affirmation of the continuity and value of the lyric tradition and of the sequence's (and the volume's) established eminence within it: "And now Propertius of Cynthia, taking his stand among these."

6

"Forth on the Godly Sea":
Hugh Selwyn Mauberley and *The Cantos*

Hugh Selwyn Mauberley

Pound's next work, *Hugh Selwyn Mauberley* (1920), has long been recognized as an important step toward the final form of *The Cantos,* and it has justly been acclaimed as one of his finest sequences. Yet although its design as an integral whole comprising a succession of smaller, interrelated units is generally agreed upon, its structure has been the subject of considerable discussion, and even some of its most enthusiastic advocates have, implicitly at least, questioned its unity.[1]

The sequence's apparently enigmatic structure will be the focus of the following discussion, since its sources have been extensively illuminated by others—notably Espey, Witemeyer, and Berryman. A culmination of Pound's Vorticist and earlier aesthetics, *Hugh Selwyn Mauberley* proceeds through a shifting succession of various states of awareness that present different facets of a single, unified consciousness. This construction makes use of a number of structural patterns developed in earlier poems and sequences. The most obvious is the sequence's movement in two main blocks, the first consisting of thirteen poems and the second of five. The bipartite arrangement of the sequence is a pattern that has already been noted in several of Pound's works as early as *A Lume Spento.* As in several volumes, especially *Lustra,* each section of this sequence unfolds through a graduated spectrum of its key tonalities and largely through the contrapuntal interplay of central oppositions, and the two sections are linked by echoing, answering, recapitulating, and rearranging a common set of tonalities, themes, images, and motifs. The complex interconnections and the resonance and development between the two sections of the sequence are the clearest indications of the essential unity of its controlling state of consciousness; as in any extended poem, such connections must either be so recognized or dismissed as ornamental elaborations.

The perspectives of the two sections are in many ways distinct, however.

The first is primarily directed outward in an examination of the age, its inadequacies, its self-destructive misdirection of resources and energy, and the mistaken demands it imposes on its artists. Its pressures are focused particularly on the poet-protagonist, who, as Witemeyer shows, is depicted partly in terms of an Odysseus figure engaged in a quest for integrity both in life and in a high level of aesthetic achievement (163–76). The second part shifts to a doubting, introspective examination of a self-destructive repression of creative and sexual energies, marked by increasing isolation, hesitancy, dislocation, and regret for lost opportunities. The first part projects an active stance and the second a passive orientation, and the social flaws acutely pinpointed in part 1 are mirrored in the second part's more subjective focus on personal inadequacies.

The controlling metaphor of an Odyssean sea-voyage in the first part is reversed in the second by presenting a state of mind whose heroism is deflated, metaphorically, by shifting from the Mediterranean to the Pacific, by replacing the Odyssean vessel with a "coracle," and by supplanting a civilizing impulse with solipsistic revery; the state of mind in part 2 is shipwrecked and ultimately dissipated altogether. In the first part there is an effort to acutely assess the age and come to terms with it constructively, but the second proceeds into a fatal withdrawal, a succession forecasted in the sequence's subtitle, "Contacts and Life": indeed, it devolves into a life without contacts. It should be clear that the two parts are carefully interrelated: the first prepares for the second emotionally and thematically, as a closer examination of the sequence will demonstrate more concretely.

The emotional preparation that takes place in the first part becomes more evident once its essentially lamentative cast has been fully assessed; the entire sequence is unified partly by its elegy for potential that has been misplaced, thwarted, and destroyed. In the first part this is only one of the central tonalities and, like the others, surfaces intermittently, but its force is crucial to the shaping of the whole. Beneath a battery of satiric jabs launched against the age, the first twelve poems lament the passing of a promising, devoted, but unrecognized poet and with him the tradition he "strove to resuscitate"; the civilization that destroys both him and itself, and the values it has lost sight of; the artists destroyed in the course of their attempts to preserve and extend the most viable dimensions of the aesthetic vortices of the past against self-appointed bastions of the "finer tradition" who are really its obstructors and against the "march of events"; vitality and talent wasted in a war brought on by the age's blindness; and experience past and irrecoverable. The second part laments a poet's failure in art and love, his lost opportunities, his exclusion, and his ultimate demise. Both parts proceed by means of rigorous analysis, first of the age's faults and failures, then of the poet's, so that this lamentative strain is voiced objectively and obliquely, largely through indignation in the first part and self-analysis and judgment in part 2.

Augmenting the sequence's bipartite structure is a proleptic organization—

a strategy operant as early as "Hilda's Book." The title of the opening poem, "E. P. Ode Pour L'Election de Son Sepulchre," is from Ronsard, and the use of the label "Ode" in this poem, as in Ronsard's, is ironic: it invokes the conventions of a triumphal encomium and then proceeds through a eulogy of defeat, with repeated reference to its heroic background (cf. Joseph 147–48). This helps to set up the sequence's key affective dichotomy, between the heroic action that dominates part 1 and the fear of defeat and collapse that takes over in part 2.

The first line of the poem reaches forward to more of what follows. "For three years, out of key with his time" already anticipates the increasing isolation and exclusion of the sequence's second part, and is sounded again in poem II of that part: "For three years, diabolus in the scale."[2] "For three years" also suggests the triadic patterning that, as we shall see, plays an important part in this sequence's design. The first line further introduces a strain of panegyric for singlehanded heroic effort against intractable obstacles (generally, against the literary and social intransigence of contemporary England), but implicit in that effort is a fear of aesthetic and psychological dissipation, anticipating the state of mind of part 2:

> For three years, out of key with his time,
> He strove to resuscitate the dead art
> Of poetry; to maintain "the sublime"
> In the old sense. Wrong from the start—
>
> No, hardly, but seeing he had been born
> In a half savage country, out of date;
> Bent resolutely on wringing lilies from the acorn;
> Capaneus; trout for factitious bait.

This opening passage is built through carefully interwoven strains of irony that, by parodying critics' charges against this anomalous poet, staunchly but subtly affirm the probity of his quest and its absolute necessity for personal survival and fulfillment and for cultural renewal. The potential for destructive failure of his effort is glimpsed in the momentary allusion to Capaneus, struck down for his defiance of Zeus, a prototype of the poet's defiance of powers he cannot match. Capaneus and the poet both display a spirit of active resistance that surges only faintly, sporadically, and with qualification in part 2.

In the third stanza, the sirens are a voice of temptation that detains but does not stop the poet from his quest. More important, however, is the fact that they sing of the fall of an advanced civilization, delineated in the poems that follow. The sirens are a collective literary and social voice that promises a fulfillment of the poet's quest, which turns out to be spurious and destructive. In particular, they represent a critical milieu whose knowledge might lead the poet to expect a responsiveness to his offerings, but whose own ears turn out to be stopped with wax (a witty reversal of the Odyssean episode) and impenetrable to both the poet's song and his social acuity. The sirens thus forecast both the demise of contemporary civilization in the first part of the sequence and the poet's self-debilitating, solipsistic revery in the second.

Against the age's and the poet's self-destructive inclinations the next quatrain sets a "true Penelope," Flaubert, who represents a standard of aesthetic achievement and, as social diagnostician, a model of constructive equilibrium between devotion to beauty and social awareness.[3] The sequence embarks on its quest partly by proceeding to diagnose the faults that led to World War I. In doing so, the poet-protagonist remains "out of key with his time," adopting "the elegance of Circe's hair" as standard rather than joining in the dissolution of the age and heeding "the mottoes on sun-dials." This heroic state of consciousness shows at least an awareness of those mottoes and takes an aggressive stance against them, as that of the second part cannot; having lost track of time and the age altogether, it ends up "Not knowing, day to day, / The first day's end, in the next noon" (part 2, poem IV).

The hostile, judgmental voice parodied at the opening ("wrong from the start") is echoed with defiant irony in the summary assessment at the close of the "Ode." But beneath the vigor of the poet's defiance are further currents of self-doubt that anticipate the "final / Exclusion from the world of letters" and the self-analytical key of part 2:

> Unaffected by "the march of events,"
> He passed from men's memory in *l'an trentuniesme*
> *De son eage;* the case presents
> No adjunct to the Muses' diadem.

This passage especially throws into relief the fear of exile and obscurity that looms over the sequence from the beginning.

The significance of the triadic pattern suggested by "For three years" begins to emerge here, glancing back over the "Ode" and forward to what follows. Daniel Pearlman has observed that the end of Canto I introduces three female figures who, he suggests, correspond to the movement of *The Cantos* as a whole: the sirens, Circe, and Aphrodite (41–45). Although there are differences in the use of this device in the two works, it is clearly operant in *Hugh Selwyn Mauberley;* for the "Ode" presents, respectively, the sirens, Penelope (whose function is of a kind with Aphrodite's), and Circe.[4] This opens out to a complex development of the triadic structural motif that is at least as crucial in this sequence as in "Cathay" and in *Lustra* as a whole. We may, first of all, think of *Hugh Selwyn Mauberley* in terms of three key movements—part 1, "Envoi," and part 2—distinct in mode, focus, and dominant affect. The first is controlled by the sirens ("Conservatrix" and Lady Valentine), who offer a specious semblance of the values that guide the poet's quest—values whose loss signals their culture's demise; the second by an ideal of feminine beauty who receives the sequence's rapturous homage in the "Envoi"; and the third by Circe, with whom the state of consciousness in part 2 fails to come to terms either aesthetically or sexually and consequently suffers ultimate diminution and destruction through metamorphosis into "an hedonist." Correspondingly, part 1 contains three poems focused on female figures—"Yeux Glauques," poem XI ("Conservatrix"), and poem XII (Lady Valentine)—and three male figures either washed up on the sirens' rocks (Verog and Brennbaum) or converted to their agent (Nixon). Only the stylist of poem X in some sense escapes, as Witemeyer notes (170–71), though he is removed from the quest and compromises in another way.

There are three strophes in the "Envoi," focused on three different qualities of ideal femininity, if not three different women (a question I shall return to), and there are three female figures in part 2: the menacing image of Messalina in poem I, the unidentified and unattained "her" in poems II and III, and the also unnamed but apparently different woman portrayed in "Medallion." Her mythic identity is another issue to be considered.

The constituent poems of the sequence fall not only into two major parts but into smaller groups as well, each one built climactically. Following the "Ode," there are three such groups in part 1, the first extending through poem V, the second through poem IX, and the third through poem XII; part 2 constitutes a single group. The first group begins, in poem II, with a somewhat detached analysis of what "the age demanded," tinged with sarcasm by its clusters of negatives (three in the first two stanzas and three in the third). This poem develops a conflict between devotion to beauty of a permanent nature ("the elegance of Circe's hair") and adherence to the taste of the age with its sacrifice of quality for speed of production ("the mottoes on sun-dials"): "an Attic grace" and the attentive vision of "the obscure reveries / Of the inward gaze" are set against an image of the age's "accelerated grimace" that can be had "with no loss of time."

Poem III picks up this opposition in its first stanza and goes on to catalogue symptoms of the decay of values that signals the doom of contemporary civilization. Inaugurated by Christianity, the process is intensified through the replacement of a well-integrated spiritual and sensual awareness with a bodiless asceticism on the one hand and a pervasive, degrading materialism on the other. The poem builds in indignation toward the climactic indictment of its last stanza. In answer to the summary judgment of the "Ode" that "the case presents / No adjunct to the Muses' diadem," it asserts that there is neither an encomium to be sung nor a character fit to receive it: "What god, man, or hero / Shall I place a tin wreath upon!"[5] (The "tin" is, of course, a mordant pun picked up from Pindar's "τίν" that both colloquializes and sharpens the poem's attack on cheap commercialism.)[6]

The loss of the classical values invoked by the allusion to Pindar is what signals the self-destruction of modern Europe, and the macabre, distorted aspect of traditional virtue in modern warfare is traced with bitter outrage in poems IV and V. The sequence reaches its highest pitch of elegiac intensity in its lament for the war dead in poem V:

> There died a myriad,
> And of the best, among them,
> For an old bitch gone in the teeth,
> For a botched civilization,
>
> Charm, smiling at the good mouth,
> Quick eyes gone under earth's lid,
>
> For two gross of broken statues,
> For a few thousand battered books.

Gaudier-Brzeska, as representative of the height of personal and artistic potential in his generation, is clearly at the focus of this poem. The outrage here is projected not as a disparagement of the "two gross of broken statues" and the "few thousand battered books" but as a lament for the sacrifice of the artist's vital potential, before it could make a mature contribution, to what already exists, which is being preserved instead for the wrong reasons.[7] Though viable in itself, the art of the past is overgrown with philology: "botched civilization" is a caustic pun (on "boche" for "German") implying not that civilization is hopeless but that the life of the art which is its highest achievement has been thwarted by a Germanic system of education against which Pound vehemently protested.[8] For that system produces the aesthetic and social insensitivity that has led Europe to war and has forced the poet of the sequence, along with Gaudier and other promising artists, into deadening obscurity. Of course, the German part in the war and the fact that a German bullet took Gaudier's life are also quite relevant to the biting indignation here.

The next group of part 1, "Yeux Glauques" through "Mr. Nixon," presents a roughly chronological overview of contemporary civilization's dissolution of values, through a series of portraits beginning with the late nineteenth century's mistaken moral censure of its art (Witemeyer 162). "Yeux Glauques," like the succeeding portraits, anticipates the state of consciousness in part 2. This portrait presents a positive exemplum of achieved aesthetic vision, yet its subject's "questing and passive" gaze and her bewilderment prefigure the enervation of part two, and "that faun's head of hers" suggests part of what is lost between the two movements of the sequence, since "faun's flesh is not to us" (part 1, poem III). Like the sirens', the song her eyes still sing recounts a culture's demise, in this case through its suppression of the positive, creative force of sexuality.

"Yeux Glauques" also supplies part of a key opposition set up in part 1; though long dead, the subject's inner life is preserved in her portrait, while the paired women in poems XI and XII are physically alive but spiritually, emotionally, and sexually moribund. This is a pattern (in reverse order) that was used before in *Ripostes,* where the same opposition is established between the living but stagnant woman of "Portrait d'une Femme" in the first group of the volume and the dead but still vital woman portrayed in the last group, in the paired poems "The Picture" and "Of Jacopo del Sellaio": "The eyes of this dead lady speak to me." In both sequences, this opposition clarifies the demarcation between the artist's vibrant and insightful vision and the age's repressive conventionality, and between the sustaining emotional vitality of art and the sterility of contemporary moeurs. In this first part of *Hugh Selwyn Mauberley,* these contrasts emerge with particular immediacy because "Yeux Glauques" and poems X–XII are in present tense, while the surrounding poems are more reflectively set in past tense. Significantly, this shift is repeated at the end of part 2, in poem IV and "Medallion."

"Yeux Glauques" is followed by a triad of negative exempla, built toward "Mr. Nixon" at its climax. Verog's reminiscences in "Siena Mi Fe; Disfecemi Maremma" attest to the constriction of sensibility the age imposes on its artists and the compensatory detours to which they are driven; denied a culture propitious to "faun's flesh" and "saint's vision" they pursue the "spirits" of alcohol, like Lionel Johnson, or the sensuality denuded of spirit in which Dowson finds recourse. If "artists are the antennae of the race" (*LE* 297) in a repressive culture, that is their destruction, since they are propelled toward its dismembered extremities. Verog is himself relegated to doing the age's morbid dirty work, cataloguing the "pickled foetuses and bottled bones" emblematic of its life-negating distortions. His exclusion serves as a link between the controlling state of mind in part 1, "out of key with his time" and offering "obscure reveries / Of the inward gaze," and that of part 2 with its "porcelain reveries":

> M. Verog, out of step with the decade,
> Detached from his contemporaries,
> Neglected by the young,
> Because of these reveries.

Verog is caught up in the past and for that reason excluded from the age, while "Brennbaum," next, is cut off from his past through assimilation to the present; both reflect the age's discomfiture with its heritage, as the fates of Jenny, Johnson, and Dowson reflect its aversion to innate human drives. All of these figures are encompassed within the sequence's awareness and are defeated or compromised in ways that prefigure the collapse of part 2.

"Mr. Nixon" is a prime spokesman for the commercialism of the age. His "cream-gilded cabin" stands in contrast to the Homeric vessel of the "Ode" and the diminutive "coracle of Pacific voyages" of part 2, and his self-complacency contrasts with the spirit of a quest for integrity of aesthetic achievement. Advocating compliance with the age's demands, he reiterates " 'Consider / 'Carefully the reviewer' " and " 'Butter reviewers.' " Against a perceptiveness of "the elegance of Circe's hair" he asserts that " 'No one knows, at sight, a masterpiece,' " and against an offering of "the sculpture of rhyme" his advice is to " 'Give up verse, my boy, / 'There's nothing in it.' " He is a mouthpiece for the attitude sardonically parodied in the "Ode"—"Wrong from the start"—and recommends application to " 'the march of events' ": " 'Take a column / 'Even if you have to work free.' " The end of the poem steps back reflectively from this encounter to observe the alliance of Nixon's commercialism with contemporary Christianity (represented by "a friend of Blougram's") as a force against both aesthetic integrity and integrated human awareness: "Don't kick against the pricks."

Poems X–XII constitute a third grouping of part 1. Prepared for by the preceding caricatures, they shift to a more ironic glance at the age and recount a sense of loss less obliquely than elsewhere, with a thinner overlay of indignation. They assess the emptiness in human relations that results from contemporary misdirection, given emphasis by the switch to present tense, and they focus especially on the destructive effects of the age's commercialism. The social and economic awareness voiced throughout part 1 and presented most acutely in this grouping is another link between *Hugh Selwyn Mauberley* and *Lustra* and clearly forecasts some of the central preoccupations of *The Cantos*.

"The stylist" is presented first: "unpaid, uncelebrated," his "sagging roof" is pointedly juxtaposed with the opulence of Mr. Nixon's steam yacht. The humility and simplicity of his withdrawal, while forecasting the solipsism of part 2, are also in contrast to Nixon's entrepreneurial assertiveness. Though he has found a comfortable retreat "from the world's welter," the stylist has sacrificed cultural advancement for isolation and, analogously, Penelope for "a placid and uneducated mistress."

The siren figures of poems XI and XII both voice the demise of contemporary life through the encroachment of its commercial spirit on relations between the sexes and between the aristocracy and the arts.[9] Poem XI tauntingly assesses the reduction of "habits of mind and feeling" to a concern with material values and the resulting emotional anemia. The first lines of poem XII, "Daphne with her thighs in bark / Stretches toward me her leafy hands," drive home a perception of encrusted female passion and reverberate with other images in the sequence. The sense of immobility and entrapment here reaches back to the "Ode"— "The chopped seas held him, therefore, that year"—and forward to the despondent and rueful frustration of the "still stone dogs" into which passion is metamorphosed in part 2 (poem II). But the momentary hopefulness projected by the image of Daphne recalls, first of all, the "Muses' diadem" of the "Ode," since

Daphne's leafy hands are laurel. Following the abrupt dismissal of this possibility with the ironic "Subjectively," however, the Lady Valentine comes to mind, a pathetically hollow parody of both the muse and Aphrodite, offering neither inspiration nor love but "well-gowned approbation / Of literary effort"; even her motives as a prospective patroness are dubious and superficial.[10] Here (as in much of Yeats's work) the aristocracy is condemned for its loss of values and the abnegation of its support for the arts. However, the poem denounces not only the Lady Valentine but also the malaise of which she is symptomatic, and it shifts at its close (like the end of "Mr. Nixon") to note that her attitude is not a specifically upper-class phenomenon, for "the sale of half-hose has / Long since superseded / The cultivation / Of Pierian roses."

Here, as in the other poems of part 1, the sensibility that observes, diagnoses, and satirizes the age does so partly because what it encounters calls into question the values that motivate its effort. It responds partly to the judgment echoed in the "Ode"—"Wrong from the start"—and partly, too, to the tacit rejection and exclusion in this series of contacts. While all of them prepare for the isolation of part 2, the immediacy of these last encounters, focused on women who have relinquished their feminine grace and their capacity for emotional, spiritual, and aesthetic engagement, helps to set up the shift in perspective in the "Envoi."

That the "Envoi" does shift dramatically is made clear by the use of italics, a device that, in Pound's work, detaches a poem, or part of a poem, from its context and enables it to reflect back on that context. Italics signify not that a passage is "spoken by a different voice" but that it adopts a different perspective or is projected at a different pitch of awareness. Notable instances in Pound's work are the frequent use of italics in epigraphs, where poem and epigraph clarify or comment on one another, often ironically (poem II of part 2 is a convenient example); or as an indication of an ironic, self-reflective shift, as in the middle section of "N.Y." and in the pivotal interlude, *"Translator to Translated,"* in "Translations from Heine"; or as the signal of a departure to a gentler and more rapturous mode than in preceding or surrounding poems, as in "Piccadilly," the lyrical envoi to *Personae* that stands in much the same relation to that volume as "Envoi" does to *Hugh Selwyn Mauberley*.

While the "Envoi" is detached from its context, it is also in some ways continuous with it. First, it picks up the present tense and the focus on women in the preceding poems, and it launches forward toward the future, the only poem of the sequence that does so. The richness of appreciative vision projected in "Envoi," the womanly graces it commemorates, and its urge to preserve these against time's ravages represent a partial consummation of the poetic quest announced in the "Ode" and an achievement wrought in spite of the age's demands and the pressures that its dissolution imposes upon its artists. It also presents a pointed contrast to the sterility of the women portrayed in poems XI and XII. Thus the poem's sensibility escapes from the welter analyzed in the preceding poems. But there is also much that adumbrates the solipsistic, self-judgmental, enervated orientation of part 2. There are, first, the self-deprecia-tive implications of the "dumb-born book" and the "faults that heavy upon me lie." In the second verse unit, the enduring monument the poem offers to a woman's beauty is set against the encroachment of time, but in the third it is set against dissolution through change, glancing ahead through "Siftings on siftings in oblivion" to the "Tawn fore-shores / Washed in the cobalt of oblivions" where the state of mind in part 2 (poem IV) is washed up. Most important is the urge to contain the sensual offerings of love's moment—Aphrodite emerging from the chaos-driven tide of the age, as it were—within an aesthetic artifact, in anticipation of the sexual indolence and "porcelain reveries" of part 2.[11]

The three verse-units of "Envoi" are probably addressed not to one woman but to three, a structural recapitulation of the three female figures of the "Ode" and the three portraits of women in part 1, and a further development of the sequence's triadic patterning. "Her that sang me once that song of Lawes" in the first verse unit is, after all, unlikely to be the same woman as "her that goes / With song upon her lips / But sings not out the song" in the third.[12] The important point is that the poem develops a key structural motif either by ad-dressing three different women or by celebrating three distinct feminine quali-ties: "her glories," "her graces," and her unvoiced song.

In its structural and tonal continuities with parts 1 and 2, then, "Envoi" serves as a pivot helping to focus and direct the movement of the sequence as a whole. But the fullness and vibrancy of vision in the poem are lost to the state of consciousness in part 2, which merely languishes, seizing opportunities nei-ther for love's moment nor for an aesthetic commemoration of it.

The five poems of part 2 constitute a single group arranged, like the group-ings of part 1, climactically. This part traces the progressive dissolution of an increasingly hesitant, disjunct, self-doubting and depressive awareness, follow-ing its decline from a failure of artistic vision (poem I), through a closely related sexual anaesthesis (poem II) and social and literary exclusion (poem III), to a final, encompassing incapacity (poem IV). Although there is a shift to the last poem, "Medallion," it is, for the most part, continuous with the poems before it.

Part 2 is an emotively congruent development of part 1 and is built through the reinforcement and refocusing of some elements already introduced and the suppression of others. The judgment and dismissal of the "Ode," for instance, become introspection and self-dismissal here, and the diagnosis of the age in part 1 becomes self-analysis. The "final / Exclusion from the world of letters" toward which part 2 moves is already implicit in part 1, and the sexual hesitancy and passivity of this part are developed from an undercurrent of suggestion in part 1, which Espey and others have traced quite thoroughly. The active artistic quest of the first part is replaced by indolent revery, and the acute analysis of contemporary moeurs and attitudes and the loss of essential values, along with an apprehension of how the present state of affairs has evolved from the past, collapses. Part 2 is dominated instead by "a consciousness disjunct" that can connect nothing with nothing, desiring only to "present the series / Of curious heads in medallion" such as the portraits of part 1, but ultimately incapable of it. Like the first part, the second focuses on three female figures—and in this respect is structurally as well as emotively continuous with it—but while part 1 launches forward from observing "the elegance of Circe's hair" to confrontation with these female figures and recognition of their inner natures, in part 2 there are only languid regret for lost opportunity, a faint urge to transform apprehended beauty into aesthetic artifact, and a final sense of paralysis in both sexual and aesthetic realms of awareness and action.

The first poem throws into relief both this part's departures from the first and its continuities. The epigraph—*"Vacuos exercet in aera morsus"*—enforces the ensuing sense of futility and suggests the aesthetic vapidity at the focus of the poem. The first two stanzas augment this suggestion:

> Turned from the "eau-forte
> Par Jacquemart"
> To the strait head
> Of Messalina:
>
> "His true Penelope
> Was Flaubert,"
> And his tool
> The engraver's.

In turning from Jacquemart "To the strait head / Of Messalina," there is a redirection from a full presentation that captures the life of its subject to a representation that merely sketches the lineaments of its subject's outer form.[13] It is, as Berryman notes, a turn from "richly detailed" portraiture to "inadequate representations" of inferior statuary (91). But "the strait head / Of Messalina," "the most licentious woman in Rome" (Espey 99), is also the first of a series of images that project a kind of sexual horror and a fear of betrayal through violent metamorphosis or destruction in the Circe-dominated movement of part 2.[14] Thus, when the second stanza ironically echoes the object of the quest in part 1, "'His true Penelope / Was Flaubert,'" it is clear that neither the aesthetic standard represented by Flaubert nor the devotion and the fruition of love represented by Penelope is an attainable object for this state of consciousness. "His tool" carries an obvious sexual entendre, and "The engraver's" is, similarly, a pun that reinforces the connection between sexuality and destruction; the sensibility of part 2 is in any case buried by doubts and incapacities, and in poem IV is "engraved" with an epitaph engraved on an oar, an ironically diminutive counterpart to the extended eulogy of the "Ode."

The resulting anaesthesis occupies the focus of poem II, beginning with the epigraph, which explicitly links aesthetic obtuseness to inadequacy in love. The poem unfolds in three sections, separated typographically by a line of dots that indicates (as at the end of "Mr. Nixon" and poem XII) shifts in perspective and levels of reflection. The first section retrospectively summarizes the failure of a potential relationship dissipated by inaction, beginning with an ironic echo of the opening line of the "Ode": "For three years, diabolus in the scale."[15] Regret for lost possibility is projected here with almost epigrammatic restraint, objectified by the galactic imagery, but the next two sections advance climactically toward an increasingly subjective recognition of failure. The elliptical beginning of the second section recreates the sexual hesitancy and aimlessness that have culminated in "the final estrangement"; the last four stanzas relate that failure to an obsession with maintaining an aesthetic distance and with converting love's offerings into "verbal manifestation; / To present the series / Of curious heads in medallion." The mounting regret in the last stanza of this section gives way to the despondent paralysis and terrifyingly desperate futility of the closing image:

> Mouths biting empty air,
> The still stone dogs,
> Caught in metamorphosis, were
> Left him as epilogues.

Poem III, "The Age Demanded," sets out from the mode of the preceding poem's summary, but shifts from its focus on sexual failure to an incisive self-analysis of social failure, of a lack of response to what "the age demanded," and of an inability to confront and assess its demands and either to accept or to eschew them. Rather, "an Olympian *apathein* / In the presence of selected perceptions" results in imperviousness to the surrounding welter, and even the details of the Arcadian retreat become a disruptive imposition. Hence, a full half of the Flaubertian balance in part 1 is lost here. The poem becomes increasingly self-accusatory, overlaid with clinically latinate diction that recalls the tone of the critical voice echoed in the "Ode," and poem IV goes on to trace the process of dissipation and destruction of "a consciousness disjunct," tossed up on "Tawn foreshores / Washed in the cobalt of oblivions":

> "I was
> And I no more exist;
> Here drifted
> An hedonist."

This image of ultimate inanition is built upon a sense of horror in a series of three images interspersed through part 2, a further development of the sequence's triadic structural motif. The first image, as noted, is Messalina in poem I; the second, in poem II, is the closing image of the "still stone dogs"; and the third, suggested in poem III and reiterated in "Medallion," is Minos. Minos, like Capaneus in the "Ode," was punished for defiance of the gods: while Capaneus was struck down for challenging Zeus, Minos suffered for failing to fulfill his vows to Zeus's brother, Poseidon. Thus, like the momentary interjection "Capaneus" in the "Ode," the "Minoan undulation" of poem III suggests an impulse to resistance. But Minos, whom Homer calls "destruction-hearted" in Book XI of the *Odyssey*, occupies an established place similar to Messalina's in the legendary tradition of sexual betrayals. His punishment through the grotesque passion of his wife, Pasiphaë, for a bull is only the best-known episode in his story.[16]

The significance of Minos's legendary background becomes clear, in the context of sexual trepidation built up steadily through part 2 of the sequence, when we arrive at the final poem, "Medallion."[17] This poem is generally read as a production "by" the fictional "Mauberley" because its title suggests a desire to "present the series / Of curious heads in medallion," and it is usually considered a vision of Aphrodite because of the *comparison to* Anadyomene in the second stanza. But the entire second part of the sequence has traced an increasing inability to come to terms with love both sexually and aesthetically, culminating in the complete collapse of poem IV; there is nothing to suggest that a vision of Aphrodite is to be vouchsafed in the closing poem, and everything to imply, on the contrary, that it cannot be. The "gold-yellow" of the frock in the second stanza and the "topaz" of the closing stanza are also assumed to herald Aphrodite, but these are Hymen's colors and signify nuptial rites in a more general sense. The third stanza provides further suggestions:

> Honey-red, closing the face-oval,
> A basket-work of braids which seem as if they were
> Spun in King Minos' hall
> From metal, or intractable amber.

The "basket-work of braids" recalls the only similar image in the sequence, the "elegance of Circe's hair" in the "Ode." (This suggests a circular return to the sequence's opening, as does the mention of Minos, linked to the Capaneus allusion.) And the braids most likely to be spun in Minos's hall probably belong not to Aphrodite but to Pasiphaë's sister—Circe—who is depicted in Homer as "the beautifully-braided goddess" (*Odyssey* X.220). Of course, Aphrodite and Circe are not unrelated figures and are often presented in similar terms in *The Cantos;* as Surette explains, "the Goddess appears in various aspects. Aphrodite is her most sublime aspect, and Circe is a more threatening and chthonic aspect" (*Light* 49). The imagery of "Medallion" suggests a conflation or confusion of the two aspects that is entirely consistent with the sense of sexual dislocation built up steadily through part 2 of the sequence and brought to a climax in this poem by its focus on a disembodied head (like Messalina's), and one that signifies an opening to a book, not to the richness of love or the fulfillment of desire; and the sterility with which she is perceived is reinforced by setting her behind a glaze, kept at an aesthetic remove. Clearly, although a comparison with "Envoi" is invoked by a use of similar color motifs and by depicting the woman as singing in both poems, the image in "Medallion" is in sharp contrast to the full-bodied, rapturous vision of "Envoi."[18] The final affect of the sequence, projected by the suddenly but dimly illumined eyes, is thus a mixture of desire and admiration with a kind of sexual terror:

> The face-oval beneath the glaze,
> Bright in its suave bounding-line, as,
> Beneath half-watt rays,
> The eyes turn topaz.

(This is strongly reminiscent of a similar affect in one of Eliot's best-known images: "(But in the lamplight, downed with light brown hair!)" [*Poems* 5].)

When "Medallion" is viewed in relation to the rest of the sequence, there is no need to posit authorship "by" a fictive Mauberley. It clearly stands in climactic relation to the rest of part 2, and its slight distancing in perspective suggests not the detached but connected positioning of "Envoi," but rather the observational stance, at an aesthetic remove, from which Jenny is presented in "Yeux Glauques" and Messalina is presented in poem I of part 2. "Medallion," then, while serving as the climax of part 2 and the culmination of the sequence, helps to draw its various parts together through its connections with them in affect, perspective, imagery, and allusion.

Glancing back over the structure of *Hugh Selwyn Mauberley* as a whole, its continuities with the arrangements of forms used in earlier poems, sequences, and volumes are immediately apparent. First, its essentially bipartite structure with a shift in the dominant tone between the first part and the second (through the intermediary "Envoi") is a pattern common to several works, including *A Lume Spento, Ripostes,* and "Cathay," and has important implications in *The Cantos.* As in earlier works, this arrangement helps to reinforce connections between different sections of the sequence (notably, for instance, between the "Ode" and part 2, poem IV, and between "Envoi" and "Medallion") and to attain a complex balance in the sequence as a whole. The related pattern of circularity, a linkage of the final poem with the first, is also used in both *Hugh Selwyn Mauberley* and the *Homage to Sextus Propertius,* and a variation of this by drawing connections between the beginning of a sequence and the end is a device common to most of Pound's volumes. The way the "Ode" proleptically traces much of what follows has been noted in a number of works, especially "Cathay" and the *Homage to Sextus Propertius*. As early as "Hilda's Book," Pound seems to have recognized the utility of a guiding initial matrix both as a compositional strategy and as a means of imparting unity and coherence to an extended work. The roughly chronological progression of the portraits in part 1 of *Hugh Selwyn Mauberley* is reminiscent of patterns used in *Canzoni* and *Quia Pauper Amavi*, though these sequences never rely on strict chronology as a structural foundation. The construction of *Hugh Selwyn Mauberley* in "blocks" or groups, another device that helps to point up the emotional unity of constituent poems, is characteristic of all the longer sequences and the volumes, though less fully exploited in *Lustra* than in the others; a coordination of this structural technique with more complex development through emotive and thematic interplay and gradations of intensity is common to this sequence and the volume preceding it, *Quia Pauper Amavi*.

Finally, the use of a triadic pattern as a key organizational strategy and as a recurrent structural motif appears as early as "Piazza San Marco" and functions prominently in subsequent sequences and again in *The Cantos*. In *Hugh Selwyn Mauberley*, as in "Cathay" and *Lustra*, triads serve to sharpen contrasts among different poems and groupings, and they help to direct the movement of the sequence, usually climactically. *Hugh Selwyn Mauberley*, then, uses a compendium of organizational devices that were developed steadily in Pound's work, beginning "in 1904 or 1905," and in this respect, as in others, it anticipates the final form of *The Cantos*.

When Pound published *Hugh Selwyn Mauberley* together with other sequences in *Poems, 1918–1921*, he positioned it according to a roughly chronological scheme and called the volume his "first formed book":

> It contains the Imperium Romanum (Propertius)
> > The Middle Ages (Provence)
> > Mauberley (today)
> > and cantos IV–VII,
> It is all I have done since 1916, and my most important book, I at any rate think canto VII the best thing I have done. . . .
> At any rate the three portraits, falling into a Trois Contes scheme, plus the Cantos, which come out of the middle of me and are not a mask, are what I have to say, and the first formed book of poem [sic] I have made. (qtd. in Pearlman 301)

But it was in reference to this volume as well as *Quia Pauper Amavi* that Pound wrote, "We are just getting back to a Roman state of civilization, or in reach of it; whereas the Provençal feeling is archaic, we are ages away from it" (*Ltrs* 179). Hence this arrangement follows not simply a historical progression but also a circular movement, returning in *Hugh Selwyn Mauberley* and the four cantos at the end to the sophisticated irony and the critique of contemporary values infused through the *Homage to Sextus Propertius*. The arrangement itself is apparently part of what makes this a satisfying volume for Pound, and his letter points to the abandonment of the persona as another reason for the volume's success.

Yet the device of the persona had been supplanted by a conception of the poem in terms of a state of consciousness long before this—as Pound had pointed out in *Gaudier-Brzeska* in 1916—so that this advancement hardly seems to apply to the contents of *Poems, 1918–1921* as a whole. Rather, this particular reference to the cantos that close the volume attests to a movement beyond the mask that had been obstructing the development of the first three Ur-Cantos since their conception in 1915. By the time this volume was published, the first three cantos had already been revised at least twice, and they were not to attain their final form until almost 1925 (Slatin and Bush, *Genesis*). The announcement of a breakthrough in *Poems, 1918–1921* indicates the direction of the structural revamping that was taking place in the first cantos and, indeed, in the formation of *The Cantos* as a whole.

"It All Coheres": Observations and Speculations on *The Cantos*

It has often been remarked that the composition of *Hugh Selwyn Mauberley* contributed to, or at least paralleled, the reconception of *The Cantos* following the publication of the first Ur-Cantos in 1917. The organizational strategy most often pointed to as a link between them is the use of an Odyssean sea-voyage as a controlling metaphor. The potential latent in this device as a lattice-work for an extended poem may have been glimpsed, as critics have often suggested, in Joyce's *Ulysses*, though Pound need not have gone to Joyce's work for the idea. In fact, the controlling metaphors of both the Ur-Cantos and *The Cantos* are strongly anticipated in Pound's earlier volumes. The showman and shaman who attempts to lead us garrulously into the Ur-Cantos, first, is a natural development of other self-conscious prefatory announcements, such as "Grace Before Song" at the outset of *A Lume Spento* and *Personae;* "Over the Ognisanti," the preamble to the "San Trovaso Notebook" and *A Quinzaine for This Yule;* and "Tenzone" at the opening of *Lustra*. A number of early poems are also built upon the sea-voyage metaphor, such as "Beddoesque" and "Purveyors General," and *Exultations* opens with an invitation to an Odyssean quest in "Guido Invites You Thus": "Lo, I have known thy heart and its desire; / Life, all of it, my sea, and all men's streams / Are fused in it as flames of an altar fire!"[19] Also like *The Cantos, Canzoni* begins with a descent to the underworld (Korè's), and *A Lume Spento, Personae,* and *Exultations* all proceed, after their opening strains, through the presentation of a series of factive heroes, notably de Born, Villon, and Browning.

Similarly, although Pound's initial plans for his long poem were based on models drawn from his predecessors, the final form of *The Cantos* is primarily the result of his earlier structural experiments and innovations. The first drafts of the Ur-Cantos, following abortive attempts at Byronic satire in "Redondillas" and "L'Homme Moyen Sensuel," began with aspirations to an extended narrative work. As Schneidau notes, some of them "contain stretches of narrative material . . . that proved intractable and could not be fit in. Usually this was because the condensation needed to get the effect Pound strove for . . . reduced the narrative to skeletons but not to 'luminous details'" ("Cross-Cuts" 519).

The Ur-Cantos published in *Poetry* in 1917, using *Sordello* as a model, aspired to a continuity built on the recognizable framework of the dramatic monologue. This model provided a source of material for the poem, which unfolds through a colloquy to Browning, as well as a means of controlling its movement. The Ur-Cantos begin by talking *about* the writing of the poem rather than moving forward with it directly. The process of their revision embodies, in miniature, the full course of Pound's poetic development, especially his recasting of the dramatic monologue into the persona and its compression and intensification: "In my own first book I tried to rid this sort of poem of all irrelevant discussion, of Browning's talk *about* this, that and the other" (YC). Canto LXXVI records Pound's impulse to drop his first book, *A Lume Spento,* into a Venetian canal. The inclusion of this reminiscence may not be arbitrary, for the decision to salvage the volume was made again when its achievement was repeated by redirecting the Ur-Cantos away from Browning's model and, most significantly, by adopting the early book's structure as a model for that of *The Cantos.*

Of course, the most striking of Pound's revisions of the Ur-Cantos are stylistic, based on the replacement of argumentation with fragmentation, juxtaposition, and ellipsis, and the replacement of conversational sequence with parataxis. For precedents to this reconception we may look not to others' works but to Pound's earlier experiments.[20] The style of *The Cantos* is the culmination of a steady course of development that can be traced from at least as early as 1912. "The Return" and "Effects of Music Upon a Company of People" in *Ripostes* and "The Coming of War: Actaeon" in *Lustra,* for instance, evidence an increasing reliance on parataxis in the interests of nondiscursive modes of development. And the contributions of Imagism and Vorticism to the "sense of construction" in *The Cantos* may readily be glimpsed in the superpositional poems and other works such as "The Game of Chess" and "Cathay" in *Lustra,* and later in the allusive, juxtapositional, and elliptical technique of *Hugh Selwyn Mauberley.* As previous chapters have shown, the ideogrammic method, the unity of image, the progression through alternating contrasts, and the establishment of rhythms of recurrence, among other stylistic and structural devices of *The Cantos,* were already implicit in Pound's method from the beginning. Clearly, at this stage Pound did not need to look to others' long poems (or novels) to "get a form" for his own. The variety of his materials, their compression, and the rapidity of transition needed to achieve the sustained intensity of *The Cantos* did, however, necessitate the abandonment of *Sordello* as a model; how much further the poem could have gone in its original mold, and how successfully it could have done so, are questions open to speculation.

It is quite reasonable to conclude, then, that when models drawn from his predecessors proved untenable, Pound looked to his own earlier works for other possibilities; the exploratory descent and consultation with Tiresias in the present Canto I certainly suggest this sort of probing of one's own poetic past as much as of the tradition behind him. And choices made in opening the poem also required a seer's glimpse into the future, for its beginning depended largely on the overall structure of what was to follow.

Nonetheless, vestiges of conventional long poem precedents are much in evidence in *The Cantos:* the classical epic, the menippean satire, the Dantesque spiritual epic, and the Romantic autobiographical narrative, for instance, all contribute to the final form of the poem. Just as its sources and background are eclectic and enter the poem paratactically, so, too, its structure is eclectic, incorporating and coordinating a range of strategies successively or simultaneously and drawing upon a number of different traditions but adhering strictly to none. This is not to say that Pound created a structural pastiche, but that he recognized the techniques these traditions made available and used them freely as the poem's composition demanded. This is precisely the method we have observed in Pound's reconception of shorter, conventional forms, such as the sonnet, the canzone, and the dramatic monologue, in earlier stages of his development.

As suggested in chapter 2, another line of antecedents for Pound's method may be traced through a number of works, each of which is built up from smaller units—usually lyrical but often quite varied in mode—and implies a dynamic relation among its parts. These include Theocritus's *Idylls,* Ovid's *Metamorphoses* and *Heroides,* Propertius's *Elegies,* and several of Browning's collections (*Dramatis Personae* and *Men and Women,* among others).[21] Pound's experiments along these lines in his earlier sequences and volumes suggest that the final form of *The Cantos* evolved partly from his awareness of this tradition, and, as we shall see, *The Cantos* attains an emotional unity by deploying the same devices and key patterns whose development has been traced in the preceding chapters. The following discussion will briefly examine the major direction of the first cantos in order to show, by way of conclusion, how the structural patterns of earlier works are brought to bear on *The Cantos* as a whole.

The clearest continuity between *The Cantos* and Pound's earlier method, first, is the longer work's development through blocks of movement. The major blocks are immediately apparent in the publication history of *The Cantos*, evolving through the addition of successive volumes over the course of nearly fifty years. But within each of these larger segments, smaller movements are "blocked in"; Pound refers to these units as "blocks," "hunks," or "chunks" no less than thirteen times in letters written between 1919 and 1924.[22] The blocks in *A Draft of XVI Cantos* are readily discernible: Cantos I–III provide the initial matrix; IV–VII, sent as a unit to the *Dial* and published together in *Poems, 1918–1921*, are unified both in mode and through the use of Lorenzo Medici as a source of thematic continuity in Cantos V–VII; VIII–XI, similarly, are held together by a focus on Sigismundo Malatesta, by their sense of futility ("for all the good that did" and "the poor devils dying of cold" are their key leitmotifs), and by a steady downward emotive sweep tracing Malatesta's decline but bolstered by partaking of his strength of character. Cantos XII and XIII comprise a pair, presentatively offering contrasts between the economic and sexual perversion of XII and the dignity, insight, and justice of Confucius in XIII, and this section ends with the hell cantos, XIV–XVI, unified in context and imagery and in their horrified, scatological vision.[23] This first volume, beginning with the directed will of Odysseus's descent to the underworld and ending with perverters of will in the hell of contemporary England, is clearly arranged in a circular pattern, as is *A Draft of XXX Cantos*. This is another recurrent design we have noted in Pound's works, particularly in the *Homage to Sextus Propertius*.

Like several earlier works, such as *Canzoni*, "Cathay," the *Homage to Sextus Propertius*, and *Hugh Selwyn Mauberley*, *A Draft of XVI Cantos* is strongly proleptic, anticipating in its initial matrix, Cantos I–III, the curve not only of these first sixteen cantos but of *A Draft of XXX Cantos* and to a great degree of *The Cantos* as a whole. There is very little, tonally and thematically, in subsequent cantos that is not at least implicit in the first three, although everything introduced at the outset is developed through the poem's unfolding toward a broadened and deepened awareness, by means of a process of psychic and emotive growth. With this concentratedly proleptic order in mind, which I shall discuss in greater detail, the coherence of *The Cantos* as an integral whole is readily conceivable. It seems extremely unlikely that Cantos I–III, among the last to reach their final form in *A Draft of XVI Cantos*, could have been shaped, arranged, and placed so strategically without a view, however approximate, of the longer stretch and ultimate destination of *The Cantos* in its entirety.[24] It was in the process of revising these three cantos that, drawing on his earlier practices, Pound "got a form" for an extended poem that would allow its full development without limiting its scope or impeding its movement. The mode of the poem is experiential, however, so that while its direction is projected at the start, its exact course had to be determined as it unfolded. Its use of form as discovery thus provides a modern parallel to the quests of Odysseus, Aeneas, and Dante, each of whom was aware of his destination and assured of its attainment without an exact knowledge of the route that his journey and its exigencies would demand.

Before focusing more closely on Cantos I–III, it should be noted that the essential principles of the poem's unfolding, both in smaller segments and as a whole, are not strictly linear but cyclic as well. The two most prominent cycles, both described by Pound, guide (but do not determine) the development of the poem, sometimes in tandem and sometimes contrapuntally. The first of these is a cycle among "the permanent, the recurrent, the casual" (*Ltrs* 239), and the second also consists of three movements:[25]

> A. A. Live man goes down into world of Dead
> C. B. The "repeat in history"
> B. C. The "magic moment" or moment of metamorphosis, bust thru from quotidien into "divine or permanent world." Gods, etc. (*Ltrs* 210)

These cycles are repeated throughout *The Cantos,* gathering depth and significance as the poem unfolds. Their stages succeed one another in varied order and at different paces, alternating rapidly within a single line or more slowly through the course of several cantos. The fact that both cycles are triadic is also significant and points to another unifying structural motif in this work that has been carried over from earlier poems and sequences.

In Cantos I–III, these two cycles are introduced together. In Canto I, "Live man goes down into world of Dead"; Canto II presents the "'magic moment' or moment of metamorphosis"; and Canto III unfolds through a series of "repeats in history." Canto I, entering the realm of Proserpine, who governs yearly cycles of growth and decay, is dominated by the principle of recurrence; Canto II enters through metamorphosis into the permanent world of the gods, specifically Dionysus and Poseidon; and Canto III is focused on the casual, a series of distinct but related temporal experiences, from Pound's to the Estes'. Partly by means of presenting these two cycles together, the first three cantos are able to embody all of the archetypes for the subject rhymes of the rest of the poem and to introduce its key emotive patterns. These three cantos also open the poem with a strong narrative thrust, each one built upon a central tableau framed by fragments of other narratives and by moments of observation and revery. In subsequent cantos, this is largely dispersed through the fragmentation and interweaving of narrative, lyric, document, satire, anecdote, reminiscence, visionary moments, and so on. Finally, citing the first lines of these three cantos, Davenport has noted that they "epitomize the three modes in which the poem will proceed: action, literature, and contemplation" (*Cities* 10).

Much has been written, of course, about these three cantos, and my commentary is intended not to provide exegesis or comprehensive explication, but to explore the relationships between these sections and further developments in the poem. Canto I begins with a grippingly urgent plunge into man's collective cultural and spiritual history as well as a personal history, launching forth intrepidly into the terrifying, chaotic realm of the dead—of the past and of all that the consciousness of the present has suppressed—in order to discover the bases for renewal of sensibility and for a psychic, cultural, and social reordering that the rest of the poem will continue to seek. Thus Odysseus's roles as a leader, as a fertility figure, as an active spirit among others less energetic, and as a social reformer—for he almost singlehandedly establishes a new social order upon his return to Ithaca—are brought to the fore in the cantos that follow through a series of heroes, all of whom, with Odysseus, are refracted dimensions of the poem's unified sensibility.[26] The primal terror and revulsion, the quality of ritual awe combined with the insistent, directed will of the *polumetis* Odysseus, and the poem's tragic awareness along with the visionary capacity glimpsed in its last few lines are key tonal patterns deepened as the work progresses. The voyage of the live man into the world of the dead here becomes, in the course of the poem, a metaphor for the lively sensibility exploring the past and the death-in-life of both the past and the contemporary world.

Canto I also introduces the motif of the sea-voyage of discovery, the periplum that uncovers various dimensions of the past and present "not as land looks on a map / but as sea bord seen by men sailing" (Canto LIX), which plays into the structuring of *The Cantos* as various heroes successively undertake this sort of journey; here, as in the overall movement of the work, the direction of travel follows the course of the sun, "over sea till day's end." Its often-noted conflation of several cultural layers—the pre-Homeric nekuia, Homer, his Renaissance translator, the Anglo-Saxon poet latent in the poem's rhythms, and the controlling modern sensibility—is a palimpsest that supplies a paradigm for subsequent explorations. The canto's urgency and rapidity of movement also suggest the freedom from limits of time and space in further voyages, especially in Cantos I–XXX, and its movement between human and immortal realms toward a vision of the divine (Aphrodite), as well as its ritual conception of the relations between those realms, are keys to the direction and quality of movement in the rest of the poem.

The various episodes encompassed by the sweep of this canto suggest other tonalities and structural patterns that come into play more fully later. There is, first, the encounter with Elpenor, followed immediately by the gruff dismissal of Anticlea, Odysseus's mother:

> But first Elpenor came, our friend Elpenor,
> Unburied, cast on the wide earth,
> Limbs that we left in the house of Circe,

> Unwept, unwrapped in sepulchre, since toils urged other.
> Pitiful spirit. And I cried in hurried speech:
> "Elpenor, how art thou come to this dark coast?
> "Cam'st thou afoot, outstripping seamen?"
> And he in heavy speech:
> "Ill fate and abundant wine. I slept in Circe's ingle.
> "Going down the long ladder unguarded,
> "I fell against the buttress,
> "Shattered the nape-nerve, the soul sought Avernus.
> "But thou, O King, I bid remember me, unwept, unburied,
> "Heap up mine arms, be tomb by sea-bord, and inscribed:
> "*A man of no fortune, and with a name to come.*
> "And set my oar up, that I swung mid fellows."
>
> And Anticlea came, whom I beat off . . . .

This passage introduces, first of all, a note of compassion ("Pitiful spirit") developed later, though not fully, perhaps, until the *Pisan Cantos,* and a note of wry humor—"Cam'st thou afoot, outstripping seamen?"—that recurs again and again: in Malatesta's mock contract at the end of Canto XI, for instance, and in the reminiscences of Canto XX and especially Cantos XXVIII and XXIX. This becomes the *hilaritas* of later cantos and in all cases is a sustaining force that helps to offset without really mitigating a darker, tragic awareness, as here; in this function it, too, plays a crucial role in the *Pisan Cantos.* Second, Elpenor is another, unheroic dimension of Odysseus (the analogy between the relationship of these two figures and that of the two parts of *Hugh Selwyn Mauberley* is obvious), who arrives at the same destination *by accident,* lacking Odysseus's active, controlling will. His ultimate fate, emblematized in his epitaph, " '*A man of no fortune, and with a name to come,*' " is also linked to the key sensibility of *The Cantos* which adopts it in the *Pisan Cantos,* and to a number of heroes, antiheroes and nonheroes in the poem, beginning with Pentheus in Canto II— "And you, Pentheus, / Had as well listen to Tiresias, and to Cadmus, / or your luck will go out of you"—and Malatesta in Canto XI, "he with his luck gone out of him." Aside from indicating the unity of the key figures in *The Cantos,* this also demonstrates the manner in which connections are to be established among them, through analogy and contrast, by dramatic encounter, juxtaposition, and motivic linkage. And finally, Odysseus's repulse of Anticlea is an expression of the obsessively directed, pragmatic disposition that occupies much of the poem; the circularity of Cantos I–XXX, for instance, is effected partly by the dominance of this disposition in the "compleynt to pity" in Canto XXX.

As Dekker notes, Odysseus's voyage to consult Tiresias is the first of many such consultations with men of the past who have knowledge to offer (168–69). And Tiresias's prediction, " 'Odysseus / 'Shalt return home through spiteful Neptune, over dark seas, / 'Lose all companions,' " of course, forecasts the ensuing struggle with a world antithetical to the values of the controlling sensibility, as well as the intractable isolation to be dealt with, especially at Pisa. The gold of Tiresias's wand, of Aphrodite's crown, girdle, and breast bands, and of the "bough of Argicida," is here a sacred emblem of otherworldly power, setting up the potential for profanation and abuse pointed out in the next canto and intermittently through the next 115.

The canto's division into two parts, the driving, explorative descent of the first and the resplendent, affirmative vision of the second with, as Rosenthal notes, its continuing dark overtones ("Structuring" 6), also prefigures the starting and ending points of Cantos I–XXX and of *The Cantos* as a whole and suggests the essentially bipartite structure of both.

As mentioned earlier in connection with *Hugh Selwyn Mauberley*, Pearlman has observed that these closing lines present a triadic sequence of female figures—the sirens, Circe, and Aphrodite—that does not correspond to the order in which they are encountered in the *Odyssey*. He proposes that each of them controls one of three major phases of *The Cantos* as a whole; although this is arguable, without question each one does dominate at various moments in the poem. This observation is especially useful if the figures are considered in terms of their Homeric associations: a tempting but menacing element of destruction (the sirens); a compelling but perilous engagement leading to transformation that results in either destruction or renewal (Circe); and an exultant element of divine harmony and creative and procreative richness (Aphrodite). This outlines the range of the poem's psychic events and suggests the natural cycles with which it interacts, focusing on instances of creative cooperation with them or destructive attempts to appropriate or disrupt them. There is also a similar female triad in the first part of the poem—Circe, Proserpine, and Anticlea—who may readily be seen to correspond to the permanent ("the 'magic moment' or moment of metamorphosis"), the recurrent seasonal cycles, and the casual or transient realm of mortals, respectively.

Canto I, then, moves from the forward thrust, the solemnity, the terror, and the tragic awareness of its first part to a brief glimpse of the "mirthful" Aphrodite, in the setting of a hymn: similarly, Cantos I–XXX move with increasing *hilaritas* toward Artemis's "compleynt to pity," and the final movement of *The Cantos* is through *hilaritas* toward the hymn of Canto CXX and its serenity.[27]

Canto II emotively picks up and extends the closing note of I, and opens with a certainly more lighthearted view of the past, followed immediately by the first moment of visionary stillness in the poem, before plunging back into confrontation with forms of living death. Canto II also carries over the first-person experiential mode of Canto I, as does Canto III; although this is broken in Canto IV, it persists implicitly through the rest of the poem and becomes intermittently dominant.

The canto begins with a lively bantering with Browning, then courses over a series of figures—Sordello, So-shu, Picasso, and Homer—all of whom, like the questing poet-hero, are concerned with realizing an ordered vision amid chaos. The object, of course, is beauty—the image of Aphrodite toward which Canto I moves—but this is viewed here in its more threatening, Circean aspect in the figures of Eleanor and Helen. This equivocal disposition toward beauty, seen as at once rich in creative potential and dangerously imposing, is a prevalent pattern in *Lustra* (and of course *Hugh Selwyn Mauberley*), and one that resonates throughout *The Cantos*. Even amid the stillness of the visionary seascape that follows the opening passage of this canto, the element of sexual violence and betrayal persists in the figure of Tyro, ravished by "spiteful Neptune."

Destructive betrayal is also a key element in Acoetes' account at the center of the canto. Like Odysseus in Canto I, Acoetes shows proper reverence for the gods and is rewarded by their alliance: "Aye, I, Acoetes, stood there, / and the god stood by me." Like Odysseus, too, he is a live man among the dead—the spiritually dead, "Mad for a little slave money"—and confronts them singlehandedly, "the whole twenty against me." And in recounting his experience as a warning to Pentheus, Acoetes first introduces the reforming spirit that comes to dominate later sections, notably the Jefferson, Adams, and Chinese dynastic cantos. But the would-be pirates who attempt to disrupt social and natural order, to appropriate the sacred (Dionysus) and convert it to lucre, are archetypes for the bankers and other usurers and the military industrialists pinpointed as a cultural blight in the rest of *The Cantos*. Their effort is reversed, however, and they are transformed into beasts instead. The implication is that this is their true inner form; or at the very least, now in the form of the beasts who are Dionysus's attendants, they, like Pentheus, are given a lesson in proper reverence for the sacred. The vividness of Acoetes' account, with its tone of awe, terror, and dark knowledge—drawing, as Quinn notes, on all five senses for its effect (82)— gives the canto much of its power and links it with Canto I; but it also indicates the pedagogic method of the poem as a whole, piling detail upon detail of observed misdirection and its consequences, and projecting the full experiential and psychic impact of these observations upon the dominant sensibility. "I have seen what I have seen": this is the voice of *The Cantos*. The way Acoetes turns from his tale to make his point, "And you, Pentheus, / had as well listen to Tiresias, and to Cadmus," is paralleled much further along in the poem by the way *Rock-Drill* shifts from the ideogrammic compilation of observed evils, their origins and their consequences, to an ideogrammic succession of apothegms, driving the points home.

But Acoetes breaks off from his lesson to point out, with elated wonder, a vision of beauty captured and rendered permanent by sacred powers, a point of stillness amid the flux of the waters about it:

> And of a later year,
>   pale in the wine-red algae,
> If you will lean over the rock,
>   the coral face under wave-tinge,
> Rose paleness under water-shift,
>   Ileuthyeria, fair Dafne of sea-bords,
> The swimmer's arms turned to branches,
> Who will say in what year,
>   fleeing what band of tritons,
> The smooth brows, seen, and half seen,
>   now ivory stillness.

This passage opens out in *The Cantos* to all of the succeeding images of sculptural achievement, artifacts of permanent beauty wrought in the face of intractable circumstance (in this case tritons). We might compare, for instance, the "marble trunks out of stillness" in Canto XVII, or the way " 'the sculptor sees the form in the air . . . / 'As glass seen under water' " in Canto XXV. As in the transformations effected by the gods, the sculptor's power brings forth the inner form latent in the stone.[28] Excited discovery and the drawing of creative energy from undercurrents of terror and tragic awareness are key, related affective patterns developed in the rest of *The Cantos*.

From here the canto shifts, returning to the visionary seascape and the "glass wave over Tyro" that precedes Acoetes' tale, with a circularity that we have observed as a common structural device for attaining a sense of closure in a number of Pound's earlier works, from "Silet" to the *Homage to Sextus Propertius*. Here this device helps to unify the canto but is not used to close it, since the canto moves on to an image of the phallic, sacred tower that "like a one-eyed great goose / cranes up out of the olive grove"—which becomes the sacred tower of *The Cantos*' ideal cities, Ecbatan, Wagadu, and so on—and ends with the Aristophanic "frogs singing against the fauns / in the half-light."[29] Even this last cadence is dissipated by the final ellipsis "And . . . " that carries the momentum of this canto into the next.

Canto II uses at least two other structural devices that recur frequently in the poem. One is the pattern of ring composition, where a passage or an entire canto is built around a key, unifying image. This canto is focused on Dionysus's sacred power of transformation, and the rings of affect, imagery, and verbal motifs move inward from a vision of order to a revelation of godhead (see figure). It will be noted that this patterned repetition and symmetry of arrangement are natural developments from earlier works, beginning with the roundels of the "San Trovaso Notebook" and some of the sonnets, the canzoni, and the sestinas, and that similar organizational strategies play a central role in some of the sequences and volumes, notably "Laudantes Decem," *A Lume Spento, Personae,* and *Ripostes*. Applied somewhat less rigorously, ring structure accounts

Ring Structure of Canto II[30]

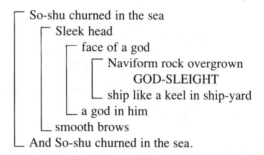

```
┌─ So-shu churned in the sea
│  ┌─ Sleek head
│  │  ┌─ face of a god
│  │  │  ┌─ Naviform rock overgrown
│  │  │  │  GOD-SLEIGHT
│  │  │  └─ ship like a keel in ship-yard
│  │  └─ a god in him
│  └─ smooth brows
└─ And So-shu churned in the sea.
```

for the shape of the *Homage to Sextus Propertius,* which builds inward toward the intensely erotic focus and the tragic awareness of its central sections, V–VII.

The other key device of Canto II is the triadic structural pattern, already noted in Canto I but applied more densely here. The canto as a whole, first of all, splits into three main sections, Acoetes' tale and the passages before and after it. The canto opens with a triad of poets—Browning, Sordello, and Homer —and three female figures: Eleanor, Helen, and Tyro. The seal (perhaps a fourth female figure, Eidothea) is decribed as first "daughter of Lir," then as the "lithe daughter of Ocean," and Helen is given the "voice of Schoeney's daugh-ters."[31] And Eleanor is refracted into the triad "Eleanor, 'ελέναυς and 'ελέπτολις!" The canto closes with two more triads: "Olive grey in the near . . . / Salmon-pink wings of the fish-hawk . . . / The tower. . . ," then "And we have heard . . . /And the frogs . . . / And. . . . " Canto III is similarly built in three sections, with the Cid tableau at the center; among the opening images is the triad panisks, dryas, and maelid, and the canto closes with the diminishing triad of Ignez da Castro, the flaking Schifanoia frescoes, and the fall of the Este family. This device proliferates throughout *The Cantos,* sometimes, as here, supplying a framework, helping to unify a canto or a passage, or to establish connections among images or tonal patterns, and at other times simply echoing a recognizable leitmotif, as in Canto LXXXIII:

> sea, sky, and pool
> alternate
> pool, sky, sea.

Triad can answer to triad subtly, sometimes across groups of cantos: "et ter flebiliter, Ityn" ("and thrice with tears") in Canto IV, and "ter pacis Italiae auctor" ("thrice peacemaker of Italy," applied to Borso d'Este) in Canto XXIV, for instance.[32] The triads are often built on traditional groupings, like the three graces of Canto XXVII, or they can present an idiosyncratic linkage, such as the "Poundian trinity" of Maia, Delia, and Korè, unfolding out of Aphrodite, that

Dekker notes in Canto LXXIX (73). Wilhelm, too, points out significant triads in Cantos XCIV, CIV, and CXIII (57), and Pearlman observes that Cantos XLVII and XLIX are both developed triadically, which he suggests is part of a key triadic structural pattern guiding the development of *The Cantos* as a whole (172–92). Although a tripartite development based on *La Divina Commedia* has been extensively debated, the poem's cyclic phases, recurrent/permanent/casual and descent/metamorphosis/repeat in history, are crucial triadic modes of proceeding. Again, we have observed the evolution of this device from its appearance as early as the "San Trovaso Notebook," in the triadic structure of "Piazza San Marco" and in the unfolding of "Matri Dei," in the poem "Lotus-Bloom," into Mary, Isis, and Demeter, toward its use as a central pattern in "Cathay," in *Lustra* as a whole, and in *Hugh Selwyn Mauberley*. These and the other strategies we have traced through Pound's work, such as the ideogrammic method, the use of subject rhyme, and the unifying image, are employed in *The Cantos* as devices that help to guide the poem's development and to reinforce its unity.

Canto III, completing the initial, triadic matrix of *The Cantos,* supplies the balance of the archetypal images and themes and the key tonal patterns to be developed in the rest of the work. The account of the Cid at the center picks up the forward drive and the experiential immediacy of the first two cantos, but much of this canto's proleptic groundwork is achieved through the rapid, fragmentary allusions at the beginning and end. It starts off with a personal account, the first truly anecdotal passage of the book, but this hovers only briefly before opening out to what follows:

> I sat on the Dogana's steps
> For the gondolas cost too much, that year,
> And there were not "those girls," there was one face,
> And the Buccentoro twenty yards off, howling "Stretti,"
> And the lit cross-beams, that year, in the Morosini,
> And peacocks in Koré's house, or there may have been.

This passage supplies, first of all, the observational perspective of much of the poem—whose sensibility is not always that of the actively engaged, factive hero—as well as a sense of exile ("lose all companions") and especially economic exile: the deprivation and exclusion here rhyme, of course, with the plight of the Cid later in the canto, with the circumstances to which Malatesta is reduced in Canto XI, and with the defeat of other heroes in the course of the poem, especially in the *Pisan Cantos*.[33] There is also a sense of social exclusion and nostalgia introduced here that persists through the poem, and a tinge of revulsion at the one face "howling 'Stretti.'" This siren figure, typifying the sexual debasement of her age, resonates with gruesome irony at the end of the canto through the contrast between her song, "In close embrace . . . / The

Spanish girl is that way when in love" (Terrell 8), and the murdered Ignez da Castro, whose story, with its implications of devotion, treachery, and necrophilia, is clarified in Canto XXX as a luminous detail that throws into relief her context of cultural collapse.

Against the mixed tones of these opening recollections are set a sylvan vision populated with the healthy fecundity of wood spirits (panisks, dryas, and maelid), and Poggio's observations of nymphlike bathers—earthly figures who are seen to embody something of the sylvan genii's restorative life impulse. It hardly needs to be said that this contrast between female figures representing "the cult of beauty" and those who belong to "the cult of ugliness," developed through *Ripostes, Lustra,* "Moeurs Contemporaines," and *Hugh Selwyn Mauberley,* guides much of the development of *The Cantos* and resonates with other key dichotomies, such as that between cultivation of the arts and their neglect. The promise of an earthly paradise is also introduced briefly in this canto through the motif "the grey steps lead up under the cedars" and is clarified through its repetitions in subsequent cantos (for instance, when Kung walks "into the cedar grove" in Canto XIII).

The Cid, in the following tableau, is another *polumetis* Odyssean hero, tricking the usurers Raquel and Vidas at their own game, and, like Dionysus in Canto II, revealing the emptiness of their nature by satisfying their lust for gold with a "big box of sand." Their perverted desire rhymes with the debasement of the howling siren at the start of the canto and with the perversion in Ignez da Castro's story at the end, and the link established here between sexual and economic corruption, along with the censure and revulsion directed at both, also continue throughout the poem and become the explicit focus, first, of the series of tales in Canto XII and the lurid hell of usurers and sodomites in Cantos XIV–XVI. The Cid's banishment, his threatened dismemberment, and the pomp of the indictment against him, with the "big seals and the writing," set up a rhyme with the Pope's interdict against Malatesta in Canto X and with the whole series of bureaucratic obstacles that confront successive heroes in *The Cantos,* and they contrast with the lively sensibility of the Cid and the ingenuous courage of the nine-year-old girl who reads him the writ with "voce tinnula." Canto III ends with the Ignez da Castro allusion and allusions to the fall of the Estes and the surrounding cultural decay; a sense of circular closure is attained in Cantos I–XXX by echoing this sequence with the da Castro story and the decline of the Borgias, and thus of the arts they patronized, at the end of Canto XXX.

It should now be clear that the structure of *The Cantos* is concentratedly proleptic, that the foundation for all that follows is solidly established in the first three cantos. I do not wish to oversimplify the poem's complexities by insisting that nothing new enters after this first segment, but rather to point out that all of the subsequent materials "fit" because they have been anticipated by the patterns of this initial matrix and enter the poem as further developments of them. It is not unreasonable to conclude that Pound "got a form that wouldn't exclude something merely because it didn't fit" in the arduous process of bringing these first three cantos to their final state between the first drafts in 1912 or 1915 and the publication of *A Draft of XVI Cantos* in 1925.

In the course of this process, Pound clearly drew less on the structural models offered by traditional genres and others' innovations than on the patterns and techniques he had been developing and employing from the beginning of his efforts in "1904 or 1905." Like the various structuring devices carried over from earlier works into *Hugh Selwyn Mauberley* and *The Cantos* that have been noted so far in this chapter, the overall design of both sequences is evidently based on a pattern that recurs frequently in Pound's sequences and volumes. Specifically, we have observed that a characteristic arrangement is a bipartite structure with a notable shift in the dominant state of consciousness between the first part and the second. In *A Lume Spento,* for instance, Pound's first published volume, this shift occurs almost exactly midway and is signalled by the two transitional pieces, "Ballad Rosalind" and "Malrin," which recapitulate the movement anticipated in the volume's framework, from the bleakness of "this grey folk" and the opening strains of nostalgia and loss to a more buoyant resurgence of life force at the close. Again in *Personae,* there is a movement from the same opening state of consciousness to a concluding affirmation of the sustaining power of art, with a final, poignant note in "Piccadilly," pivoting through the key third group at the center of the volume. The shorter sequence, "Laudantes Decem," in *Exultations,* shifts through the sensual immediacy of its seventh poem toward the resolution of thwarted passion and the sense of stillness at its close. "Translations from Heine" in *Canzoni* similarly pivots on its central interlude, *"Translator to Translated,"* offering Heine as a standard to partially resolve the sequence's conflicts, and "Und Drang," in the same volume, turns in poem IV toward its final cadence, where it reaches an acceptance of the transience it confronts, and the values it searches for are to some degree established. *Ripostes* is also constructed in this manner, shifting from its more confrontative and satiric first part to a more positive focus on the power of art and vision in the second; and, again, the shift is signalled by refuting the opening poem, "Silet," midway through the book in "The Seafarer." We have also observed how "Cathay" develops through a building sense of wastage, decay, and depredation by war to a climax in "Lament of the Frontier Guard," and from there works through an aesthetic reenvisioning toward acceptance of isolation, loss, and displacement as universal facets of experience in the closing poem, "To-Em-Mei's 'The Unmoving Cloud.'" A related pattern also informs the *Homage to Sextus Propertius,* pivoting about its central sections, V–VII, and *Hugh Selwyn Mauberley* shifts dramatically after the "Envoi," though in the opposite direction, from futility to collapse.

The frequent recurrence of this pattern in Pound's earlier works can hardly be coincidental, and it has apparently been applied to the structuring of *The Cantos* as well. In 1959, the year of *Thrones,* Pound remarked in an interview with D. G. Bridson that "There is a turning point in the poem towards the middle. Up to that point it is a sort of detective story, and one is looking for the crime" (172). Pound goes on to specify that he means the usura cantos and that the crime identified and defined explicitly—in Canto XLV and its neighboring cantos—is usury (whose presence is clear well before that, to be sure). A glance at the surrounding poems reveals that Cantos XLV, XLVII, and XLIX constitute a second matrix in the poem, in many ways recapitulating that of the first three cantos, with significant differences. The incantatory rhythm of an exorcism in Canto XLV, first, works toward freeing the poem from the evil already identified in Cantos II and III and persisting from then on. Canto XLVII traces a second major explorative descent to the underworld, more explicitly linked to sexuality than in Canto I and more specifically directed in search of bases for psychic renewal, as Canto I delves into the collective spiritual past in search of bases for cultural renewal. And the moment of stillness attained at the start of Canto II is considerably deepened in Canto XLIX, "the emotional still point of the *Cantos*" (Kenner, *Poetry* 326). This progression and its minor repetitions throughout the poem very strongly anticipate the tremendous affirmation of Cantos XC and XCI and the final cadence in Canto CXX:

> I have tried to write Paradise
>
> Do not move
>   Let the wind speak
>   that is paradise.

Like *A Lume Spento* and a number of Pound's other early works, then, *The Cantos* uses a roughly bipartite structure whose development from beginning to end is refocused and directed through a key grouping at approximately its center.

Although the degree to which a triadic, Dantesque progression of Inferno, Purgatorio, and Paradiso applies to *The Cantos,* if at all, is open to question, the poem does progress with a similar sense of inevitability from its strident, opening movement to the paradisal stillness of its close, and, like Dante's poem (and some of Pound's earlier works), it "recount[s] an increasing ritual perception of the light, beginning with the Nekyia . . . and ending with the sun visions of *Thrones*" (Bush, *Genesis* 100). Unlike Dante's poem, but very much like *A Lume Spento* and Pound's other sequences, the progression from stridence to serenity, from darkness to light, takes place not in terms of steady thematic development or through a continuous progression along an abstractable route that can be charted on an "Aquinas map," but haltingly.

Indeed, the sense of inevitability we find in *The Cantos* as a whole is not that of a philosophical or thematic development—although both sorts of development do take place and contribute to the progression of the poem—but the inevitability of a course of psychic and emotional growth. A lack of uniformity and rational sequence in *The Cantos,* of continuity in time, space, voice, context, theme, and form, is often the central reason for questioning its integrity as a whole. Of course, all of Pound's sequences and volumes exhibit the same kinds of discontinuity, yet, as we have seen, his practice has its traditional precedents, from Theocritus to Whitman and Browning, and Pound's primary departure from them is toward the integrity of a nondiscursive "arrangement of forms" with an inherent emotional unity. This is, in fact, the basis of *The Cantos'* structure: not a steady and determined progression from acorn to oak leaf (though with a similar inevitability), but the halting movement of *psychic* growth, by leaps and lapses, disjunctions, digressions and regressions, periods of constriction and others of expansion, surges forward and obsessive suspensions (hence the dilatory insistence of some stretches of *The Cantos,* which nonetheless contribute poetically to the movement of the whole).[34] Part of the lasting achievement of the poem, whatever its flaws, is that in its movement toward the deepened awareness and the increased sense of integration, acceptance, and harmony with natural process at its close, it has embodied the dynamic order of psychic, spiritual, and emotional realization with archetypal accuracy and richness, speaking for both past and present as a "tale of the tribe."

Notes

Introduction

1. The themes of Pound's early poetry are discussed at length in Christine Brooke-Rose, *A ZBC of Ezra Pound;* N. Christoph De Nagy, *The Poetry of Ezra Pound: The Pre-Imagist Stage;* Thomas Jackson, *The Early Poetry of Ezra Pound;* and Hugh Witemeyer, *The Poetry of Ezra Pound: Forms and Renewal, 1908–1920.* All of these are accomplished and valuable studies of Pound's work to which this one is much indebted.

   Valuable discussions of Pound's early theoretical bearings include Herbert N. Schneidau, *The Image and the Real* and Ronald Sieburth, *Instigations.*

2. Notable exceptions include Witemeyer's study and Thomas McKeown's unpublished dissertation, "Ezra Pound's Experiments with Major Forms, 1904–1925: *Directio Voluntatis.*"

3. Cf. De Nagy, *Decade* 26–27 and *passim.*

4. All previously unpublished materials marked "YC" are printed here with the permission of the Beinecke Rare Book and Manuscript Library of Yale University and New Directions as Agent for the Trustees of the Ezra Pound Literary Property Trust. All such materials are quoted as they appear in manuscript or typescript; editorial corrections, where necessary, are enclosed in brackets.

5. Cf. *ABCR* 113.

6. See, for instance, *LE* 268 and 324 n.; *SP* 130 and 360; and *ABCR* 47–48, 63, and 96.

7. For a full discussion of the connection between Pound's poetics and Longinus's, see Korn, *Purpose passim.*

8. Witemeyer, citing Mario Praz, suggests that Eliot's theory may have been derived from Pound's ideas in *The Spirit of Romance* (29).

9. See especially *LE* 68, 180, 265, 267, 340, and 415; *SP* 424; and *LRA* 166.

Chapter 1

1. Unless otherwise noted, all poems are quoted from *The Collected Early Poems of Ezra Pound.*

2. The improvements in this version of the poem over an earlier draft included in "Hilda's Book" and entitled "The Banners" suggest some of the directions Pound's developing poetics was to take. Foremost among these is the elimination of a great deal of verbiage, pointing the way to

the compression we find in later works. The borrowed epithet in line 3, "proud-pied gold," for instance, heightens the sense of exuberant brightness in the season past, in this version, and replaces the glaring tautology of "September's yellow gold"; similarly, "King-Oak" was actually worse in the earlier draft: a "king oak tree" whose panoply was there a "brave panoply." More important, the later version of the second line, "Driving his leaves upon a dust-smit air," is syntactically clearer and metrically more interesting than the earlier "October whirleth leaves in dusty air." "Dust-smit" carries a latent metaphor that gives it greater vividness than "dusty," and the continuing active motion of "Driving" is more forceful than the staid "whirleth." Clearly, the compression, the vividness, and the directness resulting from these revisions anticipate the stylistic and structural reorientations of later work.

3. Its one archaism is "harsh northwindish time," translated from Arnaut Daniel (Ruthven 221).

4. The word "may" here probably refers to the flower of the hawthorn and not, as Witemeyer suggests, "May weather," which would make this merely redundant with the previous line (106). Other meanings—"maiden" and "bloom, prime, heyday" (*OED*)—may also be applicable and Pound would almost certainly have been aware of them. The definition is important not only because of Pound's insistence during this period on *le mot juste*, but also because the word's convergence of meanings carries much of the emotive charge of the phrase and of the poem as a whole; this is a notable early instance of "logopoeia."

5. Kenner has observed that in the Provençal canzone God is conventionally invoked in stanza 4 or 5 (*Era* 373). Pound's adaptation answers this convention by reversing it and subordinating religious ritual to the ritual of devotion.

6. Cf. George Wright, *The Poet in the Poem:*

    Both reader and poet must be aware that the historical virtues of old personae are currently meaningful, must recognize that Cino and Bertran de Born were struggling against a vice and corruption that are still part of the human world. The mask that the poet assumes must carry with it a meaning unavailable to the persona. The twentieth-century poet speaks through the twelfth- or fourteenth-century poet, augmenting the consciousness of the latter with his own superior awareness. The speaker is aware only of his own world, but his words have reference to much more (134).

7. This is a characterization common to several critics; see, for instance, Brooke-Rose 45; De Nagy, *Poetry* 119; and Witemeyer 80.

8. Cf. Rosenthal and Gall 14. Also, as Bornstein notes, unlike both Browning and Yeats, "Pound builds his monologues from separate poetic bits, each itself a moment of intense perception or creation, so that the poem's unity derives as much from associative links in the material as from the speaker's psychological progression" (*Consciousness* 35).

9. The poem is printed as an appendix in Read, *One World* 448–52. Cf. George Bornstein's edition and commentary in Bornstein, *Ezra Pound Among the Poets* 106–27.

10. This volume was written during the period 1905–7, compiled for presentation to Hilda Doolittle in 1907, and unpublished until 1979 (Michael King in Doolittle 67–68).

11. "Inner form" is Pound's term, used, for instance, in an early letter to Floyd Dell: "Now as to my rhythmic principles. There is in every line a real form & an apparent. By the inner form ye shall know them. I, as often as I like, dispense with the other" ("Two Early Letters" 116). Elsewhere Pound explains:

Yet it is quite certain that some people can hear and scan "by quantity," and more can do so "by stress," and fewer still feel rhythm by what I would call the inner form of the line. And it is this "inner form," I think, which must be preserved in music; it is only by mastery of this inner form that the great masters of rhythm—Milton, Yeats, whoever you like—are masters of it. (*EPM* 32–33)

12. See especially De Nagy, *Poetry* 13 and 147; Jackson 119ff.; Kenner, *Era* 80–81; and Schneidau, *Image* 4.

13. Qtd. in Kenner, *Poetry* 253.

14. Of course, Pound objected to Wordsworth's being "so intent on the ordinary or plain word that he never thought of hunting for *le mot juste*" (*LE* 7). But neither poet actually employed a purely conversational language, if such a thing exists; Pound's diction was modified by his emphasis on *le mot juste*, Wordsworth's by other concerns.

15. Pound's formulation of absolute rhythm came at a relatively early date—1910, in the "Preface" to *Cavalcanti Poems*.
    Two analyses of absolute rhythm seem to me to work quite valuably together toward an understanding of the premises and practice of this technique. First, Kenner's:

    > As a structural relation . . . "absolute rhythm" provides at once a psychological and an objective correlative of emotions and shades of emotion transcending both exegesis and vocabulary. The structural principle of Gregorian chant, the exact and indissoluble union of the music, phrase by phrase and rhythm by rhythm, with the sacred text, is obviously related to *vers libre* as the opposite conception of a tune to which words are fitted is related to the stanza form. (*Poetry* 115)

    And more recently, Sally M. Gall has demonstrated that this involves actual, measurable musical patterns: "much of Pound's verse is metrical in the musical sense: it has a temporal order that can be expressed by a time-signature—4/4 or 6/4, for example. . . . In practice, fundamental to these 'absolute rhythms' (made up, one imagines, of successive musical phrases), are regular, analyzable ones that can be put into rhythmic notation" (36).

16. Pater's relevant aesthetic is that of the "hard, gemlike flame" at the end of *The Renaissance*.

17. Rosenthal, *Modern Poets* 54; Rosenthal and Gall, *Poetic Sequence* 187.

18. See, for instance, Kenner, *Poetry* 194.

19. This is spaced as Pound specified it should be when printed in the "Contemporania" series in *Poetry*, April 1913. In an unpublished letter to Harriet Monroe, Pound directs her to center the poem within whatever white space remains on the final page of the series, and to "group the words" as shown (UCL).

Chapter 2

1. This is not to conclude that the *Idylls* are intended as an integral long poem; but there is a continuity among them that strongly suggests such an arrangement, as do their clear derivation from and reaction to the epic. On their relation to epic see, for instance, Halperin 238ff.

2. For illuminating discussions of classical poetic collections, see Fraistat, *Book;* and Anderson.

3. From *Homage to Sextus Propertius,* V,2, *Personae* 217.

4. Cf. Fraistat, *Book* 10; Miner, "Some Issues" 19–21 and *passim;* and Patterson *passim.*

5. Qtd. in Foerster 122. Foerster considers these observations irreconcilably contradictory, but they seem, rather, premonitory of later developments that resolve the apparent contradictions.

    The passage quoted is strikingly parallel to many of Pound's remarks, and offers an interesting correspondence between Carlyle's "virtue" and Pound's conception of "*virtù.*"

6. Pearce, James E. Miller, and Woodward, for instance.

7. For a discussion of Rimbaud's important influence in modern reconceptions of poetic structure and poetic reference, see Perloff, *Poetics* 3–44 and *passim.*

    While Pound justly denied a direct connection between his aesthetics and the Symbolists', Mallarmé's and others' ideas were already well assimilated by the English literary milieu he entered in 1908 (Pondrom 9–10, 20–21).

8. For further discussion of these reorientations, see, for example, Foerster 164–72 and 213–20; Perkins 30–32 and *passim;* Rosenthal, *The Modern Poets* 3–10; de Sola Pinto *passim;* and Spender *passim.*

9. "Song of Myself" began (in the 1855 version) with the appearance of a traditional long poem aspiring to a surface unity that its rhythms, its "sheer variety of tonalities," and the rapidity of shifts among them militated against, ultimately giving rise to the fragmentation of the later (1892) version (Rosenthal and Gall 25). Yet even from the first, the poem was allied with the alternate tradition of the long poem, grounded in the lyric mode with the experiential self at its center rather than a conventional hero and a conventional epic struggle: "I celebrate myself." In the later version, the lyrical priorities the poem sets against those of traditional epic are even more explicit in the allusive opening, "I celebrate myself, and sing myself" (Rosenthal and Gall 35). The poem's attainment of epic breadth without sacrificing its essentially lyrical movement is precisely what makes it a central prototype of the modern long poem.

10. See Rosenthal and Gall for a more extended consideration of Tennyson's, Henley's, and Housman's poems as lyric sequences. Also, as Miner points out, in the composition of *In Memoriam* "it is quite clear that Tennyson originally started writing the separate lyrics without thought of publication, much less of ordering" ("Some Issues" 35). The correspondence between this working method and the assemblage of Pound's sequences and volumes will become clear in the following discussion.

11. YC; qtd. in McKeown 138. Emphasis added.

12. This also applies to the construction of "Portrait d'une Femme," which is what makes it specifically a "portrait": "The portrait painter's liberty runs just as far as is compatible with leaving the centre of interest *always* in the personality, the character, the individual who is the sitter" (*EPVA* 44).

13. The movement of this section of course suggests Browning more than Shakespeare; a segment of the poem cancelled in manuscript makes this connection more explicit in its remark that "Bobbi sinned" too (*CEP* 321).

14. This passage can perhaps be glossed by Pound's comments on Villon in *The Spirit of Romance:* "Villon never forgets his fascinating, revolting self. . . . Villon's song is selfish through self-absorption. . . . Villon is a voice of suffering, of mockery, of irrevocable fact" (168).

15. In the *A Lume Spento and Other Early Poems* (1965) printing of this sequence, these two lines are curiously omitted, the previous line is broken, and the three sections are detached though printed in order, so that the sequence is entirely disbanded. A glance at the table of contents for the "San Trovaso Notebook" (*CEP* 319), however, shows that these poems were clearly

designed to work together as a whole in 1908; these two central lines are rather crucial to their unity.

16. The manuscript revisions of this poem already suggest a movement toward a harder and more concise presentation of emotion, and show Pound's removal of dramatic fixtures from the poem itself to appended notes (see *CEP* 321).

17. This sequence was intended for inclusion in *Canzoni* though all except the third of its four sonnets, "L'Art," were withdrawn.

18. In an unpublished letter at Yale dated 28 October 1925.

19. In the *Umbra* printing of the sequence, greater conciseness was achieved by changing the first "poor" to "uncertain" and deleting the second (*CEP* 303–4).

20. The sequence of colors is as follows:
      II: rose, rose, crimson; III: green, white, purple; V: red, green; VI: brown, green, purple; VII: white, rose, grey, gold; VIII: rose, rose, rose; IX: silver, crimson, white; X: rose, crimson, rose.

21. In an unpublished essay dated 31 July 1907, Pound muses on "the passion of saying in the lyric of color alone":

> I would like and will I hope in future voice praise of color for its, well not its own sake, but color itself for the exalting power of its own beauty and for its power, on canvass[,] to lead us deeper into the mystery and wonder of gods own coloring, whereof we but begin to understand the subtlety of shade and blending, and but stumble mid arcana of lights and atmosphere. (YC)

The continuity of this idea in Pound's work (as well as the marked difference in its treatment) can be glimpsed in its presence as late as Canto XC, in a quotation from John Heydon: " 'From the colour the nature / & by the nature the sign!' " As Dekker explains, "Colour is the active mode of being of an object, just as love is the active mode of being of the soul; and it is by the colour or the love that we know and value an object or the soul—that is, by its manifestations" (75).

22. In later printings it is retitled "Translations and Adaptations from Heine."

23. *LE* 25, 30, and 33; cf. Demetz 285.

24. See Longenbach 401–4; McDougal 89–101; McKeown 67–74; and Witemeyer 96–103.

Chapter 3

1. "Epilogue" was deleted from the series but is reprinted in *CEP*. The tables of contents for the three versions of "Contemporania," along with Pound's comments on them to Harriet Monroe, are transcribed from drafts in the Monroe collection at the University of Chicago and are included here with the permission of Special Collections of the Joseph Regenstein Library and New Directions as Agent for the Trustees of the Ezra Pound Literary Property Trust.
      Since much of this material is undated or has been dated by a hand neither Pound's nor Monroe's, the succession of the three phases of "Contemporania" has been inferred as follows. In what is labeled the second phase, Pound enclosed new poems that are not listed in the contents of the first, and his accompanying letter refers to several of the poems listed in the first phase as "the things you've got." Since the table of contents in Monroe's hand includes some of the poems referred to as "the things you've got" and some of the new ones, it must have been

compiled after she received the new poems and the accompanying letter from Pound. In the final phase, Pound's table of contents includes poems from both the first and second phases and lists them in the order in which they were printed.

2. The poem is "To Another Man, on His Wife," reprinted in *CEP*.

3. The contents of the November 1913 *Poetry* group:

> Ancora
> Surgit Fama
> Choice
> April
> Gentildonna
> Lustra
>   The Rest
>   Les Millwins
>   Further Instructions
> Xenia ["Song of the Degrees"]
> Ité
> Dum Capitolium Scandet

4. The original order Pound specified for the November group is as follows:

> Ancora
> Surgit Fama
> The Choice
> "Helpless few in my country"
> Albatre
> April
> Gentildonna
> The Faun
> Lesbia Ille
> As Usual
> From Chebar (UCL)

5. The contents of the December 1913 *New Freewoman* group:

> Further Instructions
> Les Millwins
> Ancora
> April
> Gentildonna
> Surgit Fama
> Song of the Degrees
> The Choice
> The Rest

6. The contents of "Zenia" (actually a misprint for "Xenia") in *Smart Set*, December 1913:

> I To Dives
> II Alba
> III Epitaph
> IV Come, let us play
> V She had a pig-shaped face

    VI Causa
    VII Bath Tub
    VIII Arides
    IX The Encounter
    X Simulacra
    XI Tame Cat

7.   The poems in *Blast* I (June 1914):

    Salutation the Third
    Monumentum
    Come my cantilations
    Before Sleep
    Post Mortem
    Fratres Minores
    Women Before a Shop
    L'Art
    The New Cake of Soap
    Meditatio
    Pastoral

    The movement of the second half of the sequence is complemented by four reproductions of paintings by Wadsworth, which open out from a jagged angularity in the first to a less dissonant overlaying of spheres and radiants in the last.

8.   All quotations of poems in the first two parts of this chapter are from *Personae* (1926), unless specified otherwise.

9.   The contents of the March 1915 *Poetry* group:

    Provincia Deserta
    Image from D'Orleans
    The Spring
    The Coming of War: Actaeon
    The Gypsy
    The Game of Chess

10.   In a subsequent letter, Pound added "Fish and the Shadow" to this group and specified the desired arrangement:

    Cabaret
    Homage to Flor. Ch.
    Pagani's
    3 Poets
    Fish (UCL)

    The sequence as published ran as follows:

    Fish and the Shadow
    'Ιμέρρω
    The Three Poets
    Pagani's, November 8
    The Lake Isle
    Impressions of François-Marie Arouet (de Voltaire)

Homage to Quintus Septimius Florens Christianus
Dans un Omnibus de Londres

11. Pound also expended considerable effort on shaping sequences for other poets. In April 1916, for instance, he sent Harriet Monroe an arrangement of poems by Joyce:

> Here are the rest of the Joyce poems. I think you had better print all five. They are quite good in their way. It is not greatly my way, still the five of them together will convey their own atmosphere and they have a certain distinction, though it would perhaps be difficult to say why. (UCL)

Later that year he submitted a sequence by Iris Barry:

> I enclose 14 brief poems by Iris Barry. I want you to print the lot, and as soon as possible. . . .
> She certainly has something[ ]in her. More grip and sense of inner form tha[n] the generality of late-imagists. I can't see that anything in this group can be omitted. I have had a bunch of about forty poems to go over and have arranged this group out of it with a good deal of care. (UCL)

12. Three other periodical sequences that evidence the care taken in their arrangement are those published in *Poetry and Drama* (March 1914), in *Blast* II (July 1915), and in *Others* (November 1915).

13. Joseph 39; see also 51–65 in her illuminating discussion.

14. This is more explicit in the lines that followed this passage in an earlier draft, deleted, perhaps, in order to bring the poem closer to "the passionate dispassion of Villon":

> With no ornament but your heart and your eyes,
> And your bosom of flushed alabaster
> (Did any man then withstand you?)

(YC)

"Passionate dispassion" is Pound's phrase, in an unpublished commentary on Lionel Johnson's criticism, intended to accompany the Johnson essay (reprinted in *LE* 361–70) in the unpublished *Collected Prose*:

> Johnson went down into the bog of superstition from which he would seem to call "impressionism" a morass. Symons' morass is not, however, impressionism, but sentimentality. It is not because he gives us blurred light and haze at the stage-doors of theatres, but because these faces of tired and painted young women are hardly given without comment of sentiment, never, perhaps given with the passionate dispassion of Villon. (YC)

15. These details were apparently added by Pound in a late stage of the poem's composition. They are found neither in an earlier manuscript draft (at Yale) nor in the poem by Voltaire from which Pound's is adapted (Ruthven 151).

16. In the tentative first version of the sequence, "The Seafarer," adapted from the Anglo-Saxon, was somewhat redundant, in terms of the sequence's emotive pattern, in its placement between "Exile's Letter" and "Four Poems of Departure." It was also certainly discordant in its imposition of an occidental cultural context and an English poetic tradition upon the oriental context of the sequence as a whole. Contextual discontinuity was not, of course, in itself problematic for Pound, and wider, more abrupt disparities could be used effectively within the movement of *The Cantos;* the placement of "The Seafarer" here is a step in that direction. But "Cathay" is

arranged according to a more rigorously schematic framework. Within so controlled a pattern, the contrast between the strident, accentual movement of "The Seafarer" and the more subtle, presentative method of the Chinese adaptations was also inevitably obtrusive.

17. For a sensitive and insightful analysis of the differences between Fenollosa's literal rendering of the Chinese texts and the final version of "Cathay," however, see Ronald Bush, "Pound and Li Po: What Becomes a Man." Through an examination of the Fenollosa notebooks in the Yale Collection, Bush demonstrates convincingly that the final form of "Cathay" is the last of several different versions using different selections and arrangements of Fenollosa's materials (59–60 n.5).

18. This is the final ordering of the sequence in *Personae* (1926). The contents of "Cathay" in the 1917 *Lustra* version are identical in all respects except for the transposition of "Poem by the Bridge at Ten-Shin" and "The Jewel Stairs' Grievance."

19. All quotations of "Cathay" are from *Personae* (1926).

20. Fung Yu-Lan, *A Short History of Chinese Philosophy*, ed. and trans. Derk Bodde (New York, 1962), 138, qtd. in Yip 96.

21. On the use of fugue structure in *The Cantos*, see Kay Davis's comprehensive and illuminating article, "Fugue and Canto LXIII," and her later book, *Fugue and Fresco: Structures in Pound's "Cantos."*

     It should be borne in mind that Pound had strong reservations about the applicability of fugue structure to *The Cantos*. In 1936, for instance, he wrote to Ibbotson that the fugue analogy is a source of confusion:

> CONFOUND uncle Bill YEATS' paragraph on fugue/blighter never
> knew WHAT a fugue was anyhow.
>   more wasted ink due his
> "explanation," than you cd. mop up with a moose hide.

(Letters to Ibbotson 35)

A year later he was still using the analogy, but with qualifications: "Take a fugue: theme, response, contrasujet. *Not* that I mean to make an exact analogy of structure" (*Ltrs* 294).

22. Nowhere in "Cathay" is there an episode where "live man goes down into the world of the dead," though the survey of battle-horrors in "Lament of the Frontier Guard" strongly suggests such a scene:

> Bónes whíte with a thóusand frósts,
> Hígh héaps, cóvered with trées and gráss

Both the imagery and the rhythms used here approximate passages in Canto I, which was in its first stages of composition at the time (as Ur-Canto III):

> Sóuls stáined with récent téars, gìrls ténder,
> Mén mány, máuled with brónze lánce hèads,
> Báttle spóil, béaring yèt dréory árms.

23. *Descent From Heaven* 19–22. The terms are actually Percy Lubbock's and refer to different narrative foci in the novel. Greene proposes that in the traditional epic the primary emphasis is on the scenes, which alternate between moments of deliberation and moments of action. This is another cogent analogue to the alternation between the horror of battle and scenes of female desolation in "Cathay."

24. All quotations of "Langue d'Oc" and "Moeurs Contemporaines" are from *Personae* (1926).

25. "Symbolical" is a term almost always used pejoratively by Pound (Brooke-Rose 62).

26. The link between sexuality and aesthetics in Pound's thought is discussed at length in Espey 62–83; cf. Berryman 69–71 and Witemeyer 176–83.

27. See, for instance, Davie 85; Joseph 95; and Turner 247 and *passim*.

28. Cf. Bush, "Gathering the Limbs" 74, and Vincent E. Miller 458–60.

29. But see Vincent E. Miller 457–58 for a discussion of Pound's use of de Gourmont's version of the *Sequaire* of Goddeschalk as a model for the structure of the *Homage*.

30. All quotations of the *Homage to Sextus Propertius* are from *Personae*.

31. The opening of Canto VIII strongly echoes this passage—the opposition is naturally a crucial one in "a poem of some length":

> These fragments you have shelved (shored),
> "Slut!" "Bitch!" Truth and Calliope
> Slanging each other sous les lauriers.

32. Unpublished letter to Mencken, at Yale, qtd. in Joseph 81.

Chapter 4

1. Cf. Marjorie Perloff's fine analysis of the *collage* structure of *Gaudier-Brzeska* (*Dance* 50–60).

2. YC. Bracketed portions are interpolated since this letter is torn along the right margin.

3. Ackroyd 79; Valerie Eliot in Eliot, *Waste Land* xii; and Kenner, *Era* 355. In a letter dated 21 April 1916, Pound wrote to Harriet Monroe that Eliot "is to come in next week to plan a book, and I will then send you a group of his things" (UCL).

4. Following is the table of contents for this volume, now among the holdings of the Yale Collection in the Beinecke Rare Book and Manuscript Library:

> Envoi. INDOCTUS.
> Scriptor Ignotus
> The Cry of the Eyes
> Capilupus Sends Greetings to Grotus
> To E B B
> I and Thou
> Child Songs
>   Child in the Night
>   Child to the Sister of the Winds
> Lyric from "Quevedo"
> The Lord of Shallott
> Alba Belingalis
> The Borrowed Lady
> Donzelletta Mia
> MOTIFS for Music
>   Gottesruh
>   Ex Exilio
>   Search

Psalma
Return
Saxon Charm
Chant of the Admitted
The Watchman
Webs
Marcus Martialis
To R. B.
<small>OLD CHESTS</small>
  Supplementary verse for substitution or insertion
Finale
  <small>"THE SUMMONS"</small>

5. All quotations of "Hilda's Book" are from the text in *End to Torment*.

6. Cf. Davenport, "Persephone's Ezra" 145–46ff.

7. According to Gallup, the manuscript of *A Lume Spento* "had been almost completed when Pound left the United States for Europe early in 1908" (4).

8. See Anderson 46–49 and *passim*.

9. Viewed biographically, the imagery of this passage—the only instance of "whirring wings" in *A Lume Spento*—suggests a decisive caesura in the relationship that, H. D. claims in *End to Torment*, "Hilda's Book" documents.

10. The title of Pound's poem is taken from a phrase in section 48 of "Song of Myself," which celebrates God's signature in one's self and others around him. For a fuller discussion of this allusion and its significance, see my note "Whitman in Pound's Mirror," in *American Literature* 59 (1987): 639–44.

11. Boris de Rachewiltz also suggests a cogent analogue for this poem in the Egyptian *Texts of the Pyramids* (178–79).

12. "Letters to Jordan" 111. This refers to the beginning of the letter, where Pound explains that "I am interested in art and ecstasy, ecstasy which I would define as the sensation of the soul in ascent, art as the expression and sole means of transmuting, of passing on that ecstasy to others" (109).

13. Several of the poems were taken up into *A Quinzaine for This Yule* and a few more were included in *Personae* and *Exultations*.

14. See Davis, *Fugue and Fresco*, especially 17–28.

15. Pound recalls this ceremony in Gibraltar again in Canto XXII.

16. Only parts I and II of this sonnet sequence are printed, though the numerals III and IV hang on the page, suggestive but empty.

17. This poem is entitled "Motif" in *A Lume Spento*.

18. Petter reproduces the early table of contents referred to here. It is handwritten by Pound and uses long slashes to delineate the intended groupings:

    1 Cino, or La Fraisne.
    2 Ballad for Gloom.

3   For E. McC.

---

4   Night Litany
5   Sandalphon.
6   Nel Biancheggiar.

---

7   <u>Marvoil</u> [Pound's underscore]
8   Piccadilly.

Pound also jotted notes next to some of these poems concerning their sources (Petter 113).

19.   This alba, in a later translation, became the fourth section of "Langue d'Oc."

Chapter 5

1.   The contents of "Canzoniere, Studies in Form":

> Octave
> Sonnet in Tenzone
> Sonnet
> Canzon: The Yearly Slain
> Canzon: The Spear
> Canzon, To Be Sung beneath a Window
> Canzon: Of Incense
> Canzone: Of Angels
> Sonnet: Chi è questa?
> Of Grace
> Canzon: The Vision
> To Our Lady of Vicarious Atonement
> Epilogue: To Guido Cavalcanti
> [Notes]
>
> (Gallup 12)

2.   The volume is discussed here with the poems that Pound deleted at the proof stage, as marked, since he later expressed dissatisfaction with the result of the omissions. Writing to Elkin Mathews about the importance of construction in a volume, he lamented that

> I neglected it in "Canzoni" and the book has never had the same measure of success as the others. It is *not* so good as the others. I was affected by hyper-aesthesia or over-squeamishness and cut out the rougher poems. I don't know that I regret it in that case for the poems weren't good enough, but even so the book would have been better if they had been left in, or if something like them had been put in their place. (*P/J* 285)

In fact, Pound marked several more poems for deletion on the printer's review sheets (at Yale) that are included nonetheless; a different scheme for the volume was perhaps developing that it was too late to implement. Not all of the review sheets are extant, but those that are indicate omission of the following: "Era Mea," "The Tree," "La Nuvoletta," "Rosa Sempiterna," "The Golden Sestina," "A Prologue," "Maestro," and sections IV, V, and VI of "Und Drang." This appears to have been directed toward restoring the balance disrupted by deleting "the rougher poems."

3.   Cf. McDougal 100–101; McKeown 60–62; and Witemeyer 101–3.

4. Pound's use of Pater's translation in "Speech for Psyche" is discussed by Witemeyer (42).

5. This, perhaps, explains the placement of the classical world of Propertius and Apuleius between Provence and the twentieth century, and its later placement, in *Quia Pauper Amavi,* after the twentieth century both in the actual order of sequences and in the layering of language in that volume. As Pound explained, "the point of the archaic language in the Prov. trans. is that the Latin is really 'modern.' We are just getting back to a Roman state of civilization, or in reach of it, whereas the Provençal feeling is archaic, we are ages away from it" (*Ltrs* 179). As he later concluded, "We do NOT know the past in chronological sequence. It may be convenient to lay it out anesthetized on the table with dates pasted on here and there, but what we know we know by ripples and spirals eddying out from us and from our own time" (*GK* 60).

6. Cf. Rosenthal, *Sailing* 69–72.

7. This may also be Christ's inception, as Ruthven suggests (190).

8. *English Review,* June 1912.

9. "The Temperaments" is a poem that Pound was apparently satisfied with and that had the approbation of at least one critic whose opinion he valued, Yeats. Pound wrote to Harriet Monroe that "You may not like it, but even W. B. Y. who for the most part detests my slighter vein, admits that HERE I have the true quality, the real, the hellenic epigram" (UCL). But the poem was obviously out of place at the end of *Lustra,* as will readily be seen by comparing it with the closing poem of the English editions, "Fish and the Shadow," and with "Impressions of Voltaire."

10. A preliminary table of contents for part of *Lustra,* now at Yale:

> The Temperaments
> De mortuo
> Amici
> Society
> Prayer
> Not so long after
> As usual
> Preference
> A Translation
>   Liu Che
>   After Ch'u Yuan
>   Fan Piece
>   ~~(fountain)~~
>   ~~Prologue~~
> Ts'ai Ch'ai
> Prologue to Adventure
> Heather

(The deletions marked are Pound's.)
    Of the fourteen poems listed (assuming "A Translation" is a subheading for those that follow), six were never printed at all. The Chinese poems were kept together but "Liu Ch'e" and "After Ch'u Yuan" were transposed, and "In a Station of the Metro" was brought to the end of them. "Heather" retained its approximate position in relation to these, but a new group was formed around it that includes "Society." "Amici" (presumably "Amitiés") was moved to another part of the book altogether.

11. All quotations of *Lustra* are from *Personae: The Collected Shorter Poems* unless specified otherwise. Significant variations of this text from *Lustra* (1917) will be noted.

12. "Pax Saturni" is removed and replaced with "The Spring," "Albâtre" and "Causa"; "Dance Figure" is moved to the second group; and "In a Station of the Metro" is transposed to the end of the fourth group.

13. The first line of "A Pact" read "I make a truce with you, Walt Whitman" in all printings prior to its placement next to "Surgit Fama" in *Lustra*. The elimination of this potentially jarring repetition suggests, again, the importance of the poems' conception as links joined within the curve of the volume rather than as separate pieces.

14. *Lustra* (1917) 25. A slightly altered version of this poem, entitled "The Choice," is reprinted in *CEP* (279).

15. In fact, Pound instructed Harriet Monroe to subtitle the poem "A Thoroughly Sensuous Image" when it was first printed (UCL; Ruthven 56).

16. Cf. Rosenthal, "'Actaeon-Principle.'"

17. Cf. Witemeyer 151–55.

18. Though implicit throughout this poem, anguished yearning for the "lost dead" was more immediately present in the opening lines of the first printings: "Les yeux d'une morte aimée / M'ont salué" (*Lustra* [1917]).

19. Cf. Fleming 148–50.

20. "The Nekuia shouts aloud that it is *older* than the rest, all that island, Cretan, etc., hinter-time, that is *not* Praxiteles, not Athens of Pericles, but Odysseus" (*Ltrs* 274).

Chapter 6

1. Spanos conveniently summarizes the most common critical positions up to the time of his essay (1965): there is one school "which assumes Ezra Pound to be the speaker of the entire sequence," another "which claims that the 'Ode' is spoken by Pound's critics or by Pound speaking in the voice of his critics and that the rest of the sequence (with the exception of the last poem "Medallion") is spoken by Pound," and a third "which interprets the 'Ode' to be written by the old guard critics and some parts of the sequence to be spoken by Pound and some by Mauberley" (73–74). Spanos goes on to propose an alternative view that attributes the entire sequence to "Mauberley" except for the "Envoi."
    Some notable subsequent commentators on this issue include Alexander, who attributes the first part of the sequence to Pound and the second to Mauberley; Berryman, who, most recently, argues in great detail that the entire sequence, with the exception of "Medallion," is spoken by Mauberley; Bush (*Genesis*), who follows Spanos's view; Joseph and Korn, who both examine the problem insightfully but do not advance a single solution; Pearlman, who suggests that the voice of the entire sequence is Pound's, except in "Medallion"; and Witemeyer, who attributes the whole sequence to Pound, except for the collective voice of "Envoi" and Mauberley's voice in "Medallion." My own view of the sequence, dispensing with the dramatic construct of "speakers" in favor of a single, integral consciousness that passes through various phases in the course of the sequence, closely follows and is much indebted to Rosenthal (*Primer* 29–41) and Rosenthal and Gall (196–203).

2. All quotations of *Hugh Selwyn Mauberley* are from the text in *Personae* (1926; rpt. 1971). "Diabolus," as Espey notes (76 n.), refers specifically to the dissonance of the augmented

fourth in the major/minor tonal scales, but it has further implications that become clearer as the sequence unfolds.

3. Relevant here are, on the one hand, the strength of artistic effort and the qualities of directness and precision for which both Ford and Pound praised him and, on the other, Flaubert's acute diagnosis of the malaise that led the French into the Franco-Prussian war:

> Flaubert said of the war of 1870: "If they had read my *Education Sentimentale,* this sort of thing wouldn't have happened." Artists are the antennae of the race, but the bullet-headed many will never learn to trust their great artists. If it is the business of the artist to make humanity aware of itself; here the thing was done, the pages of diagnosis. The multitude of wearisome fools will not learn their right hand from their left or seek out a meaning. (*LE* 297)

4. Both Penelope and Aphrodite are objects of the poet's quest: in *Mauberley,* Penelope represents an earthly, aesthetic goal, whereas in *The Cantos* Aphrodite is given a more strongly spiritual dimension.

5. The quotation from Pindar in this stanza, it should be noted, is not contingent upon an approval of Pindar's rhetoric; it is used to invoke a set of values whose loss is fatal. Though Pound often derided Pindar's bombast, the second Olympian ode, from which this quotation comes, celebrates not only heroism but leadership, civic justice, and cooperation between men and gods:

> Lords of the lyre, ye hymns, what god,
> What hero, what man shall we honour? Zeus
>   Holds Pisa; the Olympiad feast
> Heracles founded, the first-fruits of war;
> Now for his four-horsed chariot victory
> Let Theron's name be praised, who to all strangers
>   Shows the true face of justice,
>   Of Acragas the staunch pillar,
>   Upholder of his city,
>   Of famous fathers the fine flower;
>
> They after many a labour, took
> Beside this riverbank their sacred dwelling,
>   And were the eye of Sicily;
> And an age sent of heaven attended them,
> Bringing them wealth and honour, to crown their inborn
> Merit. O son of Cronos, Rhea's child,
>   Who rules Olympus' seat
>   And the great games by Alpheus' ford,
>   Gladdened with songs, be gracious
>   To grant this soil be still their homeland. . . .

(Trans. Conway 11). The ironic contrast between the national loyalty, heroism, inborn virtue and spirit of tribute and prayer in this passage and the grotesquely distorted values and desperation of the war in poems IV and V of *Hugh Selwyn Mauberley* is immediately apparent.

6. "Tin" gives the poem a specifically American ring, as pointed out to me by M. L. Rosenthal.

7. Though no gloss is needed, the poem's specific details are clarified by Pound's remarks in his book on Gaudier and later in his interview with D. G. Bridson. Compare, for instance, "Quick eyes gone under earth's lid" with "The vivid, incisive manner, the eyes 'almost alarmingly

intelligent'" (*GB* 39). As a relevant comment on this poem as a whole: "Gaudier was the most absolute case of genius I've ever run into, and they killed off an awful lot of sculpture when they shot him. . . . which is the kind of wastage you get in a war" ("Int" Bridson 161). Dekker has also noted these connections (195).

8. For this use of the word "boche," see Gaudier's letters from the trenches, *GB* 55f., and Cantos XVI and XIX.

9. Cf. Rosenthal and Gall 199.

10. She never actually makes an entrance into her "stuffed-satin drawing room."

11. Cf. Rosenthal and Gall 197–98. This point is sharpened by the poem's allusion to Waller's "Go, Lovely Rose," a song set by Henry Lawes (Espey 98). Waller's poem is a *carpe diem* that offers the rose as an exemplum of the fate of all beautiful things, entreating the woman to "suffer herself to be desired" lest, like a sequestered rose, her transient blossoming pass unappreciated; but the focus of "Envoi" is idealized feminine beauty *per se* rather than the desire it evokes, and the poem shifts attention from love's critical moment to "some other mouth / May be as fair as hers" at some point in the distant future.

12. Also, if we accept the identification of the woman singing Lawes as Raymonde Collignon (Berryman 141–44), it is improbable that she would be unaware of whose song she sings and that she would be portrayed as one who goes "With song upon her lips / But sings not out the song."

13. The reproductions that Berryman provides amply illustrate this (89, 92–93).

14. Messalina's licentiousness led her to a marriage with Silius while still wed to Claudius, who consequently brought about both her and her lover's deaths; as the mother-in-law of Nero, she occupies a notable place in a tradition of such betrayals between the sexes (Harvey 267).

15. "Diabolus in the scale" is, of course, another way of saying "out of key with his time," but it suggests a more cutting exclusion; as Espey notes, "diabolus" also means devil (76–77 n.15), and the devil's name is emblematic of his role as a "slanderer," recalling the satiric activity of part 1 and partially accounting for the exclusion here, the recourse to "that Arcadia," and the drifting incapacity amid "ambrosia" that results (Lucifer cast into limbo, so to speak).

16. There is, first, Scylla's fatal betrayal of her father, Nisus, by handing over his charmed lock of hair and, with it, conquest of her city, to Minos, out of consuming passion for him; Minos follows up his triumph but repulses Scylla, revolted by her heinous sacrifice. Minos's punishment for betraying Poseidon was, of course, his wife's sexual perversion, whose hideous fruit was the Minotaur. Minos is in turn betrayed by his daughter, Ariadne (echoing Scylla's betrayal), who out of love for Theseus supplies the golden thread that allows him to slay the Minotaur and escape from the labyrinth where it was kept; but Theseus in turn betrays Ariadne's love and abandons her in Dia. The final episode in Minos's legend is his own destruction when, after pursuing Daedalus (the artist whom as patron he had betrayed and forced to flee) to Sicily, he is killed, perhaps by King Cocalus's daughters, by being stifled in a hot bath—a fate not unlike that of part 2, poem IV in *Hugh Selwyn Mauberley* (Ovid, Book VIII of *Metamorphoses;* Seyffert 394).

17. In criticism of *Hugh Selwyn Mauberley,* where Minos is mentioned at all, he is discussed as a patron of the arts (e.g., Berryman 163), as indeed he was, of a sort quite consistent with the age surveyed in part 1 of Pound's sequence: his master craftsman, Daedalus, after building the labyrinth where the Minotaur was kept, was detained by Minos in Crete, against his will. In order to escape, he built wings for himself and his son—described by Ovid in a passage Pound

recounts admiringly in the *Spirit of Romance* (15–16)—though his son, Icarus, was destroyed in the process.

18. Circe is first encountered in the *Odyssey* by Odysseus's men who, standing in her courtyard, hear her singing within (Book X).

19. As early as 1913, Pound claimed that "I have 'known many men's manners and seen many cities.' Besides knowing living artists, I have come in touch with the tradition of the dead" ("How I Began," rpt. in Stock, *Perspectives* 1).

20. Bush argues convincingly, however, for the influence of Aeschylus's "agglutinative syntax," among other likely precedents (*Genesis* 180–82). My point is not that Pound was indifferent to such models, but that by the time *The Cantos* assumed their final form, he had already been experimenting with and extending the possibilities they offered for some time.

21. Pound often referred to this line of succession, for instance in an unpublished letter to Henry Ware Eliot in 1915: "Browning in his *Dramatis Personae* and in his *Men and Women* developed a form of poem which had lain dormant since Ovid's *Heroides* or since Theocritus" (YC; cf. *ABCR* 78). Of course, Pound is referring specifically to the dramatic monologue, but the relations among poems within these collections are unlikely to have escaped his notice. These works are related not by genre but more loosely by their common procedure of building a longer work from poems and passages with an implicit interaction among them.

22. In an undated letter of 1919, Pound refers to a "bundle of three" cantos (qtd. in Slatin 60); in March 1920, he wrote to Thayer of the *Dial* insisting on keeping Cantos V–VII together as a unit (qtd. in Pearlman 301); in June 1922 he wrote to Quinn that he had "blocked in four cantos" (qtd. in Pearlman 302), and in July of that year that he had "got five cantos blocked out" (qtd. in Pearlman 302). That same month he wrote to Schelling that "the first 11 cantos are preparation of the palette" (*Ltrs* 180) and to Kate Buss that he had "blocked in five more Cantos" (qtd. in Slatin 62). In September of that year he wrote to his father that the Malatesta canto was in progress and may run to more than one, and "the four to follow it are blocked in" (YC), and to his mother that he had "several cantos blocked in, to follow the Malatesta section" (YC). The next month he wrote that he was "plugging on my next batch of cantos" (qtd. in Slatin 63), and early the next year he wrote Quinn that he had "blocked in 4 cantos on Malatesta" (qtd. in Pearlman 303). In 1924 he wrote his father that he had "blocked out course of a few more cantos" (YC) and later that year that he was beginning "another LONG hunk of Canti" (qtd. in Slatin 66), and wrote his mother that he was "ready for another long chunk" (YC).

23. These divisions more or less concur with Kenner's (*Era* 416–17), though for reasons slightly different from his.

24. Slatin's essay shows that the first three cantos were completed *after* the Malatesta Cantos and after the shape of the first sixteen cantos had more or less congealed. Ur-Canto III supplied the nodus for Canto I, as Ur-Canto II did for Canto III. Canto II was reshaped from Ur-Canto VIII. Cf. Bush, *Genesis* 246–54.

25. The permanent/recurrent/casual cycle has an analogue in the design of the Schifanoia frescoes at Ferrara, which has been discussed at length by Davenport (*Cities* 80–89) and Davis (*Fugue* 95–106). This analogy is illuminating but, like that of the fugue, needs qualification: most significantly, Pound pointed out that "the Schifanoia frescoes I discovered after I had done something similar" ("Int" Bridson 172). Hence it does not seem reasonable to conclude that the cycles of *The Cantos* are derived in any sense from the frescoes.

26. Cf. Carne-Ross 139 and Rosenthal, "Structuring" 7–8.

27. Canto CXX will be treated here as the final cadence of the work, since its tranquility and poise are representative of *Drafts and Fragments,* although it is very unlikely that Pound intended it to be the conclusion. See Stoicheff for a fuller discussion of the publication history of the last segment of *The Cantos.*

28. Not all metamorphosis in *The Cantos* serves this function, of course. Generally, it traces a movement among the levels of a hierarchical continuum from forms of lifelessness to the most vital forms of life, the gods of "the divine or permanent world." For fuller discussion of metamorphosis in *The Cantos,* see Dekker 73–82; Emery 6–7; and Quinn *passim.*

   The sculptural metamorphosis passage in Canto II is also echoed with comic irony in pointing out the figure of the Kansas woman in Canto XXVIII: "If thou wilt go to Chiasso wilt find that indestructable female / As if waiting for the train to Topeka."

29. The origin of this image in Aristophanes is pointed out in Carroll Terrell's *Companion* (7), a reference work to which the present discussion owes much. The first subject rhyme for this passage occurs in the series of poetasters at the end of Canto V.

30. Davis, *Fugue* 49. I have corrected the obvious misprint "GOD-SLIGHT" in Davis's text.

31. Davenport, *Cities* 116–17 identifies the seal as Eidothea.

32. The first of these phrases is in C. F. Terrell's translation (12).

33. This passage also parallels the first part of Book V of the *Odyssey,* where Odysseus sits looking out on "the barren sea" which he is prevented from crossing by Calypso. His hope is rekindled by a visitation from Hermes promising him passage, like the momentary vision that follows in this canto.

34. This is not by any means intended to imply that Pound's process of growth, psychic or other, is a determinant of the poem's structure. The poem's process of growth, its virtual life, is independent of any particular individual's development.

Works Cited

Ackroyd, Peter. *T. S. Eliot: A Life.* New York: Simon and Schuster, 1984.

Alexander, Michael. *The Poetic Achievement of Ezra Pound.* Berkeley: University of California Press, 1969.

Altieri, Charles. "Motives in Metaphor: John Ashbery and the Modernist Long Poem." *Genre* 11 (1978): 653–87.

Anderson, William S. "The Theory and Practice of Poetic Arrangement from Vergil to Ovid." In *Poems in Their Place: The Intertextuality and Order of Poetic Collections.* Ed. Neil Fraistat. Chapel Hill: University of North Carolina Press, 1986. 44–65.

Baldwin, Ralph. "The Unity of the *Canterbury Tales.*" In *Chaucer Criticism:* The Canterbury Tales. Eds. Richard J. Schoek and Jeremy Taylor. Notre Dame, IN: University of Notre Dame Press, 1960. 14–51.

Berryman, Jo Brantley. *Circe's Craft: Ezra Pound's "Hugh Selwyn Mauberley."* Ann Arbor: UMI Research Press, 1983.

Bornstein, George. "The Arrangement of Browning's *Dramatic Lyrics* (1842)." In *Poems in Their Place: The Intertextuality and Order of Poetic Collections.* Ed. Neil Fraistat. Chapel Hill: University of North Carolina Press, 1986. 273–88.

———. *The Postromantic Consciousness of Ezra Pound.* English Literary Studies Monograph 8. Victoria, B.C.: University of Victoria Press, 1977.

———. "Pound's Parleyings with Robert Browning." In *Ezra Pound Among the Poets.* Ed. George Bornstein. Chicago: University of Chicago Press, 1985. 106–27.

Brooke-Rose, Christine. *A ZBC of Ezra Pound.* Berkeley: University of California Press, 1971.

Burke, Kenneth. *Counter-Statement.* Los Altos, CA: Hermes Publications, 1953.

Bush, Ronald. "Gathering the Limbs of Orpheus: The Subject of Pound's *Homage to Sextus Propertius.*" In *Ezra Pound and William Carlos Williams: University of Pennsylvania Conference Papers.* Ed. Daniel Hoffman. Philadelphia: University of Pennsylvania Press, 1983. 61–78.

———. *The Genesis of Ezra Pound's Cantos.* Princeton: Princeton UP, 1976.

———. "Pound and Li Po: What Becomes a Man." In *Ezra Pound Among the Poets.* Ed. George Bornstein. Chicago: University of Chicago Press, 1985. 35–62.

Carne-Ross, D. S. "The Cantos as Epic." In *An Examination of Ezra Pound.* Ed. Peter Russell. New York: Gordian Press, 1973. 134–55.

Coleridge, Samuel Taylor. *Biographia Literaria.* Ed. George Watson. 1817; rpt. London: J. M. Dent, 1975.

Dasenbrock, Reed Way. *The Literary Vorticism of Ezra Pound and Wyndham Lewis: Towards the Condition of Painting.* Baltimore: Johns Hopkins UP, 1985.

Davenport, Guy. *Cities on Hills: A Study of I–XXX of Ezra Pound's Cantos.* Ann Arbor: UMI Research Press, 1983.

———. "Persephone's Ezra." In *New Approaches to Ezra Pound: A Co-ordinated Investigation of Pound's Poetry and Ideas*. Ed. Eva Hesse. Berkeley: University of California Press, 1969. 145–73.

Davie, Donald. *Ezra Pound: Poet as Sculptor*. New York: Oxford UP, 1964.

Davis, Kay. "Fugue and Canto LXIII." *Paideuma* 11 (1982): 15–38.

———. *Fugue and Fresco: Structures in Pound's "Cantos."* Orono, ME: National Poetry Foundation, 1984.

Dekker, George. *The Cantos of Ezra Pound: A Critical Study*. New York: Barnes and Noble, 1963.

Demetz, Peter. "Ezra Pound's German Studies." *The Germanic Review* 31 (1956): 279–92.

De Nagy, Christoph. *The Poetry of Ezra Pound: The Pre-Imagist Stage*. Bern: Francke Verlag, 1960.

———. *Ezra Pound's Poetics and Literary Tradition: The Critical Decade*. Bern: Francke Verlag, 1966.

Doolittle, Hilda (H.D.). *End to Torment: A Memoir of Ezra Pound, With the Poems From "Hilda's Book" by Ezra Pound*. Eds. Norman Holmes Pearson and Michael King. New York: New Directions, 1979.

Eliot, T. S. *Collected Poems 1909–1962*. New York: Harcourt, Brace and World, 1963.

———. "Ezra Pound: His Metric and Poetry." In *To Criticize the Critic*. New York: Farrar, Straus and Giroux, 1965. 162–82.

———. "The Method of Mr. Pound." *Athenaeum* 4,669 (October 24, 1919): 1065–66.

———. *Selected Essays*. New York: Harcourt, Brace and World, 1964.

———. *The Waste Land: A Facsimile and Transcript of the Original Drafts, Including the Annotations of Ezra Pound*. Ed. Valerie Eliot. New York: Harcourt Brace Jovanovich, 1971.

Emery, Clark. *Ideas Into Action: A Study of Pound's Cantos*. Coral Gables, FL: University of Miami Press, 1958.

Espey, John. *Ezra Pound's Mauberley: A Study in Composition*. Berkeley: University of California Press, 1974.

Fleming, William. "Ezra Pound and the French Language." In *Ezra Pound Perspectives: Essays in Honor of His Eightieth Birthday*. Ed. Noel Stock. Chicago: Henry Regnery, 1965. 129–50.

Foerster, Donald M. *The Fortunes of Epic Poetry: A Study in English and American Criticism 1750–1950*. Washington, D.C.: The Catholic University of America Press, 1962.

Fraistat, Neil. *The Poem and the Book: Interpreting Collections of Romantic Poetry*. Chapel Hill: University of North Carolina Press, 1985.

Gall, Sally M. "Pound and the Modern Melic Tradition: Towards a Demystification of Absolute Rhythm." *Paideuma* 8 (1979): 35–47.

Gallup, Donald. *Ezra Pound: A Bibliography*. Charlottesville: University Press of Virginia, 1983.

Greene, Thomas M. *Descent from Heaven: A Study in Epic Continuity*. New Haven: Yale UP, 1963.

Halperin, David M. *Before Pastoral: Theocritus and the Ancient Tradition of Bucolic Poetry*. New Haven: Yale UP, 1983.

Harmon, William. *Time in Ezra Pound's Work*. Chapel Hill: University of North Carolina Press, 1977.

Harvey, Sir Paul. *The Oxford Companion to Classical Literature*. Oxford: Oxford UP, 1937.

Hesse, Eva. "Introduction." In *New Approaches to Ezra Pound: A Co-ordinated Investigation of Pound's Poetry and Ideas*. Ed. Eva Hesse. Berkeley: University of California Press, 1969. 13–53.

Hutchins, Patricia. "Ezra Pound and Thomas Hardy." *Southern Review* 6 (1968): 90–104.

Jackson, Thomas. *The Early Poetry of Ezra Pound*. Cambridge: Harvard UP, 1968.

Joseph, Terri Brint. "Ezra Pound's Approaches to the Long Poem in 'Near Perigord,' *Homage to Sextus Propertius,* and *Hugh Selwyn Mauberley*." Diss. University of California, Irvine, 1981.

Kenner, Hugh. "The Broken Mirrors and the Mirror of Memory." In *Motive and Method in the Cantos of Ezra Pound*. Ed. Lewis Leary. New York: Columbia UP, 1954.

———. *The Poetry of Ezra Pound*. New York: New Directions, 1950.

————. *The Pound Era.* Berkeley: University of California Press, 1971.

King, Michael. "Go, Little Book: Ezra Pound, Hilda Doolittle, and 'Hilda's Book.'" *Paideuma* 10 (1981): 347–60.

Korn, Marianne. *Ezra Pound: Purpose/Form/Meaning.* London: Pembridge Press, 1983.

Longenbach, James. "Pound's *Canzoni:* Toward a Poem Including History." *Paideuma* 13 (1984): 389–405.

Malkoff, Karl. *Escape from the Self: A Study in Contemporary American Poetry and Poetics.* New York: Columbia UP, 1977.

Mallarmé, Stéphane. *Mallarmé: Selected Prose Poems, Essays, and Letters.* Trans. Bradford Cook. Baltimore: The Johns Hopkins Press, 1956.

McDougal, Stuart Y. *Ezra Pound and the Troubadour Tradition.* Princeton: Princeton UP, 1972.

McKeown, Thomas Wilson. "Ezra Pound's Early Experiments with Major Forms, 1904–1925: *Directio Voluntatis.*" Diss. University of British Columbia, 1983.

Miller, James E., Jr. *The American Quest for a Supreme Fiction: Whitman's Legacy in the Personal Epic.* Chicago: University of Chicago Press, 1979.

Miller, Vincent E. "The Serious Wit of Pound's *Homage to Sextus Propertius.*" *Contemporary Literature* 16 (1975): 452–62.

Miner, Earl. *The Japanese Tradition in British and American Literature.* Princeton: Princeton UP, 1966.

————. "Some Issues for Study of Integral Collections." In *Poems in Their Place: The Intertextuality and Order of Poetic Collections.* Ed. Neil Fraistat. Chapel Hill: University of North Carolina Press, 1986. 18–43.

Pater, Walter. *The Renaissance: Studies in Art and Poetry.* 1873; rpt. New York: New American Library, 1959.

Patterson, Annabel. "Jonson, Marvell, and Miscellaneity?" In *Poems in Their Place: The Intertextuality and Order of Poetic Collections.* Ed. Neil Fraistat. Chapel Hill: University of North Carolina Press, 1986. 95–118.

Pearce, Roy Harvey. *The Continuity of American Poetry.* Princeton: Princeton UP, 1961.

Pearlman, Daniel. *The Barb of Time: On the Unity of Pound's Cantos.* New York: Oxford UP, 1969.

Perkins, David. *A History of Modern Poetry: From the 1890s to the High Modernist Mode.* Cambridge: The Belknap Press of Harvard UP, 1976.

Perloff, Marjorie. *The Dance of the Intellect: Studies in the Poetry of the Pound Tradition.* New York: Cambridge UP, 1985.

————. *The Poetics of Indeterminacy: Rimbaud to Cage.* Princeton: Princeton UP, 1981.

Petter, C. G. "Pound's *Personae:* From Manuscript to Print." *Studies in Bibliography* 35 (1982): 111–132.

Pindar. *The Odes of Pindar.* Trans. Geoffrey S. Conway. London: J. M. Dent, 1972.

Poe, Edgar Allen. *Poems and Essays.* London: J. M. Dent, 1927.

Pondrom, Cyrena N. *The Road From Paris: French Influence on English Poetry, 1900–1920.* London: Cambridge UP, 1974.

Pound, Ezra. *ABC of Reading.* 1934; rpt. New York: New Directions, 1960.

————. *A Lume Spento and Other Early Poems.* New York: New Directions, 1965.

————. *The Cantos of Ezra Pound.* New York: New Directions, 1972.

————. *Canzoni of Ezra Pound.* London: Elkin Mathews, 1911.

————. *Collected Early Poems of Ezra Pound.* Ed. Michael King. New York: New Directions, 1976.

————. *Ezra Pound and Dorothy Shakespear: Their Letters, 1909–1914.* Eds. Omar Pound and A. Walton Litz. New York: New Directions, 1984.

————. "Ezra Pound: An Interview." With Donald Hall. *Paris Review* 28 (1962): 22–51.

214   *Works Cited*

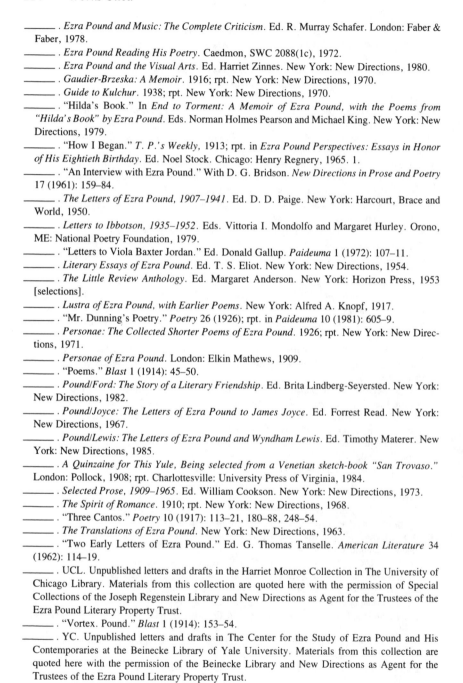

_____. *Ezra Pound and Music: The Complete Criticism*. Ed. R. Murray Schafer. London: Faber & Faber, 1978.

_____. *Ezra Pound Reading His Poetry*. Caedmon, SWC 2088(1c), 1972.

_____. *Ezra Pound and the Visual Arts*. Ed. Harriet Zinnes. New York: New Directions, 1980.

_____. *Gaudier-Brzeska: A Memoir*. 1916; rpt. New York: New Directions, 1970.

_____. *Guide to Kulchur*. 1938; rpt. New York: New Directions, 1970.

_____. "Hilda's Book." In *End to Torment: A Memoir of Ezra Pound, with the Poems from "Hilda's Book" by Ezra Pound*. Eds. Norman Holmes Pearson and Michael King. New York: New Directions, 1979.

_____. "How I Began." *T. P.'s Weekly*, 1913; rpt. in *Ezra Pound Perspectives: Essays in Honor of His Eightieth Birthday*. Ed. Noel Stock. Chicago: Henry Regnery, 1965. 1.

_____. "An Interview with Ezra Pound." With D. G. Bridson. *New Directions in Prose and Poetry* 17 (1961): 159–84.

_____. *The Letters of Ezra Pound, 1907–1941*. Ed. D. D. Paige. New York: Harcourt, Brace and World, 1950.

_____. *Letters to Ibbotson, 1935–1952*. Eds. Vittoria I. Mondolfo and Margaret Hurley. Orono, ME: National Poetry Foundation, 1979.

_____. "Letters to Viola Baxter Jordan." Ed. Donald Gallup. *Paideuma* 1 (1972): 107–11.

_____. *Literary Essays of Ezra Pound*. Ed. T. S. Eliot. New York: New Directions, 1954.

_____. *The Little Review Anthology*. Ed. Margaret Anderson. New York: Horizon Press, 1953 [selections].

_____. *Lustra of Ezra Pound, with Earlier Poems*. New York: Alfred A. Knopf, 1917.

_____. "Mr. Dunning's Poetry." *Poetry* 26 (1926); rpt. in *Paideuma* 10 (1981): 605–9.

_____. *Personae: The Collected Shorter Poems of Ezra Pound*. 1926; rpt. New York: New Directions, 1971.

_____. *Personae of Ezra Pound*. London: Elkin Mathews, 1909.

_____. "Poems." *Blast* 1 (1914): 45–50.

_____. *Pound/Ford: The Story of a Literary Friendship*. Ed. Brita Lindberg-Seyersted. New York: New Directions, 1982.

_____. *Pound/Joyce: The Letters of Ezra Pound to James Joyce*. Ed. Forrest Read. New York: New Directions, 1967.

_____. *Pound/Lewis: The Letters of Ezra Pound and Wyndham Lewis*. Ed. Timothy Materer. New York: New Directions, 1985.

_____. *A Quinzaine for This Yule, Being selected from a Venetian sketch-book "San Trovaso."* London: Pollock, 1908; rpt. Charlottesville: University Press of Virginia, 1984.

_____. *Selected Prose, 1909–1965*. Ed. William Cookson. New York: New Directions, 1973.

_____. *The Spirit of Romance*. 1910; rpt. New York: New Directions, 1968.

_____. "Three Cantos." *Poetry* 10 (1917): 113–21, 180–88, 248–54.

_____. *The Translations of Ezra Pound*. New York: New Directions, 1963.

_____. "Two Early Letters of Ezra Pound." Ed. G. Thomas Tanselle. *American Literature* 34 (1962): 114–19.

_____. UCL. Unpublished letters and drafts in the Harriet Monroe Collection in The University of Chicago Library. Materials from this collection are quoted here with the permission of Special Collections of the Joseph Regenstein Library and New Directions as Agent for the Trustees of the Ezra Pound Literary Property Trust.

_____. "Vortex. Pound." *Blast* 1 (1914): 153–54.

_____. YC. Unpublished letters and drafts in The Center for the Study of Ezra Pound and His Contemporaries at the Beinecke Library of Yale University. Materials from this collection are quoted here with the permission of the Beinecke Library and New Directions as Agent for the Trustees of the Ezra Pound Literary Property Trust.

Powell, James A. "The Light of Vers Libre." *Paideuma* 8 (1979): 3–34.

Quinn, Sister M. Bernetta, O. S. F. "The Metamorphoses of Ezra Pound." In *Motive and Method in the Cantos of Ezra Pound.* Ed. Lewis Leary. New York: Columbia UP, 1954. 60–100.

Rachewiltz, Boris de. "Pagan and Magic Elements in Ezra Pound's Works." In *New Approaches to Ezra Pound: A Co-ordinated Investigation of Pound's Poetry and Ideas.* Ed. Eva Hesse. Berkeley: University of California Press, 1969. 174–97.

Read, Forrest. *'76 One World and "The Cantos" of Ezra Pound.* Chapel Hill: University of North Carolina Press, 1981.

Riddel, Joseph N. "A Somewhat Polemical Introduction: The Elliptical Poem." *Genre* 11 (1978): 459–78.

Rosenthal, M. L. "The 'Actaeon-Principle': Political Aesthetic of Joyce and the Poets." *Southern Review* 23 (1987): 541–56.

———. *The Modern Poets: A Critical Introduction.* New York: Oxford UP, 1960.

———. *A Primer of Ezra Pound.* New York: Macmillan, 1960.

———. *Sailing Into the Unknown: Yeats, Pound, and Eliot.* New York: Oxford UP, 1978.

———. "The Structuring of Pound's Cantos." *Paideuma* 6 (1977): 3–11.

Rosenthal, M. L., and Gall, Sally M. *The Modern Poetic Sequence: The Genius of Modern Poetry.* New York: Oxford UP, 1983.

Ruthven, K. K. *A Guide to Ezra Pound's "Personae" (1926).* Berkeley: University of California Press, 1969.

Schneidau, Herbert N. *Ezra Pound: The Image and the Real.* Baton Rouge: Louisiana State UP, 1969.

———. "Pound's Book of Cross-Cuts." *Genre* 11 (1978): 505–21.

Seyffert, Oskar. *Dictionary of Classical Antiquities.* Rev. and ed. Henry Nettleship and J. E. Sandys. Cleveland: Meridian, 1956.

Sieburth, Richard. *Instigations: Ezra Pound and Remy De Gourmont.* Cambridge: Harvard UP, 1978.

Slatin, Myles. "A History of Pound's Cantos I–XVI, 1915–1925." *American Literature* 35 (1963); rpt. in *Studies in The Cantos.* Ed Marie Hénault. Columbus: Merrill, 1971. 56–68.

Sola Pinto, Vivian de. *Crisis in English Poetry, 1880–1940.* New York: Harper & Row, 1958.

Spanos, William V. "The Modulating Voice of *Hugh Selwyn Mauberley.*" *Wisconsin Studies in Contemporary Literature* 6 (1965): 73–96.

Spender, Stephen. *The Struggle of the Modern.* Berkeley: University of California Press, 1963.

Stock, Noel, ed. *Ezra Pound Perspectives: Essays in Honor of His Eightieth Birthday.* Chicago: Henry Regnery, 1965.

Stoicheff, R. Peter. "The Composition and Publication History of Ezra Pound's *Drafts & Fragments.*" *Twentieth-Century Literature* 32 (1986): 78–94.

Sullivan, J. P. *Ezra Pound and Sextus Propertius: A Study in Creative Translation.* Austin: University of Texas Press, 1964.

Surette, Leon. *A Light from Eleusis: A Study of Ezra Pound's "Cantos."* New York: Oxford UP, 1979.

Terrell, Carroll F. *A Companion to the Cantos of Ezra Pound.* Vol. 1. Berkeley: University of California Press, 1980.

Thomas, Ronald Edward. *The Latin Masks of Ezra Pound.* Ann Arbor: UMI Research Press, 1983.

Turner, Mark. "Propertius Through the Looking Glass: A Fragmentary Glance at the Construction of Pound's *Homage.*" *Paideuma* 5 (1976): 241–65.

Waller, Edmund. *The Poems of Edmund Waller.* Ed. G. Thorn Drury, 1893; rpt. New York: Greenwood, 1968.

Wilhelm, James J. *Dante and Pound: The Epic of Judgement.* Orono, ME: National Poetry Foundation, 1974.

Williams, William Carlos. *The Autobiography of William Carlos Williams*. New York: New Directions, 1951.

Witemeyer, Hugh. *The Poetry of Ezra Pound: Forms and Renewal, 1908–1920*. Berkeley: University of California Press, 1969.

Woodward, Kathleen. *At Last, The Real Distinguished Thing: The Late Poems of Eliot, Pound, Stevens, and Williams*. Ohio: Ohio State UP, 1980.

Wordsworth, William. *Literary Criticism of William Wordsworth*. Ed. Paul M. Zall. Lincoln: University of Nebraska Press, 1966.

Wright, George T. *The Poet in the Poem: The Personae of Eliot, Yeats, and Pound*. Berkeley: University of California Press, 1960.

Yeats, William Butler. *A Packet for Ezra Pound*. Dublin: The Cuala Press, 1929; rpt. in *A Vision*. New York: Macmillan, 1965. 1–30.

Yip, Wai-Lim. *Ezra Pound's "Cathay."* Princeton: Princeton UP, 1969.

Zimmermann, Hans-Joachim. "Ezra Pound, 'A Song of the Degrees': Chinese Clarity Versus Alchemical Confusion." *Paideuma* 10 (1981): 225–41.

Index